DEVELOPING THE MULTICULTURAL PROCESS IN CLASSROOM INSTRUCTION

Competencies for Teachers

H. Prentice Baptiste, Jr.
Mira Lanier Baptiste

UNIVERSITY
PRESS OF
AMERICA

LANHAM • NEW YORK • LONDON

ISBN: 0-8191-0855-3 (Perfect)

Library of Congress Number: 79-89993

PREFACE

As students of multicultural education, we have had a strong interest in identifying competencies and appropriate instructional strategies which would facilitate in-service teachers and other educators acquisition of functional skills and the spirit of multiculturalism. During the past five years in numerous workshops, conferences, seminars, and universities, we have worked with hundreds of in-service educators which provided the opportunity for the identification of those knowledges and skills deemed important by in-service educators for effective implementation of multiculturalism.

This was followed by the forming of competency statements and strategies for their implementation. The competencies have undergone several reviews and modifications. The strategies have been revised several times during the five years of experimenting. Subsequently, the competencies and strategies presented in this module are the results of five years of development with the help and support of many in-service educators and dedicated students of multiculturalism.

We would like to acknowledge the many contributors whose work has helped to make this book a reality. We also extend our appreciation to the many teachers and students who interacted with us and encouraged us in the development of the competencies and related strategies. Our thanks is also extended to Margaret "Peggy" Shallock who worked with us in the development of the first draft. Thanks is also extended to Lesley McAvoy and Mildred Kratovil for typing various parts of the manuscript. A deep sense of gratitude must be given to Linda McKinley who typed and provided technical editorial services for the final manuscript.

H. Prentice Baptiste, Jr.   Mira Baptiste

DEDICATED TO THOSE TEACHERS WHO BELIEVE
IN THE EDUCATION OF <u>ALL</u> AND WHO CONTINUOUSLY
SEEK TO IMPROVE THEIR COMPETENCE IN RELEVANT
INSTRUCTION FOR ALL LEARNERS.

TABLE OF CONTENTS

INTRODUCTION

This book was developed primarily for use with the in-service educator especially the in-service teacher. The competencies and strategies for their acquisition have been developed and organized to enable the learners to take advantage of both theory and application learning situations. Alternative learning strategies for both theory and application experiences are presented for all competencies. Furthermore, specific criteria for the demonstration of proficiency in a competency is presented with the competency statement. Therefore, a learner may test out of a competency immediately and proceed to the next competency. If one does not possess a competency, then he or she should proceed to the enabling activities and select those activities which would provide him or her with the appropriate skills for acquisition of the competency.

The competencies are divided into three phases. The phases are sequential. (See Diagram 1)

Phase I competencies focus on our cultural pluralistic society. The major purpose of these competencies is to focus the learner's attention on the various diverse groups of peoples which constitute our society. Competency 1 Enabling Activities provide the learner with knowledge of the contributions of specific groups to our society. These specific groups are representative of ethnic groups, racial groups, and cultural groups. Competency 2 Enabling Activities should make the learner aware of the various cultural experiences that members of various groups have encountered in this country. That group membership determines your cultural experience. Competency 3 Enabling Activities point out the unequal inclusiveness of various groups in our society. However, one major purpose of these activities is to explore and examine the underlying reasons as to why there exists a discriminating inclusiveness of various groups, when it comes to sharing of power within our society.

The goal of Phase I competencies are the achievement of a knowledge based on group diversity, particularly, the differential treatment of various racial, ethnic, and cultural groups within our society.

In Phase II, the competency statements and enabling activities focus on the process of multicultural education (multiculturalism). Demonstration of the competencies are primarily via application (see Diagram 1) in the K-12 school structure. Specifically, attainment of a competency by the learner is through one of the school's pertinent parameters, i.e. curriculum, materials, environment, strategies, testing, and language. The importance of Phase II cannot be overstressed, for here the learner must begin to demonstrate an application level of achievement of all the competencies. For example, Competencies 4, 7, and 8 require the examination, analysis, and critique of existing school curriculum and materials that the learner utilizes in her or his professional position. Competency 5 requires a scrutiny of the various assessment instruments used in his or her professional activities.

In Competency 6, an examination of bilingual programmatic models is coupled with the learner being able to constructively analyze local programs as to their extent of multiculturalism.

Competency 10 accomplishment, the last one in Phase II, represents an internalization of the other competencies by the learner at least at Bloom's application level and possibly the synthesis and evaluation levels. This individual has a sound knowledge base (Phase I), which can be transmitted and applied (Phase II) successfully to the pertinent parameters of education, and will soon evolve an operational rationale in Phase III.

Phase III Competency Enabling Activities, with Phase I and II competencies, serve as a synthesizer for the learner. Therefore, the learner evolves a conceptualization of a rationale or model for multicultural education.

ASSUMPTIONS

Three assumptions are made of the learner before entry to the competencies: the learner is cognizant of
1) lesson planning and module or unit development,
2) various curriculum resources and materials available for a grade level or/and subject area,
3) a school's educational environment.

PHASE I

PHASE II

PHASE III

CULTURAL PLURALISTIC SOCIETY

MULTICULTURAL EDUCATION

MULTICULTURALISM

GROUPS OF PEOPLE
→ Contributions
→ Experiences
→ Inclusion

KNOWLEDGE

Acquire a knowledge of the cultural experience in both contemporary and historical setting of any two ethnic, racial, or cultural groups

Demonstrate a basic knowledge of the contributions of minority groups in America to our society

Assess relevance and feasibility of existing models that afford groups a way of gaining inclusion into today's society

K-12 STRUCTURE
→ Curriculum
→ Materials
→ Environment
→ Strategies
→ Testing
→ Language

APPLICATION

Identify current biases and deficiencies in existing curriculum and in both commercial and teacher-prepared materials of instruction

Recognize potential linguistic and cultural biases of existing assessment instruments and procedures when prescribing a program of testing for the learner

Acquire a thorough knowledge of the philosophy and theory concerning bilingual education and its application

Acquire, evaluate, adapt, and develop materials appropriate to multicultural education

Critique an educational environment to the extent of the measurable evidence of the environment representing a multicultural approach to education

Acquire the skills for effective participation and utilization of the community

Design, develop, and implement an instructional module using strategies and materials which will produce a module or unit that is multicultural, multiethnic, and multiracial

RATIONALE

Develop a rationale or model for the development and implementation of a curriculum reflective of cultural pluralism within the K-12 school and be able to defend it on a psychological, sociological, and cultural basis

DIAGRAM 1. Cognitive Competencies for Acquiring Multiculturalism

Copyright — Mira Baptiste and H. Prentice Baptiste, Jr.

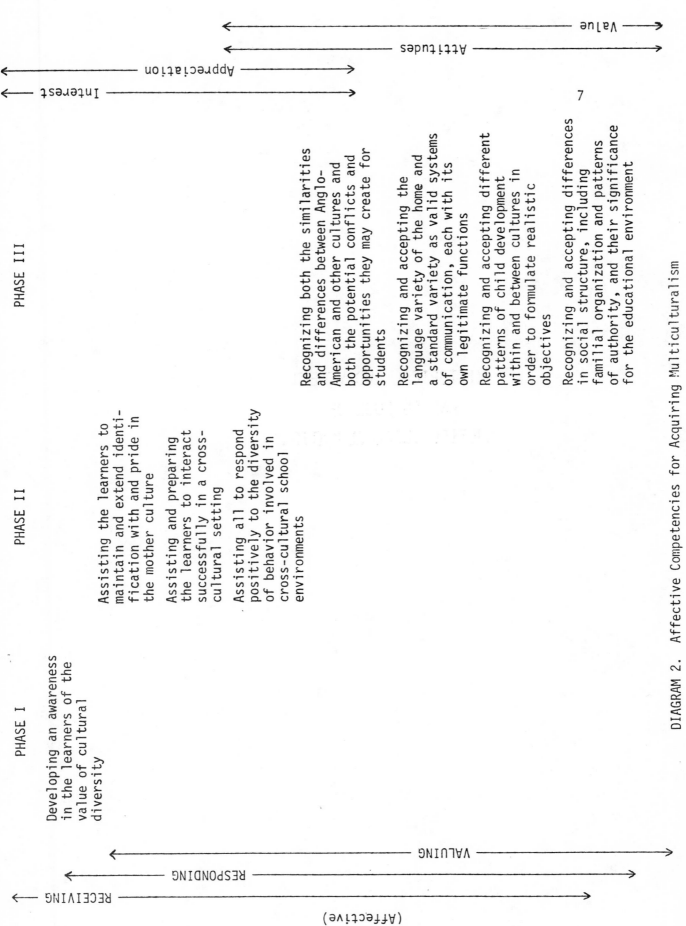

DIAGRAM 2. Affective Competencies for Acquiring Multiculturalism

The following text appears within the diagram:

Across the top (axes): Value — Attitudes — Appreciation — Interest

PHASE I

Developing an awareness in the learners of the value of cultural diversity

PHASE II

Assisting the learners to maintain and extend identi-fication with and pride in the mother culture

Assisting and preparing the learners to interact successfully in a cross-cultural setting

Assisting all to respond positively to the diversity of behavior involved in cross-cultural school environments

PHASE III

Recognizing both the similarities and differences between Anglo-American and other cultures and both the potential conflicts and opportunities they may create for students

Recognizing and accepting the language variety of the home and a standard variety as valid systems of communication, each with its own legitimate functions

Recognizing and accepting different patterns of child development within and between cultures in order to formulate realistic objectives

Recognizing and accepting differences in social structure, including familial organization and patterns of authority, and their significance for the educational environment

Along the left side (axes): RECEIVING — RESPONDING — VALUING

COMPETENCIES (Affective)

7

HISTORICAL EVOLVEMENT
AND PURPOSE OF
MULTICULTURAL EDUCATION

THE REKINDLING OF CULTURAL PLURALISM
H. Prentice Baptiste, Jr.

Introduction

Cultural Pluralism is not a new concept. As a sociological concept, it
has always existed in this country. Perhaps one would not be altogether wrong
in stating that its meaning has remained very much the same throughout its
usage.

In this chapter, I will discuss the historical evolvement of cultural pluralism, and comment on the pendulum support of the concept and its relationship
to multicultural education.

Before continuing, perhaps I should define or at least describe the concept of cultural pluralism. Cultural pluralism is a sociological concept which
describes a kind of relationship that should or does exist among several cultural groups which coexist within certain national geographic boundaries.
These cultural groups also share certain basic societal entitites such as socio-
political-economic systems, common values, and certain institutions. The primary
characteristics of this relationship are true recognition and respect for the
support of diversity among the cultural groups and within the groups. Although
cultural pluralism is thought of as describing the relationships among cultural,
ethnic or racial groups, by no means does it tend to ignore or subjugate the
individual to the group. In actuality, a recognition of the individual's group
will maximize the individual's potential and enhance his or her self-esteem
and self-worth. The cornerstone principles of cultural pluralism, i.e., equality,
mutual acceptance and understanding, and a sense of moral commitment focuses
on the intra- and intergroup relationships of individuals and their inherent
rights as ascribed by these principles of cultural pluralism (Baptiste and
Baptiste, 1977). Cultural Pluralism involves the mutual exchange of culture
within a state of equal co-existence in a mutually supportive system within
the framework of one nation of diverse groups of people with significantly
different patterns of belief, life style, color and language. Cultural pluralism
can only be achieved when there is unity through diversity.

The recognition of the cultural pluralistic nature of our nation was
espoused by Jane Addams[2] and Horace Kallen[3] and others during the 1800's. The
impetus for this recognition came from the newly arrived immigrants from southern

and eastern Europe. The approximately 40 million southern and eastern European immigrants consisting of Czechs, Moravians, Poles, Slovaks, Greeks, Jews, etc. highlighted the diversity of people constituting this country.

The concern of our national leaders during this time was how do we unify this diversity. The suggested solutions were (a) Cultural Pluralism (Addams, Kallen), (b) Assimilation (Melting Pot Idea, I. Zangwill), and (c) Americanization (E. Cubberly, T. Roosevelt).

It is my belief that each of these sociological concepts during the latter part of the 19th century had their strong proponents and followers. It is of interest that the real winner was never publicly attested to by the masses, and that the alleged winner was a psychological myth and the loser has since been strongly rekindled.

Americanization

The Americanization process (philosophy) had many distinguished individuals and national leaders as its proponents; namely, Benjamin Franklin (examine his common school philosophy),[4] Elwood Cubberly (educational historian),[5] Theodore Roosevelt (President of U.S.),[6] Madison Grant (author of The Passing of the Great Race),[7] and Henry Pratt Fairchild (sociologist).[8] The philosophy of the Americanization process was that there was only one model American - the Anglo-Saxon model. Benjamin Franklin in setting up the academic school was emphatic about English being the only institutional language. There was no debate as to what language (English), values (Anglo-Saxon), lifestyle (Anglo-Saxon) and history (Anglo-Saxon perspective or viewpoint) should be taught in school. Perhaps the essence of the Americanization process is best expressed by the following quote, taken from Cubberly's book, Changing Conceptions of Education:

> " ... After 1880, southern Italians and Sicilians, people from all parts of that medley of races known as the Austro-Hungarian Empire: Czechs, Moravians, Slovaks, Poles, Jews, Ruthenians, Croations, Servians (sic), Dalmatians, Slovenians, Magyars ... began to come in great numbers.

> "The southern and eastern Europeans are a very different type from the north Europeans who preceded them. Illiterate, docile, lacking in self-reliance and initiative and possessing none of the Anglo-Teutonic conceptions of law, order and government, their coming has served to dilute tremendously our national stock, and to corrupt our civic life ....

> "Our task is to break up their groups or settlements, to
> assimilate and to amalgamate these people as part of our
> American race, and to implant in their children, so far
> as can be done, the Anglo-Saxon conceptions of righteousness,
> law and order and popular government, and to awaken in them
> reverence for our democratic institutions and for those
> things in our national life which we as people hold to be of
> abiding worth."[9]

Cubberly's stature in the educational community led to an unquestionable acceptance of his ideas and beliefs. Educational systems operationalized his philosophy in an assimilation process of immigrants' children, which debased them of their cultural heritage as they were Americanized.

This process did not leave out their parents. Theodore Roosevelt[10] shared the xenophobic views of Cubberly and utilized his political influence to enhance the Americanization process. He denounced the idea of hyphenated Americans; i.e., Irish-Americans, Polish-Americans, etc. This he considered to be disloyal to the country, because he perceived it as holding allegiance to America and something else. His uncompromising position coerced many immigrants to forsake their heritage, their roots, for the new and "better life." The Americanization phenomenon was an assimilation process of Anglo-Saxon cultural imperialism.

Melting Pot

It only occurred on the stage and in the mind. Israel Zangwill's play, "The Melting Pot", revealed the myth which propelled the idea of creation of a new nation, a new culture, by the mutual mixing of the cultures of the diverse peoples who occupied this land. Zangwill's optimism as to what was socially occurring in this country is expressed by excerpt from his play:

> "It is the Fires of God round His Crucible. There she lies,
> the great Melting Pot - listen! Can't you hear the roaring
> and the bubbling? There gapes her mouth - her harbour where
> a thousand mammoth feeders come from the ends of the world
> to pour in their human freight. Ah, what a stirring and a
> seething! Celt and Latin, Slav and Teuton, Greek and Syrian -
> black and yellow - Jew and Gentile -
>
> "Yet, East and West, and North and South and the polar and
> the pine, the pole and the Equator, the crescent and the
> cross - how the great Alchemist melts and fuses them with
> his purging flame! Here shall they all unite to build the
> Republic of Man and the Kingdom of God. Ah, Vera, what is
> the glory of Rome and Jerusalem where all nations come to

> worship and look back, compared with the glory of America,
> where all races and nations come to labour and look forward!
> "Peace, peace to all ye unborn millions, fated to fill this
> great continent - the God of our children give you peace."[11]

Unfortunately, Zangwill's notion of the United States as a crucible for the parity mixing of the immigrants' diverse cultural ingredients, was just that: a psychological notion imprinted within the heads of the immigrants and others, thus tranquilizing them to the "Americanizing" process. The melting pot process was really a myth.

A myth because not everyone melted, and, also because there was never the intention for everyone to melt. Regardless of how you approach an analysis of the concept of the melting pot, i.e., culturally, educationally, politically, sociologically, and psychologically it was a myth. It was a myth yesterday, remains a myth today, and will continue as a myth tomorrow. Let's briefly examine this myth.

It was never the intention of the pseudo-founders of this country that the nationalistic goal would be that of a holistic culture formed from the equal contribution of the then various cultures of the diverse peoples of this land. This country was never viewed from a geo-cultural perspective (Cortes, 1976).[12] The various cultures were never dealt with on an egalatarian basis. Concomitantly, the customs, mores, norms, values and institutions of the various cultures were never treated equally by members of the emerging nation. Whereas some respective cultural parameters were accepted, others were ignored, vehemently rejected, or ridiculed.

One may ask what led to the overwhelming support of the melting pot assimilation philosophy? Perhaps it was a combination of societal and other conditions which led to its support. Approximately forty million immigrants were entering the United States searching for jobs, freedom from religious persecution and the pursuit of happiness. There was also a feeling among these immigrants of wanting to belong. Therefore, uncompromising allegiance on their part, demanded by others, was given without question. The threat of World War I further subsidized the pseudo-notions of the melting pot philosophy. Such outspoken critics as W. E. B. DuBois softened his stance during this period, and encouraged Blacks to cease their demands for civil rights as we (Blacks and whites) fight this common enemy. The brief period of postwar prosperity was followed by the Great Depression of the 1930's and then World

War II. Both of these world calamities tended to focus all our energies and attention on them. Furthermore, the political control of the "McCarthy Period" made it politically, socially, and criminally unhealthy to raise questions against the melting pot philosophy. The persecutions of some American citizens, for example - Japanese Americans as a potential wartime threat, Paul Robeson and W. E. B. DuBois for their outspokenness on civil liberties, deterred many citizens from attacking the melting pot or Americanism philosophies.

Rekindling of Cultural Pluralism

Perhaps the most significant catalysts to the emergence of cultural pluralism were the (1) 1954 Supreme Court decision, (2) the civil rights demonstrations by Black people, and (3) the civil rights legislation of 1964. The Supreme Court landmark decision on May 17, 1954 in the Brown vs. Topeka Board of Education case completely reversed the 1896 Plessy decision. The 1954 decision declared separate facilities as inherently unequal and unconstitutional. Therefore a legal death blow was dealt segregated schools.

The desegregation of public schools, perhaps unexpectedly, helped disclose the assimilation nature of the melting pot philosophy. The direct contact of Black and white students blatantly revealed the societal significance of one culture as compared to the other. Removal of the segregation veneer uncovered an anglo-centric, racist, biased educational system. The immorality of segregation, i.e., forced separation, had blinded many of us to our surreptitious assimilatory educational process. This educational system covertly and overtly stripped various groups of people of their humanity by making a mockery of their cultural customs, norms and values. It placed one group of people in a superior social position and others in an inferior position. It also systematically distributed knowledge in a manner that caused some groups to believe that they were intellectually inferior, that they had no history, no legitimate language and no worthy culture. Perhaps the realization of the educational system's pernicious character helped produce the rekindling of cultural pluralism.

However, on another front one cannot ignore the significance of Rosa Park's stance which was the spark that ignited the civil rights demonstrations. The struggles of Black people for equality in human interactions and civil rights were highlighted in the 1960's by effective conscious raising demonstrations - sit-ins, boycotts, marches, civil disobediences and revolution actions (riots). These demonstrations ran the gamut from the nonviolent bus boycott forged by the late Dr. Martin Luther King, Jr., to the violent riots which left Watts and many other ghetto areas in shambles. Perhaps the most momentous aspect of the 60's civil rights demonstrations was the emergence of a new spirit by Black people which transformed them from Negroes to Blacks or Afro-Americans. (The reader is referred to a publication entitled Black Rage by Grier and Cobbs for a thorough psychological analysis of the old Negro spirit.) The new spirit was ushered in by a conscious acceptance of self. An acceptance of Black culture was coupled with self-determination. This immediately led to a questioning of the educational process to which Black youngsters were being exposed. Thus Black people began demanding that the educational process must reflect them. Their culture, contributions and people must be included in the total educational process - i.e., curriculum, administration, policy, etc. This major attack on the educational process was another pivotal factor which contributed to the rekindling of cultural pluralism.

Accompanying this new psychological spirit of Black people was the timely passing by Congress of the Civil Right Act of 1964. The impact of the civil rights legislation cannot be overstressed for it legally provided the support for the recognition of certain rights of all individuals by stating that "No person in the United States shall on the ground of race, color, or national origin, be excluded from participation, be the benefits of, or be subjected to discrimination under any program or activity receiving federal financial assistance." This Act along with concomitant legislation, for example, the Ethnic Heritage Act and Title VII Bilingual Act led to a buttressing of cultural pluralism.

Other minority groups became caught up in the new spirit consciousness of Blacks. Cries of La Raza and Viva Chicanos were heard from some Hispanic groups. The push by LULAC and other Hispanic Groups for the recognition of Spanish as a legitimate language of instruction for their children gave credence to the existence of cultural pluralism in our society. The challenging of the Bureau of Indian Affairs by Native Americans on the education of their youth is another indicator of the acceptance of cultural pluralism over the melting pot or Americanism philosophy.

The 1970's have been characterized by the rise of ethnicity. Such popular books as Beyond the Melting Pot[13] and The Rise of the Unmeltable Ethnics[14] attest to this fact. Kenneth Clark made the following statement: "We really did not see the depth and complexity of Northern racism or anticipate that Black successes in the South would be at least partly responsible for rise of white ethnicity in Northern cities as other Americans became aware of their own inequities ...."[15] It is estimated that some sixty to eighty million Americans identify with an ethnic group. Several states have established educational agencies to study the cultural/ethnic heritage of their people. Texas[16] and Pennsylvania[17] have respectively reported thirty-one and fifty-two identifiable cultural/ethnic groups. In spite of the late sociologist Talcott Parson's prediction during the late 19th century that all ethnic groups would disappear or be melted away, this has not occurred.

Multicultural Education

The transferring of the recognition of our cultural pluralistic society into our educational system is multicultural education. The operationalizing of our educational system in such a fashion that it appropriately and in a rightful manner includes all racial, ethnic, cultural groups is multicultural education. Multicultural education must be regarded as a philosophy, as a process which guides the total education enterprise. At its most sophisticated level it will exist as a product, a process and a philosophical orientation guiding all who are involved in the educational enterprise.

CITED REFERENCES

[1]Baptiste, H. Prentice Jr. and Mira Baptiste, "Developing Multicultural Learning Activities," Carl Grant, ed. Multicultural Education: Commitments, Issues, and Applications. Washington, D.C. Association for Supervision and Curriculum Development, 1977, p. 105.

[2]Addams, Jane. Twenty Years of Hull House. New York: MacMillan Co., 1938.

_____. Democracy and Social Ethics. Cambridge, Mass.: Harvard University Press, 1902.

_____. The Second Twenty Years at Hull House. New York: The MacMillan Company, 1930.

[3]Kallen, Horace M. Cultural Pluralism and the American Idea. Philadelphia: University of Philadelphia Press, 1956.

[4]Franklin, Benjamin.

[5]Cubberly, Elwood. Public Education in the United States. Boston: Houghton Mifflin Co., 1947 (written in 1919).

[6]Roosevelt, Theodore. "Americanism" speech given in 1910.

[7]Grant, Maddison. The Passing of the Great Race. New York: Charles Scribner's Sons, 1916.

[8]Fairchild, Henry Pratt. The Melting Pot Mistake. Boston: Little, Brown and Company, 1926.

[9]Cubberly, Elwood. Changing Conceptions of Education. New York: Riverside Educational Mimeographs, 1909, as cited by Mark Krug, The Melting of the Ethnics. Bloomington: Phi Delta Kappan, 1976, p. 768.

[10]Roosevelt, Theodore. Speech "Americanism" given in 1910, as cited by Mark Krug, The Melting of the Ethnics. Bloomington: Phi Delta Kappan, 1976, p. 8.

[11]Zangwill, Israel. The Melting Pot. New York, 1909, as quoted in Oscar Handlin, Immigration as a Factor in American History. Englewood Cliffs, N.J.: Prentice-Hall, Inc., 1959, p. 150.

[12]Cortes, Carlos. "Need a Geo-Cultural Perspective in the Bicentennial," Educational Leadership, January, 1976, p. 290-292.

[13]Glazer, Nathan and Daniel P. Moynihan. Beyond the Melting Pot. Cambridge, Mass. The M.I.T. Press, 1970.

[14]Novak, Michael. _The Rise of the Unmeltable Ethnics_. New York: MacMillan
Publishing Co., 1973.

[15]"Blacks in America" in _U.S. News and World Report_, May 14, 1979, p. 49.

[16]People 5; September-October, 1975. Published by Institute of Texan Cultures,
San Antonio, Texas.

[17]Pennsylvania Ethnic Heritage Studies Dissemination Project. Bloomsburg State
College, Bloomsburg, Pennsylvania.

CHANGING CONCEPTIONS OF MULTICULTURAL EDUCATION
Geneva Gay

What is multicultural education? Is it a separate program, a unique course, a particular curriculum to be added to the other school offerings available to students? Or is it a process, a philosophical orientation, an instructional theory for the delivery of quality education? Is the most efficient way to implement multicultural education through a product or a process conceptualization?

These questions are neither trivia nor mere semantics. They are critical in that how a person or school district answers them represents a particular philosophy of education, and is indicative of their level of development relative to multicultural education. Their answers also create the parameters for the expressed forms--the programmatic articulations--multicultural education is likely to take in actual practice.

Initially, most people have conceived multicultural education as a separate program, whether it be a unit, a course, a lesson or some other particular body of content whose presence or absence is readily identifiable in school instructional offerings. Early advocates of multicultural education--and school practitioners who are faced with the daily routines and politics of implementing educational programs--tend to find this conception of multicultural education quite agreeable. They understand, only too well, the practical advantages of having "tangible" products to sell to taxpayers, politicians, parents, and other publics, as opposed to the difficulties inherent in selling educational theories and concepts that do not have sensory visibility, or are not materially tangible.

Some other people, however, conceptualize multicultural education broadly enough to encompass instructional methodologies, school climates, and assessment and evaluation procedures as well as curricula. They represent an "intermediate" stage in the conceptual development of multicultural education. Compared to the first group, these advocates are smaller in number but are more vocal in the professional arenas. Their perceptions of multicultural education tend to be more a broadening of the conceptual framework of the views

Reprinted from Educational Perspectives, December, 1977, published by University of Hawaii, Honolulu, Hawaii.

held by the pragmatists than a fundamentally different viewpoint. They talk about <u>systematic</u> change, but their targets and tools still emphasize "tangibles" --changing the composites and components of testing devices, classroom climates, curriculum alternatives, teaching styles, et cetera--such that they are inclusive of cultural and ethnic lifestyles, value systems, behaviors and habits. They function largely at a distance from K-12 classrooms, with conceptual and theoretical models as the planks of their espoused educational platforms. More frequently than not, they concentrate on <u>what</u> should be done and <u>why</u> it should be done. Their suggestions on <u>how</u> it should be done are based on ideological speculations and claims to professional judgment, as opposed to experiential data based upon insights derived from involvement in actual practice.

Still another school of thought on multicultural education is emerging. Its proponents are even less in number than the group described immediately above--but they are growing. They see multicultural education not as a single product, nor as a comprehensive program comprised of individual products, but as a certain orientation which permeates the entire teaching-learning enterprise. It is a process for changing the educational delivery system such that it excludes cultural diversity in all its dimensions and manifestations. It is a way of being and behaving in the context and act of teaching and learning that responds to the many aspects and expressions of cultural and ethnic diversity which exist in our schools and our society. To these educators, who might be described as philosophical eclectics, multicultural education is a pedagogy--a process of total educational reform--which aims to revolutionize the entire educational process, and revitalize the promise and potential of education for all students, whatever their ethnic identity and cultural backgrounds. They are evolutionary, philosophical trailblazers in that most of them have ascribed, at one time or another, to the beliefs of the other stages in the development of multicultural education, and have moved on to exploring new frontiers of conceptualization. Their current thinking is the result of developmental and progressional conceptual maturation.

These comments about the categorical conceptualizations of multicultural education are not intended to be unnecessarily critical or judgmental, or to pit one school of thought against another; they are intended merely to remind us of (1) the proverbial gap between theory and practice, between an idea conceptualized and an idea realized, in education; (2) to indicate the impracticality and impossibility of dichotomizing conceptualizations of multicultural education into mutually exclusive categories of "product" and "process" and (3) to create a more adequate contextual frame of reference for placing the wide diversity of multicultural programmatic efforts in better perspective. They also are offered as a reminder to us of the natural growth and developmental potential of educational ideas, trends and concepts.

In fact, multicultural education is both "product" and "process." This viewpoint has both descriptive and analytical utility for it can help us to understand the wide variety of programmatic activities in practice, recognize the relationship between the different theoretical conceptualizations of multicultural education, and comprehend the fact that, as a concept, multicultural education is developmental and emergent. For multicultural education to be conceived as "product" and "process" simultaneously, and to see both conceptions operating in existing programs are understandable phenomena. They are indicative of the tentativeness, the formativeness, and the differential developmental character of the concept. They also are indicative of the fact that different people enter the field of multicultural education at different points in time and with different levels of conceptual sophistication. Entry usually has occurred at the most rudimentary levels and conceptual movement beyond that point generally has been characterized by evolvement and developmental progression.

Thus, it is only natural that the conceptualizations of many of these people--and schools--who have been involved in the multicultural education movement since it began in the late 1960s have evolved from primary emphasis on the one-dimensional "product" to multi-dimensional "process." Too, some attrition has occurred, given that this is a phenomenon natural to the developmental process of educational trends and social programs; and multicultural education, when viewed from a broad operational perspective, has been characterized by staggered and overlapping differentiations, given the various developmental levels of the people conceptualizing, designing and implementing multicultural education programs.

How We Got Where We Are

The natural physiological maturation process of living organisms can be used as an analogy to explain the emerging character of multicultural education in the United States, and to understand its naturalistic conceptual movement from simple, fragmented units in the educational system, to more comprehensive

products to be incorporated in different instructional programs, to processes
for impacting upon the totality of the educational enterprise. Like living
organisms, multicultural education was "conceived and given birth;" it has
gone through the stages of "childhood," and is now into its "adolescent"
development. The time and conditions of its initial conception and "prenatal
formation" influence the subsequent character and course of the development
and implementation of multicultural education in school programs. At this
time, whether one conceives multicultural education primarily as "product" or
"process" is indicative of its "stage of development" and "age" of the idea
for that person. Although not mutually exclusive, three "stages" or phases
in the conceptual development of multicultural education are identifiable.

STAGE I

Various conceptions of multicultural education exist simultaneously among
educators throughout the country because of its differential stages of development. The idea of multicultural education was conceived initially in the
height of the 1960s civil rights movement and its demands for social and
political equity for ethnic minorities. Ethnic minorities "parented" the idea
and gave it its first "personality characteristics." In its infancy and early
childhood stage, multicultural education was conceptualized and shaped in terms
of "basic needs," one of which was: responding expediently to political
pressures. The primary purpose of the early programs was to improve self and
societal perceptions of ethnic minorities through the development of ethnic
and cultural consciousness. This stage was characterized by the appearance
of units, courses, programs and instructional materials, such as Black History,
Sociology of Mexican Americans, and Japanese-American Literature, which dealt
with factual information about the historical experiences and cultural contributions of ethnic minorities in America.

The first multicultural education programs were designed to be implemented
in only certain areas of the school curricula, and with specific student populations. Units and lessons on ethnic minorities were developed for inclusion
in secondary social studies and language arts curricula, and in university
departments of arts and sciences in the form of behavioral science, literature
and history courses. At the public-school level, the celebration of conventional holidays and heroic events was extended to encompass some of those

specific to different ethnic minority groups instead of being limited exclusively to Euro-American traditions. These changes appeared primarily as
additions and supplements to existing school programs, rather than as integral
parts of the core of the educational system.

The first multicultural education programs were student population-specific
and geographically or regionally-bound. By merely mentioning the names of
specific programs one could anticipate, with a high degree of accuracy, the
parts of the country and the ethnic composition of the student populations
where these were most likely to be found. For instance, courses in Mexican-
American History were found most predominately in public schools with large
concentrations of Mexican-American students in the Southwest, and courses about
Japanese Americans were rarely taught in schools except on the West Coast where
there were a sizeable number of Japanese-Americans students in attendance.
In higher education, though, the implementation patterns were somewhat different. Large, predominately white colleges and universities with relatively
small ethnic minority enrollments led the way in creating ethnic studies programs. Such programs usually occurred on campuses where ethnic student
organizations, such as the Black Student Unions, were politically active. It
is indeed appropriate to refer to these early experiments in multicultural
education as single-focused, product-oriented ethnic minority studies. A
cursory review of the literature on these programs of the late 1960s substan-
tiates this observation. The descriptive language used most consistently is
Black Studies, Mexican-American Studies, Asian-American Studies, et cetera.

STAGE II

The passage of time and the application of the natural laws of development
caused the conceptions, needs and purposes of multicultural education to take
on different meanings and forms. By 1970-71 a gradual shift in the conceptualization of multicultural education began to appear in the professional
literature. Like the intermediate stage of development for living organisms,
multicultural education became more "refined," its programs broadened in
complexity, and the concept became more definitive. More educators and a
greater variety of ethnic groups began to support the idea, more schools began
to participate in the venture, and emphasis began to center on incorporation
into existing programs. Advocates of multicultural education augmented their

original pleas by demanding that white students by included in the programs on
ethnic minorities, and that elementary students, too, receive instruction in
cultural diversity; that other parts of the school curricula, along with
language arts and social studies, be revised to accommodate multicultural
content; that multicultural education become an integral part of school experiences rather than being additive and supplementary; and that schools teach
about many different ethnic groups, instead of only those represented in their
student populations and immediate communities.

Therefore, the second phase of the conceptual development of multicultural
education can be described as serialized, or multiple, ethnic studies programs.
The focus of attention within the study of the separate ethnic groups was on
historical events, heroes and cultural contributions. The purposes of the
programs were to "set the historical records straight" by correcting the sins
of omission committed toward all ethnic minorities; to improve the self-
knowledge and self-concepts of students from a wide variety of ethnic groups
through the study of their historical experiences, and to help students acquire
valid information about ethnic groups other than their own as a means of combatting ethnic illiteracy, prejudices, racism and ethnocentrism, improving
social conditions, and increasing racial harmony.

STAGE III

Around 1973 some multicultural education advocates began operating on
the premise that the educative process, relative to cultural differences, must
encompass more than the mere acquisition of cognitive information, and culturally
pluralistic school programming must include more than instructional materials
and curriculum designs. Maximizing the learning potential of students requires
equal attention to instructional strategies and learning activities, the
environments in which they live and learn, the structural organization of the
school, and the institutional values, commitments and academic policy priorities
of schools. Thus, multicultural education must be conceived in gestalt or
eclectic terms.

This view of multicultural education recommends that students be exposed
to a broad range of multifaceted, interdisciplinary content and experiences
about many different ethnic groups, both minority and majority; that sensitivity and responsiveness to different ethnic lifestyles penetrate the core

and totality of the teaching-learning enterprise; and that culturally plural-istic content and perspectives be incorporated into all educational experiences, whether formal or informal, for all students in all grade levels. It argues that the effective implementation of multicultural education resides as much in teachers' attitudes, interpersonal relations with ethnic students, and instructional examples and techniques as with carefully conceptualized and well-planned multicultural curriculum designs. Similarly, the creation of classroom environments and school contexts which exhibit, prize and promote positive attitudes and values toward ethnic and cultural diversity is an indispensible component of a total or comprehensive approach to making education responsive to cultural pluralism. A "new process of education" instead of an "educational program" is a more fitting description of these conceptions of multicultural education.

The gestalt or eclectic view of multicultural education is based upon such fundamental principles as: every American belongs to some ethnic group; ethnicity is a critical determinant variable in the identification process of many Americans; America is indeed a culturally pluralistic society; pluralism is potentially a vital force in the personal and social growth of America and Americans, and the behavioral patterns, attitudes and values of individuals are reflective, to a large extent, of their ethnic experiences and cultural conditioning. It proclaims that the study of ethnicity and ethnic groups should include white ethnics--such as Polish Americans, Italian Americans, Irish Americans and Jewish Americans--as well as ethnic minorities. More atten-tion needs to be given to the cultural characteristics, value systems, the impact of socio-political problems and the status of different ethnic groups in American society in both historical and contemporary perspective. Con-certed efforts must be undertaken to change school structures, programs and processes to accommodate students from different ethnic backgrounds, and to interface school experiences with their "home experiences." School personnel need to do more careful cultural analyses of ethnic values, customs and expectations to determine and/or interpret the behavioral patterns of ethnic students within the context of schooling, and to more adequately prescribe appropriate learning experiences. The curriculum focus should be on process skill development, concept mastery, applicability of comparative analyses, and interdisciplinary, multiethnic examinations of socio-political events, problems, issues and situations. The goal of the eclectic conceptualization

of multicultural education is to develop skills necessary for facilitative
and total growth of ethnic students from different cultural backgrounds and
increase their social functional ability in our culturally pluralistic society.

Where Are We Now?

Eclectic, or process, conceptualizations of multicultural education are
on the incline today. Increasingly, it is being described as a new emergent
pedagogy that has the potential for reforming the entire educational process,
instead of as merely a separate program of studies to be taught. This pedagogy recognizes the viability of different ethnic lifestyles, and it advocates
being responsive directly to the needs and learning styles of a wide variety
of different ethnic students. It seeks to respond to demands for relevance,
developing individual potential, personalizing education, and providing equal
educational opportunities relative to ethnic students by matching teaching
styles and instructional alternatives with different ethnic learning styles,
value orientations and behavioral patterns.

Conceptualizing multicultural education as a process of educational reform
demands a systemic approach to total educational change. Changes in curricula,
staff training and professional development, instructional strategies, school
climates, and assessment/evaluation techniques are to occur conjunctively and
interactively such that each embraces multicultural content, sensitivities and
perspectives. These are implemented in relation to each other in order to
maximize their impact upon the total learning environment and experiences
available to students.

The focal point of multicultural education as instructional processing is
interpersonal interactions. How student-teacher and student-student relationships are structured, and the substantive quality of the interactions that take
place across ethnic and cultural group lines within the context of schools
form the core of multicultural teaching and learning. It is more important to
concentrate on how to teach and relate to students from different ethnic groups
than on what specific content about ethnic diversity and cultural differences
is taught and learned. Students, teachers, materials, and institutional policies
and programs are so sensitized to and embracing of cultural pluralism and
ethnic diversity that they radiate diversity as a natural modus operandi. This
diversity if reflected in communication exchanges, student-counselor relation-

ships, testing techniques, culturally-specific and ethnically-differentiated teaching strategies, learning options and alternatives, the physical plant of the school, the food served in the cafeteria, the bus ride to and from school, discipline techniques, curricular materials, et cetera.

The premises underlying these arguments are: (1) qualitative, rewarding and facilitative interethnic interactions among students and teachers require the application of multicultural knowledge and skills; (2) the natural emersion of students in multicultural contexts, environments and interactions during learning encounters broaden considerably the human growth potential of each individual; (3) the constant interweaving of ethnic and cultural diversity into all things done in the teaching-learning enterprise is a fait accompli of cultural pluralism valued, accepted and promoted, and (4) the probability of achieving instructional effectiveness with ethnically different students is heightened considerably by using data derived from cultural analyses of ethnic lifestyles and cultural conditioning to make decisions about educational programming.

The Promise of Multicultural Education as "Process"

We know that the public-school system of education in the United States has been disastrous for many ethnically-different students. It has not only been ineffective in helping them develop intellectual skills, but, in too many instances, has had a negative impact upon their self-esteem and psychological well-being. For too long schools have perpetrated the sins of society by making many ethnic students ashamed of their ethnicity and encouraging them, in both overt and subtle ways, to reject and/or deny it. Yet, emerging research indicate that however hard we may try to repress our ethnicity, it cannot be done entirely. Through life ethnicity continues to be a critical variable in our identification process, whether through affirmation or rejection. We also know that cultural conditioning and ethnic experiences are instrumental in determining the values, attitudes, behaviors, perceptions and relational styles exhibited by students from different ethnic groups. The new data emerging on ethnic lifestyles and cognitive learning patterns present convincing arguments that, although conflicts between different ethnic and cultural expectations and the normative systems of schools are inevitable, with knowledge, foresight and conscious planning these conflicts can be minimized, and ethnic experiences can be used as formative bases for instructional decision making on a broad

scale. This is the essence of the idea of multicultural education as a
process approach to educating culturally different students.

We have learned from experience that fragmented, single-dimensional
attempts at creating multicultural education programs are too limited in focus
and influence to bring about the wide-scale changes needed to have a significant impact on the quality of education available to students. Therefore, it
seems logical to posit that if we are to change the core and instructional
structure of the educational process such that they reflect and embrace ethnic
anc cultural diversity, we need to institute multifaceted, multidimensional,
comprehensive, systemic and interactive reform measures. Using a process
approach to multicultural education is a plausible strategy for guiding our
efforts in the achievement of this goal. One of its most attractive qualities
is that it demands that multicultural content and perspectives penetrate the
inner-core of all aspects of the educational enterprise, rather than multicultural education being an appendage, existing on the periphery of the institutional structures and instructional programs of our schools.

Anything less than a process conceptualization of multicultural education
as an instructional delivery system designed to affect the total educative
process, is prone to limited utility and rapid obsolescence.

The magnitude of the task of providing relevant qualitative educational
opportunities to all students, fully cognizant of their unique ethnic experiences, demands nothing less than a total approach to multicultural educational
reform. The recent explosion of knowledge on ethnic groups, ethnicity and
cultural diversity, the constant evolvement of multicultural school programming,
and the spread of the revitalization of ethnic consciousness among groups and
individuals in the United States overtax more restrictive conceptualizations
of multicultural education. Furthermore, multicultural education is still an
emergent concept and to view it as process provides the flexibility, the
elasticity and the adaptability needed to embrace new data, new analyses, new
interpretations and new experimentations which are bound to occur before it
reaches pedagogic maturity.

MULTICULTURAL EDUCATION: PURPOSE

Mira Baptiste and H. Prentice Baptiste, Jr.

Do you know anyone born in the United States -- student, friend, relative, colleague or acquaintance -- who is not glad, indeed proud, of being a citizen of this country? Do you know of anyone who has become a naturalized citizen of this country who regrets having done so? It is quite likely that you do not. This is true regardless of whether we limit the population under considertaion to black, Anglo, native, Mexican or other Americans. Surely, different people would give various reasons for their feelings about citizenship. Most such explanations however, would probably make reference to or may be explained by the Constitution of the United States, and all the rights and privileges that accrue to each of us as citizens, by virtue of that great instrument.

If the above be true, then it follows that all of us are assured and provided equal rights, liberties, freedoms, and educational as well as occupational opportunity, plus a certain measure of understanding and compassion for and by our fellow man. Do you agree? Indeed, we all know that this is not true. Our recent experiences in communication have compelled us to realize that we have to come to terms with the cultural heterogeneity of our society in the face of a massive institutional system which defies the validity of this heterogeneity if not its very existence. Ways must be devised to give the culturally different in this country honor and respect for those aspects of their own cultures which are consistent with the universal right to human dignity and self-realization and not solely a demeaning adaptation to cultural domination by the majority and the powerful.

The mono-curriculum character has historic roots in the "melting pot" phenomenon. It emanated from the beliefs and values of such men as Thomas Jefferson, Benjamin Franklin and others whose philosophy engendered the common experiences educational system which would provide the young colony with a prideful, strong culture. The purpose of this unique American culture, emanating from the diverse ethnic groups, was to fuse the loosely attached colonies into a strong confederacy. That goal was accomplished over a period of time. This phenomenon tended to glorify the contributions of other

Reprinted from Mano a Mano, Vol. 3, No. 4, August, 1974.

ethnic groups.

An example is the development of the "American dialect" which contains many phrases and words which were borrowed from other languages. Many new words were invented by the people in terms of combining words from many ethnic dialects.

Today some of these phrases and words are more acceptable than others. One can observe the majority of the unacceptable words are those emanating from minority groups. By all rights, the American myth tells us, the culturally different should have melted into the mainstream long ago. The observation of the variety of speaking behaviors in different cultures in America dispels this myth. More significant, however, is that growing numbers of people who have not melted are happy they did not, and they want an end to every sort of effort, covert as well as overt, to force them into the pot as a price for their bowlful of the American dream.

The United States is a culturally plural society, a political aggregate with a wide variety of life-styles in its midst. In such a state of cultural pluralism, the result is the subordination by one group of all others, creating great ambivalence on the part of these others in regard to their own life-styles. This ambivalence on the part of the minority group members occurs because they are constantly reminded of their subordinate status through the imposition of a negative stereotype image on them by the dominant group. This does not eliminate the culture of the subordinate groups, but it does provide socio-psychological complications.

The significance and timely relevance of this problem cannot be overstated. As Dr. Banks stated, "Our society is becoming increasingly polarized and dehumanized, largely because of institutional racism and ethnic hostility. The elimination of conflicts between the races must be our top priority for the seventies." A distinct contributor to institutional racism in education is the continuation of mono-cultural, mono-racial, mono-ethnic characterized curriculum programs for preschool learners to advanced graduate learners. This very ethnocentric nature of curricula counters Abrahams and Troike's description of the United States as a culturally plural society, a political aggregate with a wide variety of life-styles in its midst. Subsequently mono-characterized curricular programs contribute to the oppression by one group of all others, and subsequently contribute to the ambivalence of the minority as to their human worth.

Among American educators today there is a growing consciousness that revolutionary action needs to be taken to make school experiences meaningful for students whose racial, social, religious, and cultural backgrounds are different from those of so called mainstream students. But the problem of materials looms very large. Each segment of the program of studies in our schools deserves the opportunity to examine itself for the degree of diversity in its emphasis. This examination should include the nature and use of curriculum materials as well as teaching methodology. This action must be extended to content, process and evaluation.

Learners must be taught through a diversified, cultural pluralistic approach that differences are to be appreciated rather than challenged. Inclusion of minorities (of all descriptions) into the curricular program helps to bring about that appreciation. Historically, writers and publishers have excluded the records and accomplishments of outstanding Afro-Americans, Mexican Americans, and other minorities whose contributions helped to shape America and to make it the great nation our schools teach that it is. In our efforts to make instruction responsive to the needs of all learners, the total system stands to gain greater efficiency and creativity. The change will most certainly not be a painless one, for it requires deep conscious rethinking by educators. It will entail radical innovative measures, experimentation, demonstration and leadership on the part of educational agencies.

 'ENCOURAGING MULTICULTURAL EDUCATION

The ASCD Multicultural Education Commission

ASCD's commitment to multicultural education emanates from the realities of life in the United States. It also emerges from the Association's consistent affirmation of democratic processes and humanistic ideals.

We live in a culturally pluralistic society. With the increasing complexity and interdependence of economic, political, and social affairs, similarities and differences among cultural groups become more pronounced. A single national culture is no longer acceptable as a feasible concept for educational processes and interpersonal behavior. A dynamic realignment of political and economic power among various interest groups in our country and among world nations emphasizes the need for increased understanding of ourselves and others.

Attempts to understand "other" people and bases for "others'" decisions, intentions, and values must be broadened beyond historically mono-cultural perspectives. Shifting balances of power reduce abilities of adherents of the dominant culture to control their own destinies, as well as those of "others." This fact certainly necessitates a deeper reexamination of "others" if we are to understand and coexist with them. Life in a culturally pluralistic society requires fundamental changes in educational philosophies, processes, and practices. We might consider these as basic needs for human renewal.

An initial step toward human renewal must emphasize that many different cultures exist in the United States. It must also include a recognition of their right to exist, and an acceptance of the fact that they represent humanity's potential in a very altruistic sense.

Human renewal must further recognize the validity and viability of cultural diversity. As educators, we must strive to understand cultural pluralism and develop an empathy for more than the obvious "trappings" that might characterize a culture. It is therefore time to translate our concern for individual development into the more difficult task of understanding individuals within the

---

Reprinted from Educational Leadership, January 1977.

context of their cultural group experiences.

As we accept the realities of cultural pluralism, a growing recognition of the worth, dignity, and integrity of each individual becomes defined in behavior - in the cultural context of each individual. Thus, our concern for maximizing individual development of human potential must increasingly be viewed as a continually emerging and evolving one, shaped by different cultural contexts, which nourish the growth and development of the individual. There is no single criterion of human potential applicable to all. Instead, complex and varied sets of coherent values, motives, attitudes, and attributes - which determine behavior patterns - exist among cultural groups. Added to this is the effect of economic, political, and social racism toward nonwhite minority groups. All of these factors must be considered in our efforts to design opportunities for educational experiences that will maximize human dignity and potential for all individual students.

Different cultural and social environments have determining influences on individual perception and behavior. Two such environments are our early-life experiences and our technological society. The earliest associations of a child form the basis of his/her cultural heritage. Cultural heritage is the essence of relationship patterns, linguistic and expressive communication, and the fundamental values and attitudes through which each child grows. To ignore, or invalidate this living experience for any individual is, in effect, to distort and diminish the possibilities for developing that person's potential.

The growing impact of the complexity of life in our highly technological and industrialized society necessitates recognition of cultural pluralism, and should foster active efforts for its positive perpetuation. We are all in danger of being alienated, bureaucratized, and depersonalized by the rationality of the ethos of industrial technology. Not only are ethnic minorities being deculturalized and dehumanized, but _all_ of us are being sized and fitted to sets of specifications that are essentially depersonalizing, and destructive to human individuality. In a very real sense, members of the majority culture or dominant segment of society are just as invalidated as _individuals_ as are members of minority groups and cultures. All face the superstructure of technical-industrial-economic rationality. Cultural pluralism emerges not only as a social fact, but also as a positive ideal to preserve the integrity of all individuals. It is necessary for the development of a more humane society through democratic processes.

Definition

ASCD's commitment to cultural pluralism evolves from a concern for more valid educational futures, and a realization of the social and cultural changes taking place in our society. Cultural pluralism is neither the traditionalist's separatism nor the assimilationist's melting pot. It is a composite that recognizes the uniqueness and value of every culture. Cultural pluralism acknowledges that no group lives in isolation, but that, instead, each group influences and is influenced by others.

In educational terms, the recognition of cultural pluralism has been labeled "multicultural education." The essential goals of multicultural education embrace: (a) recognizing and prizing diversity; (b) developing greater understanding of other cultural patterns; (c) respecting individuals of all cultures; and (d) developing positive and productive interaction among people _and_ among experiences of diverse cultural groups.

Multicultural education, as interpreted by ASCD, is a humanistic concept based on the strength of diversity, human rights, social justice, and alternative life choices for all people. It is mandatory for quality education. It includes curricular, instructional, administrative, and environmental efforts to help students avail themselves of as many models, alternatives, and opportunities as possible from the full spectrum of our cultures. This education permits individual development in any culture. Each individual simultaneously becomes aware that every group (ethnic, cultural, social, and racial) exists autonomously as a part of an interrelated and interdependent societal whole. Thus, the individual is encouraged to develop social skills that will enable movement among and cooperation with other cultural communities and groups.

Multicultural education is a continuous, systematic process that will broaden and diversify as it develops. It views a culturally pluralistic society as a positive force that welcomes differences as vehicles for understanding. It includes programs that are systematic in nature; that enhance and preserve cultural distinctions, diversities, and similarities; and that provide individuals with a wide variety of options and alternatives.

Multicultural education goes beyond an understanding and acceptance of different cultures. It recognizes the right of different cultures to exist, as separate and distinct entities, and acknowledges their contribution to the societal entity. It evolves from fundamental understandings of the interaction of divergent cultures <u>within</u> the culture of the United States. If multicultural education is to achieve its goals, the concepts that constitute its foundations must pervade the educational experiences of <u>all</u> students.

The concepts of multicultural education seem rather familiar - and they are. What is new is contextual in nature, a sifting and winnowing to understand these goals in cultural terms. What previously seemed appropriate goals in terms of <u>individuals</u> now gain in perspective by looking at individuals in the context of cultural realities (including both origins and experiences).

The major application factor for multicultural education concerns the quality of the interaction - that which characterizes content and context of the school in relation to each child's unique cultural group reality. The critical commitment must be to <u>diversification</u>, since without this acceptance and its deliberate advancement, there is little hope of building greater understanding or greater respect for individuals. Therefore, the heart of multicultural education pertains to the interactional dimensions of human behavior, and the development of effective skills to facilitate such functioning. Multicultural education can be addressed by the type of interaction that is encouraged and structured in the schools' curricula and environment. It includes the broadest range of potential human interaction, both in content and context.

Multicultural education emphasizes the development of communication skills to enable cross-cultural and inter-ethnic group interaction. It endorses the development of perceptual, analytical, and application skills, which can be applied in both formal and informal, personal and institutional settings. It also places a high priority on developing abilities to make dependable, responsible decisions, and to gain, maintain, and exercise political power. The concern for multicultural education is fundamentally a concern for maximizing individual ability - to use communicative and interactional skills to improve the quality of life in a culturally pluralistic, multiracial, and highly technological society.

Application

In practical terms, ASCD's application of multicultural education calls for an examination of educational content and processes. ASCD's goals include the creation and advancement of understanding, along with a respect for

differences that can lead to an altruistic development of human potential.[35]
A number of suggestions are apparent at both content and process levels. The
following suggestions are clearly illustrative and are not intended to be
comprehensive:

    1. Examine text materials for evidence of racism, classism, sexism, and
realistic treatment of cultural pluralism in American society.

    2. Develop new curricula for all levels of schooling - curricula that
enhance and promote cultural diversity.

    3. Provide opportunities to learn about and interact with a variety of
ethnic groups and cultural experiences.

    4. Include the study of concepts from the humanistic and behavioral
sciences, which are applicable for understanding human behavior.

    5. Organize curricula around universal human concerns, which transcend
usual subject-matter disciplines; bring multicultural perspectives to bear
in the study of such issues.

    6. Broaden the kinds of inquiry used in the school to incorporate and
facilitate the learning of more humanistic modes of inquiry.

    7. Create school environments that radiate cultural diversity.

    8. Maximize the school as a multicultural setting, with the idea of
utilizing the positive contributions of all groups to accomplish common tasks
and not just to reduce deficiencies for the deprived.

    9. Recognize and utilize bilingualism as a positive contribution to the
communication process, and include bilingual programs of instruction for monolingual children.

    10. Examine rules, norms, and procedures of students and staff with the
purpose of facilitating the development of learning strategies and techniques
that do not penalize and stigmatize diversity, but rather, encourage and prize
it.

    11. Institute a system of shared governance in the schools, in which all
groups can enter equally in the learning and practice of democratic procedures.

    12. Organize time, space, personnel, and resources to facilitate the
maximum probability and flexibility of alternative experiences for all youngsters.

    13. Institute staffing patterns (involving both instructional and non-
instructional positions) that reflect our culturally pluralistic and multiracial society.

    14. Design and implement preservice and in-service programs to improve
staff ability to successfully implement multicultural education.

"NO ONE MODEL AMERICAN"
A STATEMENT ON MULTICULTURAL EDUCATION

In an action reflecting its commitment to alleviating social problems through education, the American Association of Colleges for Teacher Education established the Commission on Multicultural Education. The Commission, formed in the aftermath of the Kent State and Jackson State tragedies, is the outgrowth of the Association's long history of involvement in building a more effective and humane society through the betterment of teacher education.

The Multicultural Statement is a significant product of the Commission's work. The Statement, which was adopted officially in November, 1972, by the AACTE Board of Directors, was prepared for AACTE, its member insitutions, and other centers of higher learning as a guide for addressing the issue of multicultural education.

Commission members caution that the term "multicultural" is not a euphemism for "disadvantaged." Rather, the Statement encompasses broad ethnic and cultural spheres.

The Statement, a product of Commission interaction with a number of higher education institutions and personnel, is presented here in the interest of improving the quality of society through an increased social awareness on the part of teachers and teacher educators.

Text of Multicultural Statement

Multicultural education is education which values cultural pluralism. Multicultural education rejects the view that schools should seek to melt away cultural differences or the view that schools should merely tolerate cultural pluralism. Instead, multicultural education affirms that schools should be oriented toward the cultural enrichment of all children and youth through programs rooted to the preservation and extension of cultural alternatives. Multicultural education recognizes cultural diversity as a fact of life in American society, and it affirms that this cultural diversity is a valuable resource that should be preserved and extended. It affirms that major education institutions should strive to preserve and enhance cultural pluralism.

To endorse cultural pluralism is to endorse the principle that there is no one model American. To endorse cultural pluralism is to understand and appreciate the differences that exist among the nation's citizens. It is to see these differences as a positive force in the continuing development of a

---

Reprinted from AACTE brochure, "No One Model American."

society which professes a wholesome respect for the intrinsic worth of every
individual. Cultural pluralism is more than a temporary accommodation to
placate racial and ethnic minorities. It is a concept that aims toward a
heightened sense of being and of wholeness of the entire society based on the
unique strengths of each of its parts.

Cultural pluralism rejects both assimilation and separatism as ultimate
goals. The positive elements of a culturally pluralistic society will be
realized only if there is a healthy interaction among the diverse groups which
comprise the nation's citizenry. Such interaction enables all to share in
the richness of America's multicultural heritage. Such interaction provides
a means for coping with intercultural tensions that are natural and cannot be
avoided in a growing, dynamic society. To accept cultural pluralism is to
recognize that no group lives in a vacuum--that each group exists as part of
an interrelated whole.

If cultural pluralism is so basic a quality of our culture, it must become
an integral part of the educational process at every level. Education for
cultural pluralism includes four major thrusts: (1) the teaching of values
which support cultural diversity and individual uniqueness; (2) the encouragement of the qualitative expansion of existing ethnic cultures and their incorporation into the mainstream of American socioeconomic and political life; (3)
the support of explorations in alternative and emerging life styles; and (4)
the encouragement of multiculturalism, multilingualism, and multidialectism.
While schools must insure that all students are assisted in developing their
skills to function effectively in society, such a commitment should not imply
or permit the denigration of cultural differences.

Educational institutions play a major role in shaping the attitudes and
beliefs of the nation's youth. These institutions bear the heavy task of
preparing each generation to assume the rights and responsibilities of adult
life. In helping the transition to a society that values cultural pluralism,
educational institutions must provide leadership for the development of
individual commitment to a social system where individual worth and dignity
are fundamental tenets. This provision means that schools and colleges must
assure that their total educational process and educational content reflect a
commitment to cultural pluralism. In addition, special emphasis programs must
be provided where all students are helped to understand that being different
connotes neither superiority nor inferiority; programs where students of various

social and ethnic backgrounds may learn freely from one another, programs that help different minority students understand who they are, where they are going, and how they can make their contribution to the society in which they live.

Colleges and universities engaged in the preparation of teachers have a central role in the positive development of our culturally pluralistic society. If cultural pluralism is to become an integral part of the educational process, teachers and personnel must be prepared in an environment where the commitment to multicultural education is evident. Evidence of this commitment includes such factors as a faculty and staff of multiethnic and multiracial character, a student body that is representative of the culturally diverse nature of the community being served, and a culturally pluralistic curriculum that accurately represents the diverse multicultural nature of American society.

Multicultural education programs for teachers are more than special courses or special learning experiences grafted onto the standard program. The commitment to cultural pluralism must permeate all areas of the educational experience provided for prospective teachers.

Multicultural education reaches beyond awareness and understanding of cultural differences. More important that the acceptance and support of these differences is the recognition of the right of these different cultures to exist. The goal of cultural pluralism can be achieved only if there is full recognition of cultural differences and an effective educational program that makes cultural equality real and meaningful. The attainment of this goal will bring a richness and quality of life that would be a long step toward realizing the democratic ideals so nobly proclaimed by the founding fathers of this nation.

CULTURAL PLURALISM

Competency 1. Acquire a knowledge of the cultural experience in both
a contemporary and historical setting of any two ethnic,
racial, or cultural groups.

Competency 2. Demonstrate a basic knowledge of the contributions of
minority groups in America to our society.

Competency 3. Assess relevance and feasibility of existing models that
afford groups a way of gaining inclusion into today's
society.

COMPETENCY 1

Acquire a knowledge of the cultural experience in both a contemporary and historical setting of any two ethnic, racial, or cultural groups.

RATIONALE:

An individual's treatment (mistreatment), opportunity (lack of opportunity), and acceptability (nonacceptibility), are to a great extent determined by his or her racial, cultural, and/or ethnic group membership. Various racial, ethnic, and cultural groups within the United States have been treated differently. Subsequently, various coping mechanisms (cultural experiences) have evolved which are group identifiable. Thus educators must be familiar with the diverse nature of cultural experiences and the positive role these experiences may occupy in the instructional process.

An understanding of culture and its parameters is of foremost importance for teachers wanting to work effectively with diverse populations in their classrooms. Teachers must regard cultural diversity as an asset, not a problem. They must be able to respect and thus to teach all the children in their classes.

Instructional Objectives:

1. The learner will be able to identify and describe the major ethnic and minority groups in the United States.

2. The learner will identify the visible minority groups and describe the cultural experience of at least two of these groups.

3. _____

_____

_____

Enabling Activities:

1. Read: H. Prentice Baptiste, Jr., Multicultural Education: A Synopsis, Houston, Texas: University of Houston, 1976, pages 3-17.

2. View: Filmstrip "What is an Ethnic Group?" which provides a complete yet comprehensive definition of ethnicity. Educational Design, Inc., 1975.

3. *Read: Nelson Brooks, Parameters of Culture, F L News Exchange, Connecticut State Department of Education, February, 1973.

4. Participate in a Simulation Game "Bafa-Bafa" as a Learning Activity in Class. R. Gary Shirts, Simile II, P. O. Box 910, Del Mar, California 92014.

*Indicates readings that are included in the text; will be used throughout the competencies.

5. Attend and participate in class seminar on "What is Multicultural Education?"

6. _____

_____

_____

7. _____

_____

_____

Assessment of Competency:

Since Competency 1 and 2 are so closely related, the demonstration will utilize the objectives of both. Continue on to Competency 2.

Instructional Notes From Class Meetings:

Date Competency Achieved _____

PARAMETERS OF CULTURE

Nelson Brooks

. . . What is culture? For a century now, both the scientists and the humanists have been clutching this word to their breasts, each group claiming it insistently as its own, but attaching quite different meanings to it. One group, following E. B. Tylor, says that culture is everything, while the other, following Matthew Arnold, insists that culture is the best of everything. Now, it can hardly be both! Faced with such a dilemma, logic turns away in dismay. Into this field of confusion enters the language teacher who would seriously like to know what culture is so that he may teach something about it to his students. . . .

Culture. Culture is the distinctive life-way of a people, whether tribesmen, townsmen or urbanites, who are united by a common language. The dual nature of culture links the thoughts and acts of the individual to the common patterns acceptable to the group. The community provides rules and models for belief and behavior, and these cannot be disregarded by the individual without penalty. The totality of the culture is the pervading medium that gives meaning to each individual's acts, yet his capacity for innovation, choice, and rejection is never lost sight of. . . .

. . . AN ANALOGY: Culture is the root, the stem and the branch, while civilization is the branch, the leaf and the blossom. . . . . . . .CULTURE relates us to our environment, to our animal life, and to each other . . . . CULTURE establishes our emotional bonds, our beliefs and our prejudices, and imposes patterns to which we are pressured to conform. . . .

. . . The elements of culture are not countable or measurable as are the inhabitants of a town or the tax dollars on real estate. In fact, as Clyde Kluckhohn points out, we do not actually see culture at all, any more than we see the wind. What we see are its effects. Where are we to look for the expression and the totality of these effects? How can we provide a reliable general impression? This may be done by seeking out salient points in personal thought and behavior at which the effects that are of interest to us become discernible. The features they present will soon become apparent.

Reprinted from FL News Exchange, Connecticutt State Department of Education, February 1973.

Such an inventory as the one given herewith could scarcely be satisfying to specialists in the field of cultural anthropology, yet it can presume to provide a useful and reasonable perspective for the needs of the language learner.

These salient points I propose to call PARAMETERS. A brief explanation will make our use of this word clear. A PARAMETER is a constant that has a given value in one context but a different one in another. A good way to grasp our meaning of "parameter" is to consider the musical note A above middle C as written in the treble clef. This note, when played on the piano, produces one result, when played on the violin, a different one, and when sung by the human voice, still another. Yet the pitch, 440 cycles per second, remains the same. The PARAMETERS listed herewith are important focal points in the thought and life of all the communities we study, but their expression will differ accordingly to the culture being observed. We have, therefore, a single instrument that can be employed in many quite different situations.

Like language itself, culture is a double-ended nexus with an individual at one end and the social group at the other. Because of this, we need to keep in mind the various social institutions to which the individual relates. Thus we can discern the interplay of forces that makes each person into what he is. Our first list contains 25 Parameters of Culture, with emphasis upon the individual. This emphasis is, of course, congenial to the language teacher. For, apart from singing and speaking in chorus (we do relatively little of this as the weeks go by), the production of language is an individual act, though related in the most absorbing way with the effect our words have upon the person or persons addressed.

Parameters of Culture (Emphasis on the Personal)

1. Presence. How we appear, how we move about, what we sound like (regardless of what we are wearing or what we are saying) may be termed presence. Poise, glance, angle of chin, gait, voice quality, smile, laughter, all are highly personal matters, yet they are to a great extent affected by the culture in which we live and our position in it.
2. Language. Language makes culture possible. Born with the capacity for language, the infant is able to learn it only through contact with those who already know it; it soon becomes and remains an inseparable part of

himself. A person's place in his culture depends in great part upon his knowledge of and his use of language.

3. <u>Gesture</u>. Bodily movements, as of the head and hands, frequently accompany and reinforce speech and often are used alone. The meaning of gestures, like that of language, is specific to the culture in which they occur.

4. <u>Time Concept</u>. Every culture has traditional ways of measuring time: these, after language, comprise one of the earliest learnings. Whether or not the individual is ahead of time or on it or behind it generally relates to the importance attached to this concept in his culture.

5. <u>Space Concept</u>. One aspect of the space concept concerns the place of our birth and childhood and the location of our established home. Cultural patterns tend to respect and encourage this tie between self and land. Another such aspect is the distance, small or great, between persons in friendly dialogue. This distance, specific to a given culture, is learned without awareness when very young.

6. <u>Bonding</u>. Ties that bind a person to his family, to his friends, to mates of many kinds: class-, team-, room-, soul-, and others, to religion, to political party, to the home land--all these are found at the very core of culture. Bonding begins at birth and continues throughout life. Said Ruth Benedict: "Culture is that which binds men together."

7. <u>Learning</u>. Learning may be formal or informal. Although to a great extent artificial, formal learning is directly related to the refinement of culture into the high civilization we know and of which we are a part. Learning of both kinds enables the individual in the shortest possible time to understand, to become competent in and to take his place in his culture.

8. <u>Health</u>. Health, or soundness of mind and body, is both a personal and a public affair. From the commonest greetings to the most advanced medical research, concern for health is an enduring preoccupation.

9. <u>Resilience</u>. Personal recovery from adversity, from the shocks that flesh is heir to, is a reaction for which culture affords substantial and creative patterns, illustrating the interplay of self and society.

10. <u>Spirit</u>. Basically, spirit may be taken as the conscious awareness of being alive. Spirit is no doubt the ultimate inner mystery for every person, but the terms of its possible understanding are furnished by his culture.

11. <u>Play and Leisure</u>. Play is not only exercise for recreation or diversion. It is also a way for the young to learn their part in the intricate mazes of culture. Ways of spending leisure time, when one is freed from the demands of work or labor, are generously patterned by and are very characteristic of a given culture.

12. <u>Ethics</u>. Knowledge of what is right and wrong in human conduct is not innate but is learned by each person in contact with the culture about him. Models for honesty, fair play, principles, and moral thought and practice surround him, with which he is expected to comply.

13. <u>Esthetics</u>. No culture fails to provide for the expression of beauty and for pleasure in observing it. In literature, both oral and written, in painting, in music, in architecture, in the dance (apparently the oldest of the arts), man has sought gracefulness of gesture and line, harmony of color and sound, depth of feeling and nobility of idea. Ideals of beauty differ, often greatly, and the talent for its expression is unevenly shared. Yet the universal human delight in refinement of rhythm, color, mood, and thought is not to be denied.

14. <u>Values</u>. Values imply alternatives, comparison and preference. Given man's nature and his ability to symbolize, the options available to him seem to be innumerable. Values can be both positive and negative: cleanliness, freedom, education, or cruelty, crime, blasphemy. Values are manifest in ideals, in customs, and in institutions; they underlie ethics and esthetics. In no other area is the individual more sensitive to the models offered by his culture than in values.

15. <u>Religion</u>. Religion is always to be found at the base of social structure. Every child begins his encounter with the divine and the supernatural very early in life. No matter how his reactions to these may change and modify as he grows older, religion will continue to have a distinct effect upon his thought and action.

16. <u>Heroes and Myths</u>. Typical of any culture are its unique heroes who are known to everyone. Typical also are its myths, traditional, or legendary stories about supposed beings or events, dealing with the creation of the world and of man.

17. <u>Sex Roles</u>. Awareness of whether one is boy or girl comes early in life and deepens as the years go by. The kind of life each of us leads is largely decided by sex. Although food, books and music, for example,

are virtually the same for everybody, this cannot be said of clothing or language or careers. How each individual views, understands, relates to and esteems the other sex is a matter of inner tendency and cultural codes of permission, expectation and requirement.

18. Tabu. There are places to which one may not go, words one may not say, gestures one may not make, articles of clothing one may not wear (or fail to wear) on pain of strong disapproval or severe punishment--these are tabu. Of course, tabus can be deliberately broken; this is the cheapest way to draw attention to oneself. Repeated violations can weaken a tabu. But the original force behind a tabu was very strong; a supernatural power was sure to punish. Today tabus are still to be reckoned with in any culture.

19. Grooming. Clothing, hair style, shaving, cosmetics, ornaments, uniforms, and the like are personal variables that relate to age, sex, occasion, time of day, weather, occupation and social status. Culture formulates and dictates these, permitting personal preference only within limits that are clearly established.

20. Ownership. Ownership is of the essence to the individual. To have what is one's own, whether it is an idea, or an emotion, a privilege or a thing, is of great importance to the self. Cultural patterns have a strong influence over the possession of rights and properties as well as of loyalties and beliefs.

21. Subsistence. Food, drink, sleep, shields against the weather and protection against destroyers small and great--those are the essentials of life. A prime factor in culture is to provide these for the individual in infancy and childhood, then to expect him to assume responsibility for them as he matures and, in turn, to aid in supplying them for the next generation. How this is accomplished is a most characteristic feature of any culture.

22. Precedence. Who leads, who follows and in what order, who has the first choice, who takes what is left, who is oldest, strongest, brightest, most important, most imposing, most beautiful, most popular, most honored-- all these questions must find an answer whether at a doorway, a dinner, a beauty contest, or an election. Culture tends to establish fixed patterns for these circumstances in which the individual assumes his relative position.

23. <u>Ceremony</u>. Ceremonies have long been immensely popular with human beings; culture prescribes the manner in which they are to be performed. What the individual is to say, wear, and do tends to be fixed, whether at a wedding, a graduation, a funeral, a religious service, or a new year's celebration.

24. <u>Rewards and Privileges</u>. A reward is a recompense for merit, service, or achievement. A privilege is a legal or personal advantage gained by birth, social position, effort or concession. Rewards and privileges are closely linked with motivation and a wide cultural range, from a gold star in kindergarten to a Nobel prize.

25. <u>Rights and Duties</u>. This concept formalizes the relationship of the individual to the group, stating what each expects of the other in terms of such things as the vote, taxes, licenses, military service, financial and legal rights and obligations, the demands that each person must meet and the protection he may expect in return.

This personal side of culture is stressed because it is elusive, often deeply hidden from the community members themselves and its study by us still remains unsystematic. Yet this aspect of culture is absolutely basic to an understanding of what makes a Russian a Russian, an Indian an Indian, or a Yankee a Yankee.

COMPETENCY 2

Demonstrate a basic knowledge of the contributions of minority groups in America to our society.

RATIONALE:

Teachers must possess a basic knowledge of minority groups' contributions if they are to multiculturalize their instruction. Too much of education is replete with the omission of minority groups contributions. Elimination of monocultural curricula will remain a mere notion, until educators acquire knowledge of the contributions minorities have made to our society. The role of minorities in this nation's scientific and technological advances must not be ignored. The minority experiences as recorded in their poetry, prose and fine arts are very significant in the studying of such appropriate areas as American history or literature. American history or literature ceases to be American when minorities are glossed over or completely eliminated from these subject areas.

Therefore the purpose of this competency is to enable the teacher to become aware and to acquire a basic knowledge of the vast contributions and the significant role minorities have in the accomplishments of this nation.

Instructional Objectives:

1. The learner will be able to locate various resources on a selected ethnic or minority group and compile the information to present to the class.

2. The learner will be able to describe the significance of ascertaining information about a minority group from members of the group.

Enabling Activities:

1. Read: James A. Banks, Part II, "Teaching Ethnic Cultures: Concepts, Strategies, and Materials", in Teaching Strategies for Ethnic Studies, Boston: Allyn and Bacon, Inc., 2nd edition, 1979, pages 135-422.

2. Read: Milton J. Gold, and others, Part II, "Ethnic Vignettes", In Praise of Diversity: A Resource Book for Multicultural Education, Washington, D.C.: Association of Teacher Educators, 1977, pages 34-212.

3. Read: James A. Banks, Part II, "Teaching About Ethnic Minority Cultures", Teaching Ethnic Studies, 43rd Yearbook, Washington, D.C.: National Council for the Social Studies, 1973, pages 115-253.

4. Read: James C. Stone, and Donald P. DeNevi, ed., Teaching Multicultural Populations: Five Heritages, New York: Van Nostrand-Reinhold Company, 1971.

5. Read: Anthony Gary Dworkin and Rosalind J. Dworkin, ed. The Minority Report: An Introduction to Racial, Ethnic and Gender Relations, Praeger Publishers, 1976.

6. Read: Nelson Brooks, "Parameters of Culture", FL News Exchange, Connecticutt State Department of Education, February 1973.

7. _____

    _____

    _____

8. _____

    _____

    _____

Assessment of Competency:

In order to demonstrate mastery of both Competency 1 and 2, the learner should be able to combine intellect, imagination, and creativity with other members of the class, to locate various resources on an assigned ethnic group. The small group investigation should lead to handouts that contain information that teachers would consider useable for their professional self-development, and an hour presentation to the class on your assigned ethnic group, which should be instructional in nature.

Instructional Notes From Class Meetings:

Date Competency Achieved _____

Guidelines for Ethnic Group Work
Competency 2

As a group you are expected to do the following:

I. Utilize your individual and combined intellect, imagination, and creativity
    to locate various resources on your assigned ethnic group.
    e.g. - library (city, university, school, etc.)
          - community - agencies
          - individuals
          - state, federal and regional agencies
          - other

II. Develop handouts to accompany each group's presentation that contain informa-
    tion that teachers would consider useable for the professional self development.
    e.g. - Annotated bibliographies
          - Community agencies
          - Audio-visual materials
          - Unique strategies
          - Hints and suggestions

III. Usually thirty to forty-five minutes will be allowed for each group's presen-
     tation. Please organize your presentation so that this time is utilized most
     effectively. You should view your presentation as an instructional period
     for your classmates. At a minimum you should
     (1) suggest how various resources about the assigned ethnic group may
          be legitimately incorporated in the regular curriculum with illustrative
          examples at various grade levels;
     (2) Critique where appropriate various resources;
     (3) Provide enlightening information concerning history, dominant values
          and contributions.

COMPETENCY 3

Assess relevance and feasibility of existing models that afford groups a way of gaining inclusion into today's society.

RATIONALE:

An individual's rights, privileges, and power are directly related to group membership; therefore, the status of one's group in relation to other groups in our society is of utmost significance. Subsequently, it is important to fully understand the models which afford opportunities for a group to change its relative position in our society. That is, how can they attain a more powerful position in our society?

Instructional Objectives:

1. The learner will be able to analyze the "Power Inclusion Model".

2. The learner will be able to analyze the "Shared Power Model".

3. The learner will be able to compare and contrast the "Shared Power Model" and "Power Inclusion Model" and determine the relevance and feasibility of both.

4. _____

    _____

    _____

Enabling Activities:

1.** View: Barbara Sizemore, on "Power Inclusion", Videotape, LRC Number 498.

2. Read: H. Prentice Baptiste, Jr., Multicultural Education: A Synopsis, Houston, Texas: University of Houston, 1976, pages 18-35.

3.* Read: Barbara A. Sizemore, "Is There a Case for Separate Schools?", Phi Delta Kappan, January, 1972, pages 281-284.

4. Read: Barbara A. Sizemore, "Separatism: A Reality Approach to Inclusion?" in Racial Crisis in American Education, Robert L. Green, ed., Chicago: Follett Educational Corp., 1969, pages 249-279.

5. Read: Barbara A. Sizemore, "Shattering the Melting Pot Myth", in Teaching Ethnic Studies, James Banks, ed., 43rd Yearbook, Washington, D.C.: National Council for the Social Studies, 1973, pages 53-101.

  ** This indicates that the resource is available through the Learning Resource Center at the University of Houston. Resources with an LRC number may only be available at the University of Houston.

6. *Read: James A. Banks, "Curricular Models for an Open Society", Education for an Open Society, Delmo Della-Dora, and James E. House, ed., Washington, D.C.: Association for Supervision and Curriculum Development, 1974, pages 43-63.

7. _____

   _____

   _____

8. _____

   _____

   _____

Assessment of Competency:

In order to demonstrate mastery of this competency, learners must display an understanding of existing models that afford groups a way of gaining inclusion. This can be done by describing and defending various models in a short paper (2-3 pages) or in class discussion with feedback from instructor.

Instructional Notes From Class Meetings:

Date Competency Achieved _____

IS THERE A CASE FOR SEPARATE SCHOOLS?
Barbara A. Sizemore

The 1971 U.S. Supreme Court ruling which allows court-ordered busing
to speed integration of Southern schools is an attempt to facilitate enforcement of the Court's 1954 Brown decision. The fact that such an act is necessary
indicates the magnitude of the problem which has been inaccurately defined as
segregation. Segregation is the condition of separation which occurs when
one group forces another to remain apart. It is an effect, not a cause.
What makes one group demand the separation of another group? Racism and
oppression are possible answers. Racism is the belief that race is the primary
determinant of human traits and capacities and that racial differences produce
the inherent superiority of a particular race. Oppression is the unjust and
cruel exercise of authority and power. In the U.S. most institutions promote
and protect an authoritarian decision-making hierarchy based on the values of
white European superiority, male superiority, and the superiority of people
with money. This support precludes possibilities for true integration, for
true integration demands an end to both racism and oppression.

The Integration Paradox

Handlin gives two definitions of integration.[1] One refers to an open
society, to a condition in which every individual can make the maximum number
of voluntary contacts with others without regard to qualifications of ancestry,
sex, or class. This definition demands solutions which would eradicate segregated housing, deny unequal job opportunities, eliminate inadequate medical
and educational services, and remove unequal tax assessments. If this definition had been chosen and acted upon, all barriers to association would have
been leveled except those based on ability, taste, and personal preference.
In this article the word integration should be so understood.

The other definition refers to integration as racial balance. This means
that individuals of each racial or ethnic group are randomly distributed
throughout the society so that every realm of activity contains a representative cross section of the population. For this meaning I shall use the
word desegregation. Integration affords free choice to equals with the same

Reprinted from Phi Delta Kappan, January, 1972.

limitations; desegration, like segregation, is imposed on one group by another, maintaining the super/subordinate relationship necessary for the system of oppression. Handlin says that the civil rights movement never made a clear choice between these two definitions. This failure has created enormous disadvantages for black people.

The open society definition was not adopted and models for desegration which accommodated racist and oppressive goals emerged. Using Sol Tax's model A/B, wherein A represents groups with power and B represents groups with no power,[2] A has the power to distribute and disseminate knowledge, information, and skills as well as make decisions. Power is the ability to make a person or group do something even when the person or group does not want to do it or when the demanded task is difficult to accomplish. In this model, when A wins, B loses, and when B wins, A loses. If A has the power, B will continue to be the loser unless B begins to define situations and problems. Desegregation and segregation are solutions chosen by A for B. Both are logical outcomes consistent with the competitive economic model in American society. Whether a school is segregated or desegregated, if the role for blacks is inferior, the outcome will remain the same. Simple mixing does not insure redefinition of roles, especially when the larger social order makes no such stipulations.

In most places where desegregation models have been implemented, blacks lose jobs. Most blacks have been recruited into teaching because they were systematically excluded from participation in the professional slots in the business-industrial-military complex. Recent research indicates that hundreds of black teachers have been demoted, dismissed outright, denied new contracts, or pressured into resigning because of desegregation and that new teachers hired to replace them include fewer and fewer blacks. Moreover, the black principal has been desegregation's primary prey. Desegregation, then, serves to create more jobs for whites at a time when the economy is shrinking and industry constricting.

The Power-Inclusion Model

A careful study of the goals of desegregation shows that the models are inimical to the best interests of black people. Desegregation serves A-group interests. How, then, can black people achieve inclusion in an open society? What models are available to B-group people to attain this end?

Most B-group people work toward integration into the great American "melting pot" --which does not exist. But the meaning of integration has been so muddled that another word is needed to describe these aspirations. Such a word is inclusion. Parsons defines inclusion as full participation in the American social order with complete preservation of distinctive ethnic and cultural differences.[3] Most B groups have used a separatist model to achieve inclusion. This separatist model for group mobility and full citizenship in the American social order has been called a power-inclusion model. It has two strategies, violence and nonviolence, and five stages.[4]

The first stage is the separatist stage, during which the excluded group defines its identity. This process includes the emergence of the pseudo-species declaration, "We are the chosen people made in the image of God." The unchosen are given special names, such as goya, devils, and pagans. It is during this stage that social or group identities are carefully delineated and religion is used to emphasize the "we" or "in" group feeling from which cohesion results. The identity-separation phenomenon is difficult to analyze, for it is an ongoing process. The stages of identity formation probably occur before the inclusion process but provide the necessary impetus for movement into it. The process cannot begin until identity is defined. But once this definition occurs, cohesion can develop. This cohesion is further enhanced by the attachment of a group to a land base. The separatist stage is characterized by three developments: 1) the pseudospecies declaration, 2) the identity specification, and 3) the territorial imperative. Separatism is a condition of separation which occurs when one group decides voluntarily to separate from other groups.

The second stage is the nationalist stage, in which the excluded group intensifies its cohesion by building a religio-cultural community of beliefs around its creation, history, and development. The history, religion, and philosophy of the nation from which the group comes dictate the rites, rituals, and ceremonies utilized in the proselytization of the old nationalism. Because of rejection by white Anglo-Saxon Protestants and the ensuing exclusion from full participation in the social order, the excluded group embraces its former or future nation. For the Irish Catholics, it becomes Ireland; for the Polish Catholics it is Poland; and for the Jews it is Zion-Israel. This intense nationalistic involvement increases separatism.

56

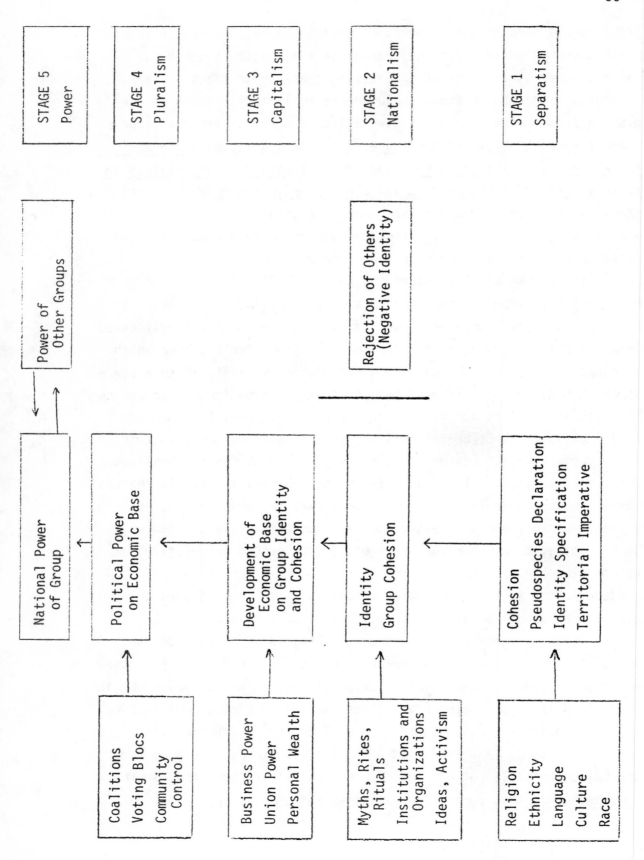

STAGE 5
Power

STAGE 4
Pluralism

STAGE 3
Capitalism

STAGE 2
Nationalism

STAGE 1
Separatism

Power of
Other Groups

Rejection of Others
(Negative Identity)

National Power
of Group

Political Power
on Economic Base

Development of
Economic Base
on Group Identity
and Cohesion

Identity
Group Cohesion

Cohesion
Pseudospecies Declaration
Identity Specification
Territorial Imperative

Coalitions
Voting Blocs
Community
Control

Business Power
Union Power
Personal Wealth

Myths, Rites,
Rituals
Institutions and
Organizations
Ideas, Activism

Religion
Ethnicity
Language
Culture
Race

Figure 1. Power-Inclusion Model for Excluded Groups

Through this model, ethnic groups plug their form of nationalism into Americanism (the common core of myths and language provided by the white Anglo-Saxon ideal) and become Irish-Americans, Italian-Americans, German-Americans, etc. The nationalism of these groups is paraded annually on holidays such as March 17, St. Patrick's Day. So intense was the involvement of the nationalistic stage that such vestiges still remain. As group cohesion and solidarity increased, development of the negative identity occurred. The negative identity of other pseudospecies is "perversely based on all those identifications and roles which are most undesirable" and "dictated by the necessity of finding and defending a niche of one's own."[5] So it becomes necessary for the well-defined pseudospecies to project its negative identities toward other groups.

The third stage of progression toward inclusion is the capitalistic stage. The cohesion developed in the separatist stage and magnified in the nationalist stage, added to the rejection of others created in the second phase, produces a need which can be the foundation for an economic base for the group. Such programs formed by active nationalism were discussed by both W.E.B. DuBois and Booker T. Washington, and were actually implemented by Marcus Garvey. The man most associated with this stage is Malcolm X, although it is the Nation of Islam under Elijah Muhammad which is the example.

In the capitalistic stage economic blocs and work niches are created for the group. Glazer and Moynihan demonstrate that the best jobs demand skills and training which tend to be kept within the "in" group.[6] Therefore, the problem is not simply discrimination against the blacks or any one group, but against all outsiders. In other words, there are Irish and Italian skilled workers in part because Irish and Italians were prominent in contracting and construction and they dominated the unions. With other groups, then, nationalism and separatism have contributed to an ethnic base for business and jobs. But when black people talk of these means they are castigated.

The fourth stage is the pluralistic stage, during which the group utilizes its cohesion-rejection powers to form a political bloc on its economic base in order to thrust its interests into the foreground of the political arena. It is this stage which gives the illusion that integration is real. For example, in the black man's drive for integration which started in housing, the white response was separation. Since identity cohesion is an important variable in four stages of the power-inclusion model, the particular ethnic group involved in integration responds to this need.

When an ethnic group is approaching or is in the nationalistic phase where identity cohesion is great, the rejection of others will be intense. Resistance to desegregation may be fierce and violent. When the ethnic group is approaching or in the capitalistic phase, where identity cohesion and rejection have formed a strong economic base, resistance may be immediate but nonviolent. In integration of housing, for example, this group could afford to relocate or to prevent the invasion.

When a group enters the pluralistic stage, integration may be a threat to its cultural institutions, but the group's high degree of participation in decision making offers abundant opportunity for control of the rate of integration. Resistance might be delayed and nonviolent. Once in the power phase, the group is then ready to control the conditions which provide impetus for integration. Bachrach and Baratz call this the silent face of power.[7] Carmichael and Hamilton indicate that coalitions are not viable when blacks are not equal partners.[8] In this capitalistic society, no partner without capital is equal.

The fifth stage is the power stage, sometimes called egalitarian and/or democratic. In this stage the economic and voting blocs and coalitions guarantee that the interests of the group have as much chance of winning as those of other groups at this level of participation. This is still utopian. Power is still held by white Anglo-Saxon Protestants, but both Jews and Catholics are trying to get it. Recent community control attempts have not changed the relationships between powerless and powerful groups in the educational system.

The Decentralization Hoax

Community control requires a change in the power relationships between A group and B group. Decentralization plans bring A-group power closer to B-group turf, but the power remains in A-group hands. The hierarchical administrative decision-making apparatus of the bureaucracy stays intact, as in the experiments at Ocean Hill-Brownsville, I.S. 201, and the Chicago Woodlawn Experimental School Project. Without a new aggregate power model, decisions are made at the top and filter down to students and parents at the bottom rather than vice versa. The Woodlawn experience provides an example.

Having embraced the hierarchical decision-making model as appropriate, the Woodlawn community had no way to actualize a community control model. (See Figure 11.) Finally, it collaborated with the city schools administration and supported unilateral decision making, which excluded students and teachers, thereby contradicting the project goals and extinguishing any chance for community control. This support affirmed the existing school bureaucratic order and all the other external offices higher than the school. The community organization, allegedly fighting for local control, actually supported more bureaucratic control and less aggregate decision-making at the grassroots level. In the end, it was pushed into the untenable position of advocating police action against its own constituency--the high school students.

Demands for community control are derived from an ideology taken on by a group because of specific theoretical elements conducive to its interests and needed by every group in social conflict to generate solidarity. Without it, B groups fall constant prey to "divide and conquer" tactics or embrace inadequate A-group models. Instead, B-group activities must consist of action and reflection or praxis.[9] Their major goal must be the transformation of the world, requiring theory and practice. Dialogue with the poeple is a necessity for the elimination of oppression, and leaders who deny praxis to the oppressed invalidate their own praxis.

The residual concern, however, is that the competitive model which is an A-group specification dictates losers and is oppressive. This is the usual predicament which prompts negative responses to separatism from B groups searching for more humane ways to live. This reaction overlooks the importance of the source and development of power needed to change the model to one which is promotively interdependent, so that whenever A group wins anything, B group wins also, and vice versa. No matter whether the goal is inclusion or revolution, B group must have the power to effect a change in the status quo. Therefore, the name of the game is power.

How does a group gain power? It either conquers land and amasses capital therefrom or it mobilizes and unifies its people. A choice is nonexistent. For B groups the only source of power is people. How does it mobilize and unify its people? This is accomplished through separatism, religion, and nationalism, all three of which speak to the cultural needs of the group when culture is the expression of the relationships between man and society.[10]

The B group must establish organizations and institutions which permit the oppressed to carry on the "critical and liberating dialogue which presupposes action."[11] Assuming that education is never neutral, B groups must make it serve their needs so that it will: 1) create opportunities for socio-economic mobility and survival; 2) maintain B-group solidarity against oppression; 3) enhance the myths, rites, and rituals which preserve this solidarity; and 4) distribute and disseminate knowledge, information, and skills which produce ideologies that make liberation possible.

Greeley and Rossi's study of Catholic Americans,[12] Erickson's work with the Amish,[13] and Essien-Udom's research in the Nation of Islam[14] show that groups separate to fight oppression. And, although in most cases the end goal seems to be inclusion, it actually is the acquisition of power. Since no revolutionary group has yet attained this power, none has used it for revolutionary change. But this possibility does exist.

Is this a case for separatism?

FOOTNOTES

1. Oscar Handlin. "The Goals of Integration," in Talcott Parsons and Kenneth B. Clark (eds.) The Negro in America. Boston: Houghton-Mifflin, 1965, pp. 659-77.

2. Sol Tax, "The Freedom to Make Mistakes," in Fred Gearing, Robert McNetting, and Lisa R. Peattie (eds.) The Documentary History of the Fox Project. Chicago: University of Chicago Press, 1960, pp. 245-50.

3. Talcott Parsons, "Full Citizenship Rights for the Negro American," in Parsons and Clark, op.cit., pp. 721-22.

4. Barbara A. Sizemore, "Separatism: A Reality Approach to Inclusion?," in Robert L. Green (ed.), Racial Crisis in American Education. Chicago: Follett Educational Corporation, 1969, pp. 249-76.

5. Erik H. Erikson, Identity, Youth and Crisis. New York: W. Norton, 1968, p. 175.

6. Nathan Glazer and Daniel P. Moynihan, Beyond the Melting Pot. Cambridge, Mass.: M.I.T. Press, 1963.

7. Peter Bachrach and Morton S. Baratz, "Two Faces of Power," American Political Science Review, December, 1962, pp. 948-49.

8. Stokely Carmichael and Charles V. Hamilton, Black Power. New York: Random House, 1967, p. 96.

9. Paulo Freire, The Pedagogy of the Oppressed. New York: Herder and Herder, 1970, pp. 119-121.

10. Sekou Toure, "A Dialectical Approach to Culture," The Black Scholar, November, 1969, p. 13.

11. Freire, op.cit., p. 52.

12. Andrew M. Greeley and Peter H. Rossi, The Education of Catholic Americans. Chicago: Aldine, 1966.

13. Donald A. Erickson, "The Plain People and American Democracy," Commentary, 1968, pp. 36-44. See also, "Contradictory Studies of Parochial Schooling," School Review, 1967, pp. 425-36, and "Nonpublic Schools in Michigan," in J. Alan Thomas (ed.), School Finance and Educational Opportunity in Michigan. Lansing, Mich.: Michigan Department of Education, 1968, p. 276.

14. E. U. Essien-Udom, Black Nationalism. Chicago: University of Chicago Press, 1962.

CURRICULAR MODELS FOR AN OPEN SOCIETY
James Banks

IT IS NECESSARY to define an *open society* before we can design a curriculum that will enable students to develop a commitment to that kind of social system, and the strategies and skills needed to create and maintain it. This is essential, because each curriculum is normative since it is designed to create and sustain a specific set of beliefs, attitudes, and institutions. In this chapter, an *open society* is defined as one in which individuals from diverse ethnic, cultural, and social class groups have equal opportunities to participate. Each individual can take full advantage of the opportunities and rewards within all social, economic, and political institutions without regard to his ancestry or ethnic identity. He can also participate fully in the society while preserving his distinct ethnic and cultural traits,[1] and is able to "make the maximum number of voluntary contacts with others without regard to qualifications of ancestry, sex, or class."[2]

In an open society, rewards and opportunities are not necessarily evenly distributed, but they are distributed on the basis of the knowledge and skills which each person can contribute to the fulfillment of the needs of his society. The societal needs referred to here consist of those systems and institutions which every society must have to function, such as a system of education, government, and the production and distribution of goods and services. The kind of society that we are proposing has never existed in the human experience. History and contemporary social science teach us that in every past and present culture individuals have had and still have widely unequal opportunities to share fully in the reward systems and benefits of their society. The basis for the unequal distribution of rewards is determined by elitist groups in which *power* is centered.

[1] Talcott Parsons. "Full Citizenship Rights for the Negro American." In: Talcott Parsons and Kenneth B. Clark, editors. *The Negro American.* Boston: Houghton Mifflin Company, 1965. pp. 721-22.

[2] Barbara A. Sizemore. "Is There a Case for Separate Schools?" *Phi Delta Kappan* 53: 281; January 1972.

Reprinted from <u>Education for an Open Society</u>, 1974, p. 43-63.

Ruling and powerful groups decide which traits and characteristics are necessary for full societal participation. *They determine necessary traits on the basis of the similarity of such traits to their own values, physical characteristics, life-styles, and behavior.* At various points in history, celibacy, sex, ethnicity, race, religion, as well as many other variables have been used by ruling groups to determine which individuals and groups would be given or denied opportunities for social mobility and full societal participation. In Colonial America, white Anglo-Saxon male Protestants with property controlled most social, political, economic, and military institutions. These were the men who wrote the Declaration of Independence and the United States Constitution. They excluded from full participation in decision making people, such as Blacks and Native Americans (Indians), who were different from themselves. Our "founding fathers" had a deep suspicion and contempt for individuals who were culturally and racially different. They invented and perpetuated stereotypes and myths about excluded groups to justify their oppression.

The United States, like all other nations, is still controlled by a few powerful groups who admit or deny individuals opportunities to participate in society on the basis of how similar such individuals are to themselves. White Anglo-Saxon male Protestants with money are the most valued persons in modern America; an individual who may be so classified has maximum opportunities to participate in America's social, economic, and political institutions. He is the "ideal" person in the United States, and all other individuals and groups are judged on the basis of their similarity to him. Black females without money are probably the least valued individuals in America.[3]

To create the kind of open society which we have defined here, we will either have to redistribute power so that groups with different ethnic and cultural characteristics will control entry to various social, economic, and political institutions; or we will have to modify the attitudes and actions of individuals who will control future institutions, so that they will become less ethnocentric and will permit people who differ from themselves culturally and physically to share equally in society's reward system on the basis of the *real* contributions which they can make to the functioning of society. We can conceptualize these two means to an open society as models.

Model I may be called a SHARED POWER MODEL. The goal of this model would be to create a society in which currently excluded groups would share power with dominant groups. They would control a number of social, economic, and political institutions, and would determine the criteria for admission to these institutions. The methods used to attain the major ends of this model would be an attempt to build group pride, cohesion, and identity among excluded groups, and help them to develop the ability to make effective political decisions, to gain and exercise political power effectively, and to develop a belief in the humanness of their own groups.

[3] Barbara A. Sizemore. "Social Science and Education for a Black Identity." In: James A. Banks and Jean D. Grambs, editors. *Black Self-Concept: Implications for Education and Social Science.* New York: McGraw-Hill Book Company, 1972.

The alternative means to an open society may be called Model II, ENLIGHTENING POWERFUL GROUPS MODEL. The major goal of this model would be to modify the attitudes and perceptions of dominant groups so that they would be willing, as adults, to share power with oppressed and excluded groups. They would also be willing to regard excluded members of groups as human, unwilling to participate in efforts to continue their oppression, willing to accept and understand the actions by oppressed groups to liberate themselves, and willing to take *action* to change the social system so that it would treat powerless peoples more justly. The major goals within this model focus on helping dominant groups to expand their conception of who is human, to develop more positive attitudes toward exploited peoples, and to foster a willingness to share power with excluded groups. (See Figures 1 and 2 for a summary of these two models.)

Model I—Shared Power

Most oppressed individuals who are acutely aware of the extent to which excluded groups are powerless in America will perceive the SHARED POWER MODEL as more realistic than Model II. This model, if successfully implemented, would result in the redistribution of *power* so that groups which have been and still are systematically excluded from full participation in America would control such institutions as schools, courts, industries, health facilities, and the mass media. They would not necessarily control all institutions within America, but would control those in which they participate and which are needed to fulfill their individual and group needs. These groups would be able to distribute jobs and other rewards to persons who, like themselves, are denied such opportunities by present powerful groups. In recent years, the Nation of Islam has used this model to create employment and educational opportunities for poor and excluded Blacks. The community control movement was an unsuccessful attempt to implement this model, and elements within this model have been used by such groups as Jews and Catholics to enable them to participate more fully in shaping public policy.

In a society in which power is shared by different groups, Blacks, Chicanos, women, Native Americans, Asian-Americans, Puerto Rican Americans, and other oppressed and colonized groups would control and determine the traits and characteristics necessary for sharing societal rewards and opportunities. IQ test scores may cease to be an important criterion, but the ability to relate to Third World peoples may become an essential criterion. A major assumption of this model is that present excluded groups, if they attained power, would, like present ruling groups, provide opportunities for those persons who are most like themselves physically and culturally. This assumption may or may not be valid, since some evidence suggests that oppressed groups have, at least in the past, idealized Anglo-Saxons with power and money, and held negative feelings toward their own cultures and groups.[4] This has been true even when previously oppressed individuals assumed power positions.

However, recent evidence reported by Arnez and Baughman indicates that this situation is changing and that exploited peoples are developing more group pride and cohesion.[5]

If the SHARED POWER MODEL is used to achieve an open society, we would have to think of ways in which such a model may be implemented without the genocide of powerless groups. We would also have to determine how essential societal cohesion may be maintained without conflict between competing and antagonistic powerful groups. There are valid reasons to believe that both of these concerns should be taken seriously by educators and policy makers if we intend to create a society in which a number of competing and alienated groups will share power.

History teaches us that people with power usually do not relinquish it without violence and bloodshed. The Black Revolt of the 1960's, which was a movement among Blacks designed primarily to attain power and influence over their lives, resulted in the murder of many Blacks who participated in protest movements and ghetto rebellions. Many of the victims were innocent bystanders. When the Black Panthers tried to

[4] See: James A. Banks. "Racial Prejudice and the Black Self-Concept." In: James A. Banks and Jean D. Grambs, editors. *Black Self-Concept: Implications for Education and Social Science.* New York: McGraw-Hill Book Company, 1972.

[5] See: Nancy L. Arnez. "Enhancing the Black Self-Concept Through Literature." In: James A. Banks and Jean D. Grambs, editors. *Black Self-Concept: Implications for Education and Social Science.* New York: McGraw-Hill Book Company, 1972.

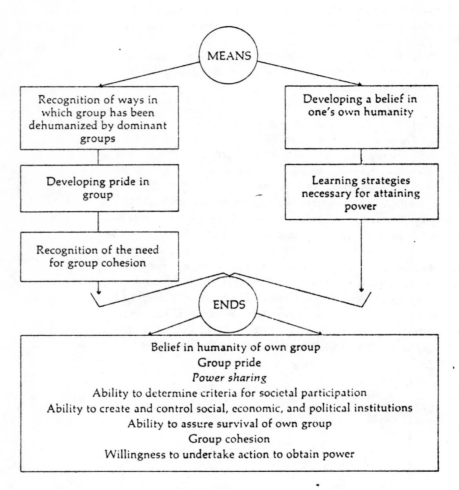

Figure 1. Model I—Shared Power Model

gain control over their communities, they were hunted down and killed by police in a number of large cities.

The Fred Hampton murder which occurred in Chicago in 1970 is perhaps the most well known and notorious of such attacks by police on the Black Panther Party. Respected white-controlled newspapers such as the *Chicago Sun Times* and the *New York Times* concluded that the Hampton murder resulted from an unwarranted police attack on the Party. Between February 1968 and December 1969, it was alleged that more than 50 incidents involving the Panther Party and policemen took place in cities throughout the nation. Twenty-eight Panthers were killed by policemen in 1969 alone.[6] Many Blacks regarded the attacks on the Panther Party as a national conspiracy. The violent assassinations of Malcolm X, Medgar Evers, and Martin Luther King also suggest that excluded groups run the risk of genocide when they try to take power from ruling groups. Thus, recent history makes it clear that powerless groups, when making a bid for power, run the risk of extermination.

When excluded groups lead movements to free their people from oppression and colonialization, they also run the risk of imprisonment or, to use the phrase of some who are imprisoned, of becoming "political prisoners." In an anguished and touching book, *If They Come in the Morning*, Angela Y. Davis tells why she feels that she is a political prisoner: "The offense of the political prisoner is his political boldness, his persistent challenging—legally and extra-legally—of fundamental social wrongs fostered and reinforced by the state."[7] James Baldwin viewed Miss Davis as a political prisoner when he wrote, ". . . we must fight for your life as though it were our own—which it is—and render impassable with our bodies the corridor to the gas chamber. *For, if they take you in the morning, they will be coming for us that night.*"[8] (Emphasis added.)

Excluded groups clearly risk genocide and imprisonment (Martin Luther King was jailed many times) when they try to take power from ruling groups. However, a dilemma is created by the fact that throughout history, power has rarely been given to oppressed peoples by ruling groups; rather it is usually taken, and power struggles often result in

[6] James A. Banks. *March Toward Freedom: A History of Black Americans.* Belmont, California: Fearon Publishers, 1970. p. 107.

[7] Angela Y. Davis (and other political prisoners). *If They Come in the Morning.* New York: Signet Books, 1971. p. 31.

[8] James Baldwin. "An Open Letter to My Sister, Angela Y. Davis." In: Angela Y. Davis. *If They Come in the Morning.* New York: Signet Books, 1971. p. 23.

violence and deaths. Notes Clark, "No human being can easily and graciously give up power and privilege. Such change can come only with conflict and anguish and the ever present threat of retrogression." [9]

However, since violent strategies by America's powerless groups will most likely result in genocide, imprisonment, and further repression, the school must help them to develop other tactics to attain power and influence. Clark insightfully points out why violent revolution is an unrealistic way for excluded groups in America to get power: "The strategy of nonviolence reflects most obviously the fact that Negroes, in the minority, could not afford to be violent—except for the unplanned Watts type of violence, itself suicidal or a reflection of racial desperation. The historical and contemporary predicament of the Negro in America provides no basis for systematic military revolution." [10]

In translating the SHARED POWER MODEL into curriculum goals and strategies, our attention would focus primarily on the victims of oppression, such as Blacks, Native Americans, Chicanos, Asian-Americans, and Puerto Rican Americans. We would try to equip exploited peoples with the strategies which will enable them to attain power, while preventing their extermination and maintaining an essential degree of societal cohesion. We would help them see, through valid content samples, how previous oppressed groups in history have attained power, and how certain nonreflective and irrational *actions* and *inactions* can result in further repression or genocide. Case studies of groups such as unionized auto workers and teachers can serve as examples of groups which have successfully attained significant amounts of power in America with little bloodshed and violence. The cases of the German Jews and Native Americans could serve to illustrate the latter point.

Model II—Enlightening Powerful Groups

Model II, whose primary goal is to *help whites develop more positive attitudes toward oppressed peoples and a willingness to share power*, rests on a number of assumptions, the validity of which we have little evidence to support. If anything, current data give us little hope in this model as an effective way to achieve an open society. It assumes that people with power feel guilty about the ways in which exploited groups

[9] Kenneth B. Clark. "Introduction: The Dilemma of Power." In: Talcott Parsons and Kenneth B. Clark, editors. *The Negro American.* Boston: Houghton Mifflin Company, 1965. p. xv.

[10] *Ibid.*, p. xvi.

are treated, or can be made to feel guilty. For example, Myrdal, in his classic study of racism in America, *The American Dilemma*, suggests that American democratic ideals vis-à-vis the treatment of Blacks in

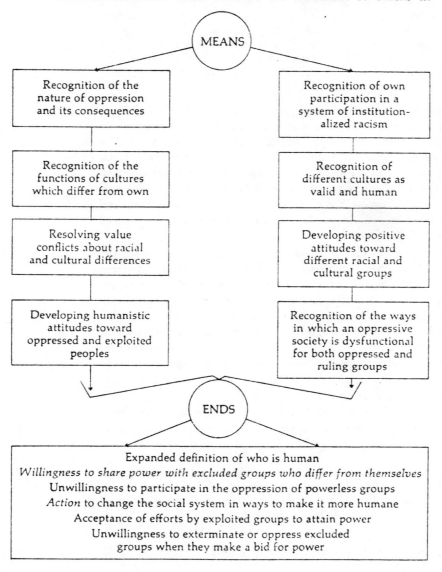

Figure 2. Model II—Enlightening Powerful Groups Model

America create a dilemma for most white Americans.[11] It may be that such a dilemma never has existed because whites have never perceived Blacks as *humans*. Writes Strom,

> . . . a new image of the Negro was created; he was for the first time endowed, by fiction rather than by God, as being somewhat less than human, a subhuman, a "nigger" whose natural inferiority to man justified his servant stature and allowed whites to see themselves as benevolent caretakers. . . . a group of enslaved people could be looked upon as subject to different rules and separate standards of conduct than real people, than human persons; these were "niggers."[12]

The differential reactions by the majority of whites to the killings of Blacks and whites in recent years suggest that many whites still do not consider Blacks and other Third World people as "human."[13] The majority of whites remained conspicuously silent when two Black students were shot by police on the campus of a Black college in South Carolina in 1969. The killing of four white students by National Guardsmen a year later at Kent State evoked strong reactions and protest by most white Americans. No similar strong reactions followed the Jackson State Massacre.

Thus, it may be unrealistic to assume that, by learning about the atrocities which have been committed against Blacks, whites will become more willing to share power with them, and to regard them as fellow human beings because of feelings of guilt. Some writers contend that the policies in our society which influence the ways in which excluded groups are treated are *deliberate* policies.[14] If this assumption is valid, then teaching whites about the brutalities of slavery, or the inhumanity of "Indian" reservations, cannot be expected to affect significantly the ways in which dominant groups treat Blacks, Native Americans, and other colonized groups in America.

This model also assumes that dominant groups may develop a commitment to change if they are helped to see the ways in which an oppressive and exploitative system is detrimental to the oppressor as

[11] Gunnar Myrdal. *An American Dilemma*. New York: Harper & Row, Publishers, 1962.

[12] Robert D. Strom. "The Mythology of Racism." Lecture delivered at Oxford University, England, Spring 1972. p. 1.

[13] James A. Banks. "The Imperatives of Ethnic Minority Education." *Phi Delta Kappan* 53: 268; January 1972.

[14] James Baldwin. "A Talk to Teachers." In: Everett T. Keach, Jr., Robert Fulton, and William E. Gardner, editors. *Education and Social Crisis: Perspectives on Teaching Disadvantaged Youth.* New York: John Wiley & Sons, 1967. pp. 263-68.

well as the oppressed. This assumption puts a lot of faith in the power
of knowledge; yet evidence is quite clear that man often rejects knowledge which is antithetical to his *perceived* self-interests, and that the
knowledge which becomes institutionalized within a society—and thus
that knowledge which is taught in school—is designed to perpetuate the
status quo, and to keep excluded groups from participating in shaping
public policy.

Purposes of Models

While these two models represent what we feel are the basic ways
by which we can create an open society, they are ideal-type constructs.
And like any ideal-type constructs or models, they are best used for
conceptualization purposes. The laws of the land, the current organization of schools, and the types of student populations in many American
schools make it difficult, in many cases, to implement either Model I
or Model II in *pure* form. However, these models can help the curriculum
specialist to determine the kinds of *emphases* which are necessary for the
curriculum for different student populations. While the curriculums
for exploited and dominant groups should have some elements in
common, we believe that the central messages which these groups
receive in the curriculum should in many cases differ. In the following
paragraphs, we will discuss, using the two models as departure points,
the kinds of *emphases* which we feel should constitute the curriculums
for *oppressed* and *dominant* groups in order to create and sustain an
open society. We intend to take into account the limitations of each
of the models in our recommendations, and to suggest ways in which
they may be reduced. In those situations in which a teacher has students
from both dominant and excluded groups, it will be necessary for him
to combine elements from both models in order to structure an effective
curriculum.

The Curriculum for Oppressed Groups:
Curricular Implications of Model I

The curriculum which we recommend for oppressed groups will
include most of the elements of Model I. However, it will also include
elements from Model II because a "pure" SHARED POWER MODEL curriculum may result in a totally fragmented and dehumanized society.

Throughout history, oppressed ethnic minority groups have been
taught by the larger society that they were less than human, and that
they deserve the low status in society in which they most often find

themselves. Notes Baldwin, "The American triumph—in which the American tragedy has always been implicit—was to make Black people despise themselves. When I was little I despised myself; I did not know any better."[15] A large body of evidence collected by the Clarks in the 1940's, and by Morland in recent years, indicates that minority groups often accept the definitions of themselves which are perpetuated by dominant groups.[16] Recent studies reviewed by Arnez and conducted by Baughman and his students suggest that the self-perceptions of minority groups may be changing, largely because of the positive results of the Black Revolt of the 1960's.[17] However, Goldschmid's intensive review of the literature indicates that ethnic minority groups often hold negative attitudes toward themselves and their race.[18] The curriculum for Blacks and other oppressed groups must recognize their feelings toward self, help them to clarify their racial attitudes, liberate them from psychological captivity, and convince them of their humanness, since the dominant society has made them believe that they are less than human. Writes Johnson:

The African descendants in America, having passed through three phases of education in America—de-Africanization, dehumanization, and, finally, an inferior caste status—through application of self-determination and the establishment of a voluntary self-separated school system, can educate themselves.[19]

Blacks and other ethnic minorities will be able to liberate themselves from psychological and physical oppression only when they know *how* and *why* the myths about them emerged and were institutionalized and validated by white "scholarly" social scientists and historians. A curriculum which has as one of its major goals the liberation of oppressed peoples must teach them the ways in which all social institutions within this society, including the schools and the academic community, have participated in a conspiracy to make them believe that they are less than human.[20]

[15] James Baldwin, "An Open Letter . . .," *op. cit.*, p. 20.

[16] James A. Banks, "Racial Prejudice and the Black Self-Concept," *op. cit.*

[17] Nancy L. Arnez, *op. cit.*

[18] Marcel L. Goldschmid, editor. *Black Americans and White Racism: Theory and Research.* New York: Holt, Rinehart and Winston, Inc., 1970.

[19] Edwina C. Johnson. "An Alternative to Miseducation for the Afro-American People." In: Nathan Wright, Jr., editor. *What Black Educators Are Saying.* New York: Hawthorn Books, Inc., 1970. p. 198. Reprinted by permission of Hawthorn Books, Inc.

[20] James Baldwin, "A Talk to Teachers," *op. cit.*, p. 268.

They must be taught how social science knowledge reflects the norms, values, and goals of the ruling and powerful groups in society, and how it validates those belief systems which are functional for groups in power and dysfunctional for oppressed and powerless groups. When teaching Black students about ways in which social knowledge has served to validate the stereotypes and myths about them, the teacher can use as examples Ulrich B. Phillips' racist descriptions of the nature of slavery, Moynihan's disastrous study of the Black family, Jensen's and Schockley's denigrating work on Black-white intelligence, and Banfield's distorted and myopic interpretations of the Black ghetto rebellions. Textbook descriptions of Asian-Americans, Native Americans, Puerto Rican Americans, and Chicanos can also be used to teach oppressed peoples about ways in which social knowledge has been used to keep them at the lower rungs of the social ladder.[21]

While studying about the ways in which they have been psychologically and physically exploited and dehumanized is necessary to help exploited groups to liberate themselves, it is not sufficient. They must be helped to develop the ability to make *reflective* public decisions so that they can gain *power* and shape public policy that affects their lives. They must also develop a sense of *political efficacy*, and be given practice in *social action* strategies which teach them how to get power without being exterminated and becoming further oppressed. *In other words, excluded groups must be taught the most effective ways to gain power.* The school must help them become effective and reflective *political activists.* We are defining *reflective* decision making and social action as those kinds of decisions and social action which will enable oppressed groups to attain power, but will at the same time ensure their existence as a group and essential societal cohesion. Opportunities for social action, in which students have experience in obtaining and exercising power, must be emphasized within a curriculum which is designed to help liberate excluded groups. Since oppression and racism exist within the school as well as within all other American institutions, students can be provided practice in shaping public policy and in gaining power within their classroom, school, or school system.

The social studies curriculum for oppressed groups must not only help release them from psychological captivity, and focus on social action, it must also help them to develop *humanistic* attitudes toward members of their own group, as well as toward other excluded groups, since

[21] See: James A. Banks. *Teaching the Black Experience: Methods and Materials.* Belmont, California: Fearon Publishers, 1970. See also: James A. Banks, editor. *Teaching Ethnic Studies: Concepts and Strategies.* 43rd Yearbook. Washington, D.C.: National Council for the Social Studies, 1973.

coalitions among Third World peoples are necessary for them to gain and exercise political power. The fact that individuals are more likely to attain power when working in groups than when working alone is a highly important generalization which must be incorporated into a curriculum which has *liberation* as its goal. Write Bailey and Saxe:

> Individualism, a Euro-American value imposed upon Blacks, is dysfunctional for us when internalized, because of our precarious position in this society. Cooperation is far more valuable and necessary. Achievement-motivation directed toward the goal of liberation, coupled with a desire to work with others in an organized fashion to end oppression, and training to do so effectively—this is what a twentieth century education for black children demands.[22]

The school must also make an effort, when teaching oppressed groups how to attain power and to develop an appreciation of their cultural identity, to prevent them from becoming chauvinistic and ethnocentric, and from developing the kinds of attitudes and perceptions about different cultural groups which present ruling groups have toward people who are different from themselves. While presently excluded groups must learn to value their own cultures, try to attain power, and develop group solidarity and identity in order to participate fully in this society, they must also learn that there are other ways of living and being, and that even though dominant groups treat them in dehumanizing ways, it would not be to their advantage to treat other groups similarly if they attained power positions. To imitate the behavior of the oppressor would be the highest compliment which powerless peoples could pay to him. The humanism which exists among oppressed groups would be killed if they, once having attained power, were to act like current ruling groups; and the opportunity to humanize this society would be lost.

We stated that a curriculum for oppressed groups should help them to develop group pride, ways in which to attain power, and humanistic attitudes toward all cultural, ethnic, and social class groups. Most of these elements are Model I components, but we feel that the *humanistic* emphasis, which is a Model II component, must be incorporated into a curriculum for oppressed groups to prevent them from developing ethnocentric attitudes that are similar to the detrimental attitudes which dominant and powerful groups have today.

[22] Ronald W. Bailey and Janet C. Saxe. *Teaching Black: An Evaluation of Methods and Resources.* Stanford, California: Multi-Ethnic Education Resources Center of Stanford University, 1971. p. 31.

Curriculum for Dominant Groups:
Curricular Implications of Model II

Since we have no reliable ways of knowing that a Model I type curriculum *would* lead to an open society as we have defined it in this chapter, the curriculum builder should also implement elements of Model II in appropriate settings; that is, in settings which contain dominant groups. What we are suggesting is that since both of these models have severe limitations, and since we know little about ways to create an open society because we have never made a serious effort to create one, we should take a *multiple* approach to the problem. Also, the two models are complementary and not contradictory. If we succeed in enlightening or changing the attitudes of dominant groups so that they become more willing to share power with excluded groups, then the struggle for power among oppressed peoples will consequently be less intense, and thus less likely to lead to violence and societal chaos.

The elements which constitute Model II have been among the most widespread methods used by educators and policy makers to create a more humane society and better opportunities for Blacks, Native Americans, Chicanos, Asian-Americans, and other powerless groups in America. This approach is suggested by such terms as *intergroup education, intercultural education, human relations,* and *race relations.* Massive efforts were undertaken by such organizations as the American Council on Education and the Anti-Defamation League of B'nai B'rith in the forties and fifties to implement workshops to change the attitudes of teachers and children toward ethnic minority groups.

Hilda Taba and her colleagues developed a theoretical rationale for intergroup education, conducted numerous workshops, and published a number of books for the American Council on Education. Taba identified four major goals of intergroup education: (a) to provide pupils with facts, ideas, and concepts basic to intelligent understanding of group relations; (b) to develop the ability to think objectively and rationally about people, their problems, relationships, and cultures; (c) to develop those feelings, values, attitudes, and sensitivities necessary for living in a pluralistic society; and (d) to develop skills necessary for getting along with individuals and for working successfully in groups.[23]

[23] Hilda Taba, Elizabeth H. Brady, and John T. Robinson. *Intergroup Education in Public Schools.* Washington, D.C.: American Council on Education, 1952. p. 36. This summary of Taba's theory is taken from: June V. Gilliard. "Intergroup Education: How, For What, and For Whom?" Unpublished paper, University of Washington, Seattle, 1971. p. 2.

Jean Dresden Grambs, another leader in intergroup education, states the assumption of the approach:

If a person can learn to hate and distrust others, he can learn to like and trust others. . . . This is the basic assumption of intergroup education. . . . Intergroup education similarly assumes that, as a result of selected materials and methods, individuals will be changed, that their attitudes and behaviors toward persons of other groups, and toward members of whatever group they themselves belong to, will be changed. The change will result in more *acceptance of persons who differ and* more *acceptance of one's own difference from others.*[24]

Other leaders in the field also assume that we can teach people new attitudes toward excluded groups. Trager and Yarrow write,

Children learn what they live; in a culture which practices and condones prejudice, one behaves and thinks with prejudice. If children are to learn new ways of behaving, more democratic ways, they must be *taught* new behaviors and new values.[25]

The seminal study by Trager and Yarrow supports the assumption that democratic attitudes can be taught to children if a *deliberate* program of instruction is designed for that purpose.[26]

The primary goal of intergroup education (Model II elements) is to "enlighten" dominant groups by changing their attitudes toward excluded groups. Attempts are made to enlighten whites by conducting workshops and courses, often called *"Human Relations,"* in which whites are told about the sins of institutionalized racism, and are exposed to readings and materials which illustrate the ways in which racism has adversely affected excluded groups. Often, in these courses and workshops, ethnic minority speakers who are perceived as "militant" by whites serve as consultants and speakers, and they "tell it like it is." Frequently in these sessions anger and hostility reign. However, there is little evidence that these kinds of sessions achieve much, except to serve as a catharsis forum for both whites and ethnic speakers.

It would be premature to say that Model II approaches have *no* value. *They have never been tried on a mass level.* Whites are not usually exposed to a Model II type experience until they are adults.

[24] Jean Dresden Grambs. *Intergroup Education: Methods and Materials.* Englewood Cliffs, New Jersey: Prentice-Hall, Inc., 1968. p. 1. © 1968. Reprinted by permission of Prentice-Hall, Inc., Englewood Cliffs, New Jersey.

[25] Helen G. Trager and Marian Radke Yarrow. *They Learn What They Live: Prejudice in Young Children.* New York: Harper and Brothers, 1952. p. 362.

[26] *Ibid.*

Such adults usually attend a workshop two or three weeks or a course in race relations for a quarter or a semester. Evidence suggests that these experiences usually have little *permanent* impact on adults' racial attitudes, although other kinds of experiences (used in conjunction with lectures and readings) seem to have *some* lasting influence on the racial attitudes of adults.[27] It is predictable that a short workshop would have limited effect on adults' racial attitudes, since an experience of 20 hours or less cannot be expected to change attitudes and perceptions which an individual has internalized over a 20-year period, especially when the basic institutions in which he lives reinforce his pre-experimental attitudes.

Because of the meager results which have been obtained from Model II approaches, many ethnic minority spokesmen feel that this model should be abandoned, and that a shared power model is the only realistic way in which to achieve an open society. As a Black person who has conducted many *race relations* workshops, I greatly respect individuals who endorse this point of view. However, I feel that Model II approaches should be continued, *but the ways in which they are implemented should be greatly modified*. They should be continued and expanded because: (a) We have no assurance that a shared power model will succeed in this period of our history (however, we also have no assurance that it will not); (b) Model II strategies have never been implemented on a mass level, rather they are usually used in experiments with children or with teachers when a racial crisis hits a school district; (c) research suggests that the racial attitudes of children can be modified by curriculum intervention, especially in the earliest years—the younger children are, the greater the impact that curriculum intervention is likely to have on their racial feelings;[28] and (d) racism is a serious, dehumanizing pathology in this society which the school has a moral and professional responsibility to help eradicate, and most schools are controlled by whites. If we recommend the elimination of Model II approaches to an open society, we will in essence be telling people in power (dominant white groups) that they should play no role in humanizing this society, and should fiddle while our ghettos are burning. This kind of advice to dominant groups would be myopic, since the widespread repression within America is a powder keg that can explode and result in bloodshed and the destruction of this nation.

Earlier we discussed the severe limitations of Model II, and the

[27] For a summary of the research on which this discussion is based, see: James A. Banks, "Racial Prejudice and the Black Self-Concept," *op. cit.*
[28] *Ibid.*

questionable assumptions on which it is based. Later we argued that elements of this model should be implemented in appropriate settings. We do not see these two positions as contradictory; rather, we feel that when the curriculum builder is aware of the limitations of his strategies, he can better use, evaluate, and modify them. A knowledge of the limitations of a curriculum strategy will also prevent the curriculum builder from expecting unrealistic outcomes. For example, a knowledge of the limitations of Model II will help a teacher to realize that a unit on race relations during Black Heritage Week will have little impact on the racial attitudes of his pupils. Rather, he will know that *only* a complete modification of his total program is likely to have any significant impact on his students' racial attitudes and beliefs, and that even with this kind of substantial curriculum modification, the chances for alteration of racial attitudes will not be extremely high, especially if he is working with older students or adults.

Despite the severe limitations of Model II as it is currently used in the schools and in teacher education, I believe that substantial modifications in the *implementation* of Model II components can significantly increase this model's impact on the racial attitudes and perceptions of dominant groups. The ultimate result of an effective implementation of a model *may be* that children of dominant groups, as adults, will be more likely to perceive oppressed groups as *humans*, and thus more likely to share power with them, and allow them to participate more fully in America's social, economic, and political institutions. All of these statements are, at best, promising hypotheses, but I base them on experience, gleanings from research, and *faith*. In the next few paragraphs, I would like to suggest ways in which the implementation of a Model II type curriculum can have maximum opportunity to "enlighten" or modify the racial attitudes, beliefs, and perceptions of dominant and ruling groups.

By the time that the child enters school, he has generally already been inculcated with the negative attitudes toward ethnic minorities which are pervasive within the larger society. Although this fact has been documented since Lasker's pioneering research in 1929,[29] teachers are often surprised to learn in workshops that even kindergarten pupils are aware of racial differences and assign different values to Blacks and whites. This fact alone gives us little hope for effective intervention. However, a related one does. The racial attitudes of kindergartners are not as negative or as crystallized as those of fifth graders. As children grow older, and no systematic efforts are made to modify their racial

[29] Bruno Lasker. *Race Attitudes in Children*. New York: Henry Holt & Company, 1929.

feelings, they become more bigoted. The curricular implications of this research are clear. To modify children's racial attitudes, a *deliberate* program of instruction must be structured for that purpose in the earliest grades. The longer we wait, the less our chances are for success. By the time the individual reaches adulthood, the chances for successful intervention become almost—but not quite—nil.

Effective intervention programs must not only begin in the earliest grades, the efforts must be *sustained* over a long period of time, and material related to cultural differences must permeate the *entire* curriculum. Also, a variety of media and materials improves chances for successful intervention. A unit on Native Americans in the second grade, and a book on Chicanos in the third grade, will do little to help majority group youngsters to understand or accept cultures which are different from their own. A "hit and miss" approach to the study of cultural differences may do more harm than good. While there may be times when an in-depth study of an American ethnic minority culture is educationally justified in order to teach a concept such as *acculturation* or *enculturation*, most often when ethnic groups are studied in this way the students are likely to get the impression that ethnic minorities have not played an integral and significant role in the shaping of this society and its institutions, and that they are not "real" Americans. Most often Blacks, Native Americans, Chicanos, Puerto Rican Americans, and Asian-Americans are studied only when they are presented as "problems" by the textbook writer or curriculum builder. Thus most information about Blacks in textbooks focuses on the topic of slavery. Substantial information about Blacks does not appear again in most textbooks until the Black Revolt of the sixties. Native Americans are discussed when Columbus "discovered" them, and when they later become a "problem" when Anglo-Saxons expand westward.

If white students are to be helped to perceive other cultures as valid and legitimate, *a totally new conceptual framework must be used to view and teach about the American experience.* Most textbooks and curriculum materials are written from a white Anglo-Saxon point of view. Books on the "American Experience" usually begin with a discussion of the Crusades, the Vikings, and other Western European institutions and movements. Native American cultures are considered only as Columbus "discovers" them and they become an obstacle to the expansion of the colonies. Not only is this approach to American studies blatantly ethnocentric, it interprets the American experience strictly as a political entity which was an extension of Western European institutions and culture into the Americas. This totally Anglo-Saxon way of viewing the American experience cannot be tolerated in a curriculum which is designed to achieve an open society. America must be viewed as a land which was made up of a rich variety of cultures centuries before Europeans arrived. The introduction to American studies should deal with the nature of these complex and diverse cultures, and the ways in which they structured institutions to meet their needs for survival.[30]

After students have studied early America as a *culture area*, made up of a wide diversity of peoples and cultures, they can then learn about the foreigners who came to America from Europe. They can study about the ways in which the Europeans renamed Native Americans *Indians* (even though whites knew that America was not India), eradicated their cultures, committed genocide against the Natives, took their land, and created the most technologically advanced nation in the world. In any serious and honest study of American culture, the tragic experience of its Native peoples must be seen from new and humanistic perspectives. The point which I am trying to emphasize is that the study of America must be seen through the eyes of the vanquished, since students now study it primarily from the viewpoint of the victors. While both views can add to our understanding of the American experience, we must stress other viewpoints since the Anglo-Saxon view of American history is so distorted and widespread within our school and the larger society. Only by trying to see this nation from the viewpoints of oppressed peoples will we be able to fully understand the complexity of the American drama.

White students must also be helped to expand their conceptions of what it means to be human, since many whites assume that people who possess physical and cultural traits which differ markedly from their own are less than human. One promising way to help dominant group children to understand that there are many ways to be human is to expose them to a wide variety of cultures both within and outside the United States, and point out the similar needs which all groups have, and illustrate how they have used a wide variety of ways to satisfy them. Cross-cultural studies will help students understand that all cultures find ways to satisfy the needs of their members, and that a culture can be evaluated only within a particular social context. Thus, a cultural trait that is *different* does not mean that it is nonhuman or inferior, but rather it is different because it is functional for a different group of *human* beings.

Majority group students must also be helped to come to grips with the value dilemmas which are pervasive within our society and with

[30] See: Alvin M. Josephy, Jr. *The Indian Heritage of America.* New York: Bantam Books, Inc., 1968.

their own interpersonal value conflicts. Many students verbally claim that they value freedom for oppressed groups, but harshly condemn efforts by these groups to liberate themselves from oppression. Teachers must help students to see why these two feelings are contradictory and inconsistent. They have a professional responsibility to help students to see the contradictions and conflicts in their beliefs, to analyze reflectively their values, and to express a willingness to accept their implications. Some beliefs are inherently contradictory, and education should create men who have clarified, consistent beliefs which can guide meaningful and purposeful action of which the individual will be proud. A number of valuing inquiry models and strategies are available for use by teachers to help students to confront and analyze value problems and conflicts.[31]

The contradictions between the values expressed in our national documents and the ways in which minority groups are treated in our society should constitute an important part of a curriculum which purports to enlighten dominant groups. By reading case studies and documents on the experiences of ethnic minority groups, students will be able to conclude that only the wealthy persons within our society enjoy the "best" of America. The schools, the courts, and medical institutions respond best to the needs of the powerful groups in society. Poor people get an inferior education, little justice in the courts, and minimal medical care.

These facts about American life may or may not cause future powerful individuals to share power with the poor. However, many people in powerful positions today have never had to confront these issues in the school or elsewhere. *If for no other reasons, these facts need to be taught to students in order for them to obtain a sound education and liberated minds.* The school must help to liberate the minds of both dominant and exploited groups; both have been victimized by the myths and illusions which are rampant within America. Writes Paynter,

It should be obvious today that few American youth, black or white, will settle for illusions over reality where the past is concerned. By continuing to put forth a mythology in our history books which has little basis in fact, we shall be teaching contempt for history and for the white world which is its purveyor, as well as contributing to the already considerable degree of cynicism among many American young people today. . . . in studying various atrocities, some students would have trouble avoiding the conclusion that inhumanness

---

[31] A number of such strategies are presented in: James A. Banks (with contributions by Ambrose A. Clegg, Jr.). *Teaching Strategies for the Social Studies.* Reading, Massachusetts: Addison-Wesley Publishing Company, 1973. pp. 445-75.

was a necessary consequence of whiteness. . . . these students should be helped to see that simply to condemn the past has no more merit than mindless celebration of it.[32]

In summary, we have argued that in order to create an *open society* it is necessary to define clearly such a social system, and to design a curriculum specifically to achieve and perpetuate it. We have defined an open society as a social system in which individuals from diverse ethnic, cultural, and social class groups can freely participate, and have equal opportunities to gain the skills and knowledge which the society needs in order to function. Rewards within an open society are based upon the contributions which each person, regardless of his ancestry or social class, can make to the fulfillment of the society's functional requirements.

We conceptualized two models by which we may achieve and maintain an open society. Model I, or the SHARED POWER MODEL, focuses on helping oppressed groups to attain power so that they can control a number of social, economic, and political institutions, and determine who may participate in these institutions. These groups would also determine how rewards would be distributed. A second model, the ENLIGHTENING POWERFUL GROUPS MODEL, focuses on changing the attitudes of dominant and ruling groups so that they will share power with excluded groups, regard them as *human*, and take action to eliminate institutionalized racism within America.

The complexity of our society makes it impossible for either of these models to be implemented in *pure* form. Also, both models are ideal-type constructs which are based on a number of unverified assumptions. However, these models can help the curriculum builder to determine the kinds of focuses which should constitute an open society-curriculum for excluded, dominant, and mixed groups, for planning programs, and for ascertaining the effectiveness of various curriculum strategies. The urgency of our current racial crisis demands that we take decisive steps to create a more open society if we are to prevent racial wars and chaos and the complete dehumanization of the American Man.[33]

[32] Julie Paynter. "An End to Innocence." In: James A. Banks and William W. Joyce, editors. *Teaching Social Studies to .Culturally Different Children.* Reading, Massachusetts: Addison-Wesley Publishing Company, 1971. pp. 333, 336. Reprinted by permission. *Journal of Current Social Issues* 7 (4); January 1969. Published by the United Church Board for Homeland Ministries.

[33] James A. Banks, "The Imperatives of Ethnic Minority Education," *op. cit.,* p. 269.

MULTICULTURAL EDUCATION

Competency 4. Identify current biases and deficiencies in existing curriculum and in both commercial and teacher-prepared materials of instruction.

Competency 5. Recognize potential linguistic and cultural biases of existing assessment instruments and procedures when prescribing a program of testing for the learner(s).

Competency 6. Acquire a thorough knowledge of the philosophy and theory concerning bilingual education and its application.

Competency 7. Acquire, evaluate, adapt, and develop materials appropriate to multicultural education.

Competency 8. Critique an educational environment to the extent of the measurable evidence of the environment representing a multi-cultural approach to education.

Competency 9. Acquire the skills for effective participation and utilization of the community.

Competency 10. Design, develop and implement an instructional module using strategies and materials which will produce a module/unit that is multicultural, multiracial, and/or multiethnic in character.

COMPETENCY 4

Identify current biases and deficiencies in existing curriculum and in both commercial and teacher-prepared materials of instruction.

RATIONALE:

It is a known fact that a vast majority of curricula and instructional materials contain a plethora of ethnic, racist, and sexist biasness, cultural ethnocentrism, and sins of omission and commission. For the most part, progress has only been in the deceitful sophistication which publishing companies have dealt with the complaints of racism, etc. in their materials. Subsequently, educators must become more astute in applying multicultural criteria in the evaluation of these materials. They must be able to apply various criteria in a very sophisticated manner.

Instructional Objectives:

1. The learner will be able to find examples of racism, sexism, distortion and omission in school textbooks.

2. The learner will be able to identify examples of racial, sexual, or cultural bias in commercially prepared materials.

3. The learner will be able to identify examples of racial, sexual, or cultural bias found in sample lessons brought by classmates, and then recommend changes.

4. The learner will be able to compile a bibliography of other sources with criteria for evaluating educational materials in their subject area or grade level.

5. The learner will be able to describe similarities and differences between Anglo-American and other cultures, and be able to point out areas of potential cultural conflicts and opportunities.

6. _____

_____

_____

Enabling Activities:

1. Read: National Council for the Social Studies, Curriculum Guidelines for Multiethnic Education, Arlington, Virginia: National Council for the Social Studies, 1976, pages 18-41.

2. * Read: Gloria Grant, "Criteria for Cultural Pluralism in the Classroom", Educational Leadership, December, 1974, pages 190-192.

3. Read: Carl A. Grant and Gloria W. Grant, "Instructional Materials in Multi-cultural Education", Multicultural Education: Commitments, Issues, and Applications, Washington, D.C.: Association for Supervision and Curriculum Development, 1977, pages 113-120.

4. *"Criteria for Evaluating the Treatment of Cultural/Ethnic Groups in Textbooks and Other Learning Materials", modified from Educational Leadership, November, 1973.

5. Read: Booklet on "Sexism and Racism in Popular Basal Readers, 1964-1976", Council on Interracial Books for Children, 1976.

6. View: Filmstrip "From Racism to Pluralism", in class, and participate in class discussion. Council on Interracial Books, 1841 Broadway, N. Y., N.Y., 10023.

7. Review: Special Issues of Interracial Books for Children "Bulletin" which singles out literature on specific racial and ethnic groups, and evaluates them.

8. *Read: "What To Do About Sex Bias in the Curriculum", American Education, April, 1977.

9. _____

_____

_____

Assessment of Competency:

The learner is expected to demonstrate mastery of this competency by presenting to the class a ten minute critique on chosen curriculum materials and resources, relevant to their subject area or grade level. The learner is to present examples of teacher prepared and commercially prepared materials (including textbooks and audio-visual material) and be able to identify examples of racial, sexual, and cultural bias. The learner should be able to do this by creating her/his own appropriate checklist with criteria for evaluating educational materials.

Instructional Notes From Class Meetings:

Date Competency Achieved _____

CRITERIA FOR CULTURAL PLURALISM IN THE CLASSROOM
Gloria W. Grant

Men are made of the same stuff, are destined for the same cycles of birth and death, love and hate, happiness and tragedy. This universality of thought expressed in social law is not one that demands sameness of all of man's actions, or claims that talent and weakness are uniformly distributed. Men need not share the same symbols of language, religion, and culture to be worthy of human treatment.[1]

From preschool to college, schools play a vital role in molding the attitudes and beliefs of the youth of our society. The curriculum and and teachers within the schools serve as the primary instrument for facilitating and implementing this molding process. The teacher's role is that of diagnostician, prescriber, and interpreter within the learning environment, using the curriculum to provide the content, learning experiences, and activities needed to meet the school's goals. The importance of having a curriculum that is capable of responding to the diverse needs of a pluralistic society is most essential because such a curriculum has as one of its primary goals the enhancement of individual self-esteem by helping members of various racial and ethnic groups to retain and value their cultural identity.

A culturally pluralistic curriculum must be consistent with the goals of our culturally diverse society. Such a curriculum should be characterized by mutual understanding and respect, equal worthiness of all cultural groups, and recognition of important contributions to society which each of these groups has made. Cultural differences are prized and given full expression to the extent that students of all ages, from all cultures and socioeconomic groups, learn and interact together. Students learn respect and trust for one another by receiving respect and trust.

Black psychiatrist Alvin Poussaint bluntly points out the need for a culturally pluralistic curriculum:

> Students should not be viewed as some homogeneous, monolithic group that can be fitted into a rigid educational machine designed to service yesterday's model of a white middle-class

Reprinted from <u>Educational Leadership</u>, December, 1974.

child. A curriculum designed to meet the needs of a child
in white suburbia may fail miserably if foisted unmodified
on black youth in the ghettoes. Variations in experiences
and lifestyles mean that different people need different
things at any given time. No single approach or method works
effectively with everybody. Schools should have the flexibility
of styles and approaches to work with a variety of classes
of youth.[2]

For too long the curricula have prepared students to perceive society
as composed of unequals, equals, and more equals.

The Evaluative Criteria

The development of a curriculum, or the modification of an existing
curriculum to be consistent with the goals of a culturally pluralistic
society, places a tremendous responsibility on the teachers. The teachers
must be able to evaluate the curriculum to decide if it meets criteria
for a pluralistic society and to determine what curriculum changes are
needed.

A first step that can be taken by teachers to meet the goal successfully
is the development of comprehensive criteria for evaluating a culturally
pluralistic curriculum. Evaluation criteria would facilitate the systematic,
comprehensive, and objective review of curricula in an attempt to identify
concepts or areas that do not adhere to the goals of cultural pluralism.
Evaluation criteria will also help teachers and other concerned individuals
to become aware of their subjectiveness, as well as their own biases
and prejudices.

The development of evaluative criteria can be an excellent project
for an in-service program. However, to be relevant to the needs of the
local community and society at large, any evaluation group should include
wide representation from the educational community, such as teacher
associations, and the general community, such as parents of the students.

Although no evaluative criteria will satisfy all situations, there
are some areas of general concern that can be met. The following list
hopefully can encourage teachers and other concerned individuals to examine
their school curriculum to ascertain its responsiveness to a culturally
pluralistic society.

A culturally pluralistic curriculum should:

1. Reflect the pluralistic nature of our society, both past and
present

2. Present diversity of culture, ethnicity, and custom as a strong positive feature of our nation's heritage

3. Present the cultural, sexual, and racial groups in our society in a manner that will build mutual respect and understanding

4. Portray people--boys and girls, men and women--whatever their culture, as displaying various human emotions, both negative and positive. Individuals of different cultural groups should be described working and playing together

5. Provide a balanced representation of cultural groups

6. Present members of various cultural groups in positions of authority

7. Examine the societal forces and conditions which operate to optimize or minimize the opportunities of minority group individuals

8. Help students to gain knowledge and appreciation of the many contributions to our civilization made by members of various cultural groups

9. Show that every cultural group has many individuals, such as educators, scientists, artists, writers, architects, and others, who have made important contribution to society

10. Portray cultures other than from a "special occasion" point-of-view. For example: Is there usually a "piñata" when studying Mexico? Are Native Americans presented mostly around Thanksgiving? Is the study of Blacks confined to Black History Week? Are Asian Americans usually studied around the Chinese New Year?

11. Present a wide representation of the many cultures in the world in the total curriculum from kindergarten to twelfth grade

12. Include an equal representation of the cultures presented in the United States in the total curriculum from kindergarten to twelfth grade

13. Examine real problems and real people of the various cultures and not just heroes and highlights

14. Provide experiences that will help build positive attitudes of a student's own cultural group and acceptance of other cultural groups

15. Use words and phrases that are complimentary and honest for the culture

16. Make certain that cultures are not presented separate or in

isolation from each other. A pluralistic curriculum should provide experiences that show how people of one culture have adopted food, clothing, language, etc., from other cultures.

17. Present all sides of an issue utilizing primary resources whenever possible.

The curriculum plays a paramount role in influencing the attitudes of the students. As educators, we must make certain that the curriculum respects the dignity of <u>all</u> people.

FOOTNOTES

[1] Seymour W. Itzkoff. <u>Cultural Pluralism and American Education</u>. Scranton Pennsylvania: International Textbook Company, 1969, pp. 105-106.

[2] Alvin F. Poussaint. "The Black Child's Image of the Future." In: Alvin Toffler, editor. <u>Learning for Tommorow</u>. New York: Vintage Books, Random House, Inc., 1974, p. 71.

CRITERIA FOR EVALUATING THE TREATMENT
OF CULTURAL/ETHNIC GROUPS IN TEXTBOOKS AND
OTHER LEARNING MATERIALS

Does this textbook or learning material in both its textual content and illustrations:

	Yes	No	Unclear
1. Evidence on the part of writers, artists, and editors of a senstitivity to prejudice, to stereotypes, to the use of material which would be offensive to any cultural/ethnic group?			
2. Suggest, by omission or commission, or by overemphasis or underemphasis, that any sexual, racial, religious, or ethnic segment of our population is more or less worthy, more of less capable, more or less important in the mainstream of American life?			
3. Utilize numerous opportunities for full, fair, accurate, and balanced treatment of minority groups?			
4. Provide abundant recognition for minority groups by placing them frequently in positions of leadership and centrality?			
5. Depict both male and female adult members of minority groups in situations which exhibit them as fine and worthy models to emulate?			
6. Present many instances of fully integrated human groupings and settings to indicate equal status and nonsegregated social relationships?			
7. Make clearly apparent the group representation of individuals--Caucasian, Afro-American, Indian, Chinese, Mexican American, etc.--and not seek to avoid identification by such means as smudging some color over Caucasian facial features?			
8. Give comprehensive, broadly ranging, representation to minority groups -- in art and science, in history and mathematics and literature, and in all other areas of life and culture?			
9. Delineate life in contemporary urban environments as well as in rural or suburban environments, so that today's city children can also find significant identification for themselves, their problems and challenges, and their potential for life, liberty, and the pursuit of happiness?			

Modified from Educational Leadership, November, 1973

	Yes	No	Unclear

10. Portray sexual, racial, religious, and ethnic groups in our society in such a way as to build positive images-- mutual understanding and respect, full and unqualified acceptance, and commitment to ensure equal opportunity for all?

11. Present social group differences in ways that will cause students to look upon the multicultural character of our nation as a value which we must esteem and treasure?

12. Assist students to recognize clearly the basic similarities among all members of the human race, and the uniqueness of every single individual?

13. Teach the great lesson that we must accept each other on the basis of individual worth, regardless of sex or race or religion or socioeconomic background?

14. Help students appreciate the many important contributions to our civilization made by members of the various human groups, emphasizing that every human group has its list of achievers, thinkers, writers, artists, scientists, builders, and political leaders?

15. Supply an accurate and sound balance in the matter of historical perspective, making it perfectly clear that all racial and religious and ethnic groups have mixed heritages, which can well serve as sources of both group pride and group humility?

16. Clarify the true historical forces and conditions which in the past have operated to the disadvantage of minority groups?

17. Clarify the true contemporary forces and conditions which in the past have operated to the disadvantage of minority groups?

18. Analyze intergroup tension and conflict fairly, frankly, objectively, and with emphasis upon resolving our social problems in a spirit of multiculturalism?

19. Seek to motivate students to examine their own attitudes and behaviors, and to comprehend their own duties and responsibilities as citizens in a pluralistic democracy-- to demand freedom and justice and equal opportunity for every individual and for every group?

20. Help minority group (as well as majority group) students to identify more fully with the educational process by providing textual content and illustrations which give students many opportunities for building a more positive self-image pride in their group, knowledge consistent with their experience; in sum, learning material which offers students meaningful and relevant learning worthy of their best efforts and energies?

WHAT TO DO ABOUT SEX BIAS IN THE CURRICULUM

In July of 1975, the Education Division of the Department of Health, Education, and Welfare, under the leadership of then Assistant Secretary for Education Virginia Y. Trotter, undertook a National Project on Women in Education. The project was to assess current practices in sexrole stereotyping throughout the educational process and at the same time to link experts and practitioners in the field of sex roles with policymakers, with the objective of planning for change. The following article was prepared for the project by Adeline Naiman of EDC's Role of Women in American Society Project. It is reprinted from the April, 1977, American Education.

There are a number of issues on sexism that schools face, and in so doing they must take into account the guidelines set by their own systems and communities. One such issue arousing controversy is sex-fair versus sex-affirmative teaching materials. In the light of the great inequalities to be overcome, do schools need a more aggressive stance on sex bias in curriculum? Should schools make do with the often sexist materials they own and expect teachers to provide the disclaimers and cautions, or should new materials be prepared or bought? How can schools deal with the impact of television, and what should an individual teacher or school do about biased educational programs beamed into the classroom? Even the most spohisticated and egalitarian curriculum is not "teacher proof"; thus, how can teacher training contribute to a teacher's successful use of non-sexist--or even biased materials?

A particular question for schools is whether it is better to institute courses in women's studies, particularly on the secondary level and for teachers, or to revamp as extensively as possible the whole curriculum, giving attention to language, role models, stereotypes, and balanced historical and cultural perspectives. Should studying and eliminating sex bias remain the province of a particular component of the school structure or curriculum, or should this effort pervade the entire curriculum (mainstreaming)? Should a women's studies course be an elective, and if so, under which department? Courses on women's issues are currently taught in high-school departments as diverse as media, history, English, home economics, social studies, guidance, and health.

Schools must also recognize pressures from the community, which may challenge federal legislation on the ground that its beliefs and right of free speech are being threatened. Parental uproar has already been provoked

---

Reprinted from the April 1977 American Education.

by the Title IX requirements which eliminate sex discrimination in school athletic programs. How does a school or school board handle the diversity of values, the fears, and the expectations of parents? How particularly can schools help students to make their own life choices free from the a priori constraints imposed by traditional socialization. Girls "choose" limited options, not realizing that their choices are heavily conditioned by the expectations of others. Where does "curriculum" leave off and society begin?

Perhaps there is a curriculum for the school and the larger society to pursue in combating sex bias. Through the schools, parents, teachers, and administrators can be helped to increase their own awareness of the process and costs of sex bias. Schools can extend participation in curriculum development to the users and provide curriculum materials, training, and support systems to teachers. Colleges and teacher-training institutions have a special responsibility to attend to the preservice curriculum and to offer resources to inservice teachers who seek retraining. There are also ten general assistance centers around the country to further these efforts, and other projects have been funded under the Women's Educational Equity Act. The higher-education establishment can work with public and private research and development agencies to develop materials, programs, and guidelines for bias-free and sex-affirmative materials. Publishers can be encouraged to go beyond the letter of the law in preparing and revising curriculum materials. Guidelines, such as the ones developed by the National Council of Teachers of English ("Guidelines for Non-sexist Use of Language," single copies of which may be had by writing to the Council, 1111 Kenyon Rd., Urbana, IL 61801), should be standardized and shared across the educational publishing industry and throughout schools. Ultimately, however, the responsibility for assuring bias-free curriculum belongs to governing bodies: school boards and state boards.

What are the realistic constraints on instituting bias-free curriculums in schools at this time? Parental pressures and the traditional social attitudes as expressed in the all-pervasive media are obvious, albeit hard to track down. Other constraints are easier to pinpoint: Budgets are tight and shrinking. How can schools allocate funds for new curricular materials or teacher training when declining enrollments, tenured faculties, and a depressed economy are squeezing the already strangled dollar? For example, in many systems where school budgets are supported by real-estate taxes, most of the operating costs of government are assignable to the schools yet only a small percentage of those costs is subject to debate over use. Teacher contracts, building mortgages, and fixed expenditures can take 85 percent or more of the total school budget. With limited options, how is a school system to set priorities? Title IX calls for an immediate expenditure of already limited funds. Will schools see curricular reform as an equally high priority?

Important, too, is the problem of affecting teachers and others in an area not easily reached by programs or legislation: attitudes. Attitudinal change in any population is hard to achieve and hard to measure. How can regard for the rights of individuals be maintained while carrying out the broader obligation of respect for statutory and moral law?

In the face of this hard task, policymakers in education need to set their own priorities for helping the schools. With regard to curricular materials in particular, policymakers should implement selection policies for new materials that will ensure bias-free curriculums. Where complete revision or replacement is not possible, they should provide supplemental materials to balance those currently in use. They should express their concern for consistent observation of bias-free guidelines to the commercial sector and to public and private agencies. They should enlist the support of teachers in using these guidelines in the classroom and in monitoring all acquired materials. Above all, policymakers should support the development of new materials that will meet the present need for addressing sex bias and that, over time and with use, will help to bring about the change in attitudes necessary to guarantee an end to sex bias in schools.

Recommendations

The following are suggestions for actions that can be taken by school boards and administrators:

1. Develop a policy statement outlining your concern about the elimination of racist and sexist stereotypes in textbooks and library books.

2. Appoint a task force to investigate the racist and sexist problems in your community and make recommendations for action.

3. Develop guidelines for all personnel to follow in purchasing and using textbooks and other instructional materials.

4. Earmark a proportion of funds to be used for the purchase of nonracist, nonsexist supplementary materials.

5. Develop and implement a plan for inservice training of all personnel who select, purchase, recommend, or use textbooks and other instructional materials.

6. Direct supervisors and curriculum specialists to develop resources and materials for assisting classroom teachers in reducing the impact of biased materials.

7. Call on state departments of education, teacher-training institutions, and professional associations to provide materials, workshops, and technical assistance.

8. Interpret the problems of biased textbooks and materials to parents, community groups, and policymaking boards. Let them know of your concerns and how they may assist in solving the problem. Hold book fairs that offer nonracist, nonsexist books to parents.

State boards and education departments can be instrumental in implementing the above recommendations. In addition, they can assist local systems by providing centralized resources, both for the state as a whole and for regional centers. The following are some particular supports the state can provide:

1. Compile a reference library of bias-free materials for supervisors and teachers.

2. Provide a centralized lending library of books, periodicals, audio-visual materials (particularly films), curricular materials, documents relating to legislation and guidelines for implementation. (Many of these documents are available from the Office of Education as a result of the Women's Educational Equity Act.)

3. Mandate workshops for teachers and administrators on dealing with sex bias in the curriculum, in existing materials, and in the media. Provide funding for workshop leaders who can act as resources to local schools on a continuing basis.

4. Communicate concern about bias in textbooks and other educational materials to publishers and to legislators.

5. Establish a review committee in state adoption and recommendation procedures to monitor curricular materials for bias.

6. Support the local development of new curricular materials for use in local schools and classrooms. Encourage innovative solutions on the part of the classroom teachers, curriculum specialists, and local administrators.

7. Involve community groups and parents in the effort to eliminate sex bias.

RESOURCES

The following is a sample of materials available to educators.

Association for Childhood Education International, Growing Free: Ways to Help Children Overcome Sex-Role Stereotypes, Washington, D.C.: ACEI, 1976.

Dick and Jane as Victims: Sex Stereotypes in Children's Readers. Princeton: Women on Words and Images (P. O. Box 2163, Princeton, New Jersey 08540), 1972.

Federbush, Marcia. Let Them Aspire! A Plea and Proposal for Equality of Opportunity for Males and Females in the Ann Arbor Public Schools. 4th edition, November 1973. Pittsburgh, Pa.: KNOW, Inc., (Box 86031, Pittsburgh, Pa. 15111).

Frazier, Nancy, and Sadker, Myra. Sexism in School and Society. New York: Harper and Row Publishers, Inc., 1973.

Golden, Gloria; Hunter, Lisa; and Morine, Greta, The Process of Change: A Handbook for Teachers on the Concept of Changing Sex Role Stereotypes, San Francisco: Far West Laboratory, 1974.

Greenleaf, Phyllis Taube. Liberating Young Children From Sex Roles: Experiences in Day Care Centers, Play Groups, and Free Schools. Somerville, Mass.: New England Free Press (60 Union Square, Somerville, Mass. 02143), 1972.

Guidelines for Equal Treatment of the Sexes. New York: McGraw-Hill Book Co. (1221 Avenue of the Americas, New York, N.Y. 10020, Attn: Public Information and Publicity Department).

Guidelines for Nonsexist Use of Language in NCTE Publications, Urbana, Illinois: National Council of Teachers of English, 1975.

Harrison, Barbara G. Unlearning the Lie. New York: Liveright, 1973.

MacLeod, Jennifer S., and Silverman, Sandra T. You Won't Do: What Textbooks on U.S. Government Teach High School Girls. Pittsburgh, Pa.: KNOW, Inc. (P. O. Box 87031, Pittsburgh, Pa. 15221), 1973. With "Sexism in Textbooks: An Annotated Source list of 150 + Studies and Remedies."

Moberg, Verne. A Child's Right to Equal Reading: Exercises in the Liberation of Children's Books from the Limitations of Sexual Stereotypes. Washington, D.C.: National Education Association.

Report on Sex Bias in the Public Schools. New York: National Organization for Women, New York City Chapter (28 East 56th Street, New York, N.Y. 10022).

Role of Women in American Society. Teacher and student guides to Girls at 12 and Clorae and Albie, Newton, Mass.: Education Development Center, 1975.

Self-study Guide to Sexism in Schools. Harrisburg, Pa.: Pennsylvania Department of Education (Box 911, Harrisburg, Pa. 17126).

"Sex Discrimination." Special issue of Inequality in Education, October 1975. (Quarterly publication of the Center for Law and Education at Harvard University, Harvard University, Larsen Hall, 14 Appian Way, Cambridge, Mass. 02138).

Thomas, Marlo and Friends, Free to be ... You and Me, (book and record), New York: Ms. Foundation, Inc., 1974.

Weitzman, Lenore J., and Rizzo, Diane, Biased Textbooks: Action Steps You Can Take, Washington, D.C.: The Resource Center on Sex Roles in Education, 1974.

Women on Words and Images, Help Wanted: Sexism in Career Education Materials, Princeton, N.J.: WWI, 1974.

COMPETENCY 5

Recognize potential linguistic and cultural biases of existing assessment instruments and procedures when prescribing a program of testing for the learner(s).

RATIONALE:

Assessment is a vital part of education. Every learner during the course of her/his schooling is exposed to hundreds of teacher and commercially prepared tests. It is important to understand the various biases that characterize assessment instruments.

Instructional Objectives:

1. The learner will be able to identify examples of cultural bias in Intelligence Tests and Standardized Tests.

2. The learner will be able to identify areas of conflict, such as language and culture, in certain testing programs.

3. The learner will be able to detect examples of cultural bias in both teacher and commercial made tests used in his/her subject area or grade level.

4. _____

   _____

   _____

Enabling Activities:

1. Attend and participate in class seminar on "Assessment and Multicultural Education".

2. For a better understanding of cultural biasness in testing, take "The Barriology Exam" and "The Black Intelligence Test of Cultural Homogeneity".**

3. *Read: Sheldon White, "Social Implications of I.Q.", The National Elementary Principal, Vol. 54 #4, 1975, p. 4-14.

4. *Read: "The Score Against I.Q.: A Look at Some Test Items", The National Elementary Principal, Vol. 54, #4, p. 42-43.

5. *Read: Jeffrey Blum, "Ethnic Minorities and I.Q. Tests: The Problem of Cultural Bias in Tests", Pseudoscience and Mental Ability, 1978, p. 98-109.

** May be purchased from Robert Williams, Professor of Psychology, Washington University, St. Louis, Missouri.

6. *Read: R. Samuda, "Consequences of Ability Grouping for Blacks and Other Minorities", <u>Psychological Testing of American Minorities</u>: <u>Issues and Consequences</u>, 1975, p. 107-115.

7. *Read: G. Weber, "Elementary and Secondary Achievement Tests", <u>Uses and Abuses of Standardized Testing in the Schools</u>, #22, 1977, p. 10-21.

Assessment of Competency:

In order to demonstrate mastery of this competency, the learner will be given sample items from assessment instruments, including teacher made, commercially prepared, standardized achievement, and I.Q. tests and must be able to identify linguistic and cultural biases that exist on the named test(s).

Instructional Notes From Class Meetings:

Date Competency Achieved _____

SOCIAL IMPLICATIONS OF IQ

Sheldon H. White

Existing instruments (for measuring intellect) represent enormous improvements over what was available twenty years ago: but three fundamental defects
remain. Just what they measure is not known, how far it is proper to add,
subtract, multiply, divide, and compute ratios with the measures obtained is
not known; just what the measures obtained signify concerning intellect is
not known. We may refer to these defects in order as ambiguity in content,
arbitrariness in units and ambiguity in significance.

Edward L. Thorndike

The meaning and wisdom of intelligence testing is much debated today.
This is as it should be, because our ideas about intelligence and our practices
of testing for it have significant influence on the way we educate children.
Unhappily, too much of the debate stays within a kind of magic circle. We
argue about whether intelligence is given at birth or whether it can be
changed. We discuss whether or not there are culture-fair procedures for
measuring intelligence. We consider how much schools should or should not be
guided by intelligence tests. But all of these discussions are curiously re-
stricted. Staying within the magic circle, we hover about the notion that
there is a single, generalized human capability that may be called "intelligence." I say hover because I believe that most of us have serious doubts
about there being some single "it" in human ability.

The central question in intelligence testing is not whether one can give
a child some games, puzzles, and questions. Everyone knows we can do that, at
least to some extent. And everyone knows that we can predict from the games,
puzzles, and questions of the test to those embodied in school classrooms,
at least to some extent. The central question is whether the child's performance on the games, puzzles, and questions - those of the test and those
of the school - reflects some essence in the child so significant that it

Reprinted from The National Elementary Principal, Vol. 54, #4, 1975,
p. 4-14.

should be considered to be merit, general ability, or promise for society.
It is here where we have doubts. Those in the schools have some doubts about
the tests as definitive measures of intellectual ability, and those outside
the schools have some more generalized doubts about "school smartness."

Why, with our doubts, do we confine our arguments within the magic circle?
We do so, I believe, because the circle defines a zone within the mythic
structure and rationalized practices of our society. If we stay within such
a zone, we can debate means, not ends. If we step outside the magic circle,
however, we suddenly open unsettling questions about the values inherent in
our social arrangements and equally difficult uncertainties about what is
right and fair in the practices of the public and institutional side of
children's socialization.

Intelligence tests are not ordinarily discussed as components of a mythic
system. They are ordinarily addressed as technology, as instruments, or as
measuring devices. They are considered to be science, not magic. But a
consideration of the history of intelligence testing suggests strongly that
the tests have not won their way by their technological merits - indeed, that
a technology of intelligence measuring has not been invented and probably
could not be. Much of the historical sequence looks like a history of the
dissemination of an imperfect technology that moves into currency because
of its social utility.

The intelligence test was invented in the first decade of this century
at a time when American social arrangements were changing, particularly
arrangements for the upbringing of children. It was also a time when major
activity patterns of American psychology were being established. We cannot
fully understand the forms and the growth patterns of American psychology
unless we understand the emerging discipline in the social milieu of that
period.

Barbara Tuchman's book The Proud Tower[1] conveys dramatically just how
different that time was from our own. The movement of Western societies was
clearly toward industrialization, urbanization, automation, and bureau-
cratization. But the last rites in the transfer of power had not taken place;
there were still remnants of an older social order. Most of the kings and
queens of Europe were in place. There were aristocracies. The aristocrats
were dilapidated, nervous, even fatalistic, but they still had a little power.
Most of their ancient power was in the hands of the merchant princes, with
whom they shared a love-hate relationship. Of course, the United States had

no king and no titles, but it did have an establishment that could get along comfortably with the titled establishments of Europe.

One can read Nicholas Murray Butler's autobiography, Across the Busy Years, to get an impression of the life of a pillar of the American establishment at that time. Butler was active in the widespread conversions of American colleges into American universities near the turn of the century. In 1901, becoming president of Columbia University, he entered into the company of the leadership of American affairs. He enjoyed, as he delicately puts it, "worldwide contacts and associations of the greatest possible charm and importance." He visited frequently at the White House. He was offered opportunities to become a bank president, a railroad president, a governor, a senator. He traveled abroad regularly and was involved in the machinations of international affairs. His autobiography radiates a coziness and a comfort that we can hardly imagine today -- a leader born in a time when leaders could imagine they were born to lead, an American aristocrat from Paterson, New Jersey.[2]

Contrast Butler with the harassed, short-lived college president of our time and you have one aspect of the difference between then and now. Now consider another difference. There was then explosive radicalism, anarchism, the Wobblies, and the fighting trade unions. For more than a hundred years the common man had been coming, since the American and French revolutions, since 1848, since Marx. There was still something a little adventurous and dangerous about active espousäl of his cause, but the fight for the common man was in the open. The battle was engaged.

If we examine the entries in the three-volume documentary history <u>Children and Youth in America</u>, we then get a sense of what the common men were fighting about. Volume II of that history contains excerpts that describe the life of the American poor farm family, the immigrants, the blacks, the Indians, and the mining families at the turn of the century. We find chronicles of low wages, long hours, hunger, uncertain work, poor housing, child labor, and poor health. We find Eleanor Roosevelt relating how, as a little girl, she was taken by her father to help serve Thanksgiving dinner at the Children's Aid Society:

> I was tremendously interested in all these ragged little boys and in the fact, which my father explained, that many of them had no homes and lived in little wooden shanties in empty lots, or slept in vestibules of houses or public buildings or any place where they could be moderately warm. Yet they were independent and earned their own livings.[3]

Eleanor Roosevelt was being initiated into the then genteel practice of social work, in the tradition of Jane Addams. Social work was one of the few ways by which, voluntarily and on the impulse of charity, selected individuals crossed the large gulf between the haves and the have-nots.

In the first decade of this century, then, we find a social order more split than our own. The aristocrats were more clearly set off as aristocratic. The common man was a little more common. But bridges were being built between them. There were renegotiations of the social contracts of that society, and those renegotiations ultimately tended to blur together the aristocrats and the anarchists. Many of those renegotiations involved social work directed not at the individuals but the institutions of society, and those renegotiations changed the socialization of children of children in our society:

Common schooling was coming. Compulsory schooling had been argued for unsuccessfully since before the Civil War. Now a series of compulsory attendance laws were passed between 1880 and 1917, and attendance at school became a requirement. But there was still a conflict between common schooling, conceived of as a homogenizing agent, versus vocational schooling, conceived of as training and disciplining a labor force, just as there was conflict between child education and child labor. In 1900, although twenty-eight states had compulsory school attendance laws, about 1.7 million children under sixteen were still in employment. In the decades to come, however, common schooling would grow and child labor and vocational education would subside.

Child welfare was coming. There had been a long series of private, city, and state moves against abuse, neglect, and abandonment of children. In the early 1900s, the issue of children's rights became a national issue. The first of the decennial White House Conferences on Children was convened by President Theodore Roosevelt in 1909. The Children's Bureau was established in 1912. There ensued a series of state coventions in a decade of the 1910s to reconsider and strengthen state-level laws and practices concerning the treatment of children.

The "Whole child" professions were coming. There were efforts to create a science of education and on that science found a true profession of teaching. To this end, schools of education were incorporated within the universities. The young Nicholas

Murray Butler, assistant in philosophy, ethics, and psychology, was trying to teach pedagogies and trying to bring together Columbia College and Teachers College, a liaison that was effected in 1900. Notonly teaching, but other professions relevant to the care and socialization of children were being established -- social work, pediatrics, and a variety of other school or health related career lines. A new division of responsibility and labor was being established reallocating the child-rearing responsibilities of family and society. Some traditional parental rights and responsibilities were being reassigned to the professions.[4]

It was amidst the social arrangements and the social changes of that time that American psychology was born. I believe that most of us share a misunderstanding about the history of American psychology. We see it too much as something that was created in intellectual and scientific history, rather than as something that was given life and form by American social concerns in the 1900s. The new American psychology emerging at the opening of the nineteenth century took an abrupt turn away from the philosophical psychology originally imported from the German universities. A set of psychological enterprises erupted into prominence in the American universities that are not easily traced back to one lineage.

If we stick with the traditional analysis of American intellectual history, then the decade from 1900-1910 appears to be a decade of brilliance. We find within the confines of that decade the abrupt emergence of men, ideas, and enterprises that were quite distinct from the German philosophical psychology, that squelched its growth in short order, and that superseded it to become the basis of American psychology today. It was indeed a decade of brilliance, but there was something else. During this period, certain images, ideas, and inquiries were afloat in the intellectual world that were struck by the heat and light of social movement and were crystalized into institutionalized forces. Society started investing in public knowledge of human behavior because it was making a major new set of investments in public responsibility for human socialization and human development. In fact, if we examine the new psychologies that erupted in the 1900s, we find that they were stimulated by the social concerns of the time, particularly by contemporary interests in creating professional, scientific bases for children's education and socialization.

Consider learning theory. In 1898, Thorndike published his first monograph on animal associative learning. By 1904, Pavlov had announced his turn from the study of digestion toward the study of psychic reflexes, and by 1909 we find Pavlov's work under discussion in American journals in a paper by Yerkes and Morgulis. By 1913-14, Thorndike had published the three volumes of his Educational Psychology and Watson had published his "Psychology as the Behaviorist Views It." The learning theory movement was now in place.

Note that in Thorndike's mind, learning theory was the cornerstone of a science of education; in Watson's mind, behaviorism was the cornerstone of a science of child rearing. These were the themes of clinical psychology and personality theory. In 1896, Lightner Witmer founded the Psychological Clinic at Pennsylvania. In 1909, William Healy founded what was to become the Institute for Juvenile

Research at Chicago. These were the beginnings of the child
guidance movement. It was in 1909 that G. Stanley Hall brought
Freud, Jung, Ferenezi, and Jones to participate in the twentieth
anniversary celebrations of Clark University. Theories about the
importance of early human personality development, and clinical
activity related to these theories, emerge at the beginning of
American psychology.

The theme of child study began with G. Stanley Hall's
educational psychology. Hall founded the Pedagogical Seminary
in 1891. He studied the contents of children's minds from 1894
to 1903. (By the middle of the first decade of this century,
there was a sizeable bibliography on child study, which was the
work of many hands.) This movement waned during the First World
War, but took life again as the Child Development Movement in the
late 1920s and early 1930s and finally became the foundation for
the basic and applied efforts that are characteristic of psychological research with children today.

Finally, there was the theme of mental testing. The Binet
and Simon instrument, first developed in 1905, was the culmination
of a long series of efforts toward the development of mental tests.
It shortly became accepted as an intelligence test. Learning
theory, clinical psychology, personality theory, and child study
were all put in place in the dawning psychology of that day
because of the special feeling that new social sciences would help
in designing new social contracts. But nothing so instantly leaped
into use and relevance as mental testing. The relevance of mental
testing to the social needs of that period was particularly striking,
and it merits some extended discussion.

One of the most interesting things about Binet and Simon's invention is the contrast between the curious indefiniteness of the invention compared with the curious definiteness of its social acceptance. What did Binet's test measure? According to Binet and Simon:

> It seems to us that in intelligence there is a fundamental faculty, the alteration or the lack of which is of the utmost importance for practical life. This faculty is judgment, otherwise called good sense, practical sense, initiative, the faculty of adapting one's self to circumstances. To judge well, to comprehend well, to reason well, these are the essential activities of intelligence. A person may be a moron or an imbecile if he is lacking in judgment; but with good judgment he can never be either. Indeed the rest of the intellectual faculties seem of little importance in contrast with judgment . . . .[5]

Binet and Simon are here trying to discount the value of the sensory and memory mental testing that had preceded them. Their affirmation of judgment appears in a paper in which the basic items of the Binet-Simon scale are presented, and one can easily examine the items to see if they are valid according to the stated criterion of judgment. The items do not look like items that tap only judgment; one would guess they identify a complex of entities.

Binet and Simon were not completely sold on judgment as the sine qua non of intelligence. In writings before and after the above quote, indeed in the very same paper, Binet sponsored a curiously vacillating series of verbal definitions of intelligence, with little apparent relationship among them. Spearman, in his The Nature of "Intelligence" and the Principles of Cognition reviews some of Binet's definition variations and finally concludes: "It would seem as if, in thus inconstantly flitting hither and thither, Binet can nowhere find a theoretical perch satisfactory for a moment even to himself.[6]

Spearman also reviews some of Simon's writings about intelligence, independent of Binet's which only compound the problem. In the very delivery of their instrument, Binet and Simon initiated a situation with which we are quite familiar today -- intelligence testing, definite procedure, explicit test items, and countable and scorable behaviors. But this procedural definiteness is shrouded in a never ending series of feeble, wandering verbal statements of what the items and the behaviors are all about.

The development of the Binet-Simon instrument was certainly not a simple fruition of theoretical inquiry. The instrument was precipitated by a practical social problem in the selection of children. It was submitted to the minister of public instruction in France in 1905 after he requested a study of measures to assure the benefits of education to defective children. The test was submitted to assist in a question of social selection. This question was probably, then as now, one that was individually poignant and politically tricky for those individuals having to make the decision. Not all psychologists, teachers, and psychiatrists, were happy about the theory or the practice of the tests. They are not happy today. But the tests moved slowly into use.

A bureaucratic society must, for many of its activities, categorize or classify people. Those responsible for such classifications are under relentless pressure to justify their sorting of people on universal grounds that are at least argumentatively objective and fair. It seems most likely that the intelligence

tests came into use in the 1920s and 1930s for much the same
reason that they were used for preschool evaluations in the
1960s -- not because of strong belief in them, but because
there were no alternatives and something had to be used. The
public became aware of the mental testing movement at the time
of World War I, when grading men for military service was
initiated. Brought into prominence and given commercial
development, the series of offspring of the rather rudimentary
venture of Binet and Simon, became the basis of the large and
diversified enterprise of psychological testing we find in our
society today.

But, throughout this period of social growth, that seed
of paradox first visible in the Binet-Simon work remains. In
1927, when Thorndike and his colleagues reviewed the theory of
intelligence testing, they found that the tests had improved,
but they still could not determine, any more than Binet, what
was being measured by the tests or what was meant by "measurement."[7]

In 1958, David Wechsler commented on the attempts over
decades to define intelligence:

> Some psychologists have come to doubt whether
> these laborious analyses have contributed anything
> fundamental to our understanding of intelligence while
> others have come to the equally disturbing conclusion
> that the term intelligence, as now employed, is so
> ambiguous that it ought to be discarded altogether.
> Psychology now seems to find itself in the paradoxical
> position of devising and advocating tests for measuring
> intelligence and then disclaiming responsibility for
> them by asserting that "nobody knows what the word
> really means."[8]

Either Thorndike's or Wechsler's judgment could apply today.

In short, if one reviews the situation persisting from

Binet through Thorndike to the present, we find that we have in
some astonishing way managed to continuously upgrade a technology for directing an uncertain measurement paradigm toward
an undefined entity. If we look at an intelligence test as a
piece of technology, an invention, or an outcome of science,
then I do not believe we can understand this. We advance on
understanding the problem somewhat if we consider that the
growth of intelligence testing has largely come through recurrent
human needs to justify selection and classification of people.
But even this does not seem sufficient. There are a good many
practices of social classification for which we do not use tests.
And despite the fact that there are by now thousands of tests,
no test has been assigned its own magic circle quite so
decisively as the intelligence test. No test is given more
credence. No test has been implicated as deeply in usage and
in serious discussion of education and society. What we deal
with here, I believe, is an affair in which magic, science, and
myth are intermixed.

In some classic essays in cultural anthropology, Bronislaw
Malinowski has attempted to capture the place of magic, science,
religion, and myth in primitive societies. He discusses the
cultural practices of the Trobriand Islanders. Reacting against
some descriptions of primitive peoples, which would picture them
as wholly immersed in superstition and magic, he argues that the
Trobriand Islanders have scientific knowledge, and they recognize
a distinction between practice based on knowledge versus practice
that must be based on magic. The Trobrianders must contend with

natural forces, in a variety of their cultural activities --
in gardening, building boats, fishing, warfare, and in care
of the sick. Where they understand and can control what they
are doing, they use science; where they do not understand,
they are very apt to interject magic. "It is most significant,"
Malinowski says, "that in the lagoon fishing, where man can
rely completely upon his knowledge and skill, magic does not
exist, while in the open-sea fishing, full of danger and
uncertainty, there is extensive ritual to secure safety and
good results."[9]

Overriding the knowledge, magic, and beliefs of the
Trobrianders are stories -- fairy tales, legends, and sacred
tales or myths. Malinowski argues that these bring order and
unity to the Trobrianders' body of social experience, uniting and
justifying:

> The cultural fact is a monument in which the
> myth is embodied; while the myth is believed to be the
> real cause which has brought about the moral rule, the
> social grouping, the rite, or the custom. Thus these
> stories form an integral part of culture. Their
> existence and influence not merely transcend the act
> of telling the narrative, not only do they draw their
> substance from life and its interests -- they govern
> and control many cultural features, they form the
> dogmatic backbone of primitive civilization."[10]

Our culture went through some serious changes around the
turn of this century. The time was much marked by appeals to
science and reason. But is it possible that we could not have
accomplished those changes entirely on those grounds? If we
concede that the Trobriand Islanders had a little science, then
we might entertain the possibility that today we supplement our
science with a little magic. If we hold that the Trobriand

Islanders unify and justify their social practices using myths, we might also suspect that our ancestors, putting behind them the social values associated with the myth of creation, might have rebuilt social explanations and justifications around the evolutionary narratives newly offered to them by scientific work. One reason for believing in this possibility is precisely the peculiar transcendental status of the notion of intelligence during the period we are considering.

Our notion of intelligence has transcended questions of definition and proof. In all the diverse writings about intelligence, there is a curious resemblance to the medieval proofs of God. Hundreds strive to define or measure its ineffable essence, sometimes with epic labors such as those of Piaget or Guilford. Who sanctified intelligence and made it prior to proof? The likelihood is that Herbert Spencer gave the term "intelligence" ideological santification. The likelihood is that subsequently changing American social practices at the turn of the century wove intelligence testing in as part of a new act of procedures for assigning social status.

More than a hundred years ago, Spencer stated that the be-all and end-all of human evolution was the growth of intelligence, sentience, and elaborated knowledge of the world. He argued that, if one arranges the phylogenetic tree in the way we usually do, with natural history moving toward man and culminating in man, then the basic dimension of phylogenesis is intelligence. To evolve is to become more intelligent; to become more intelligent is to evolve.

Spencer had an enormous vogue as the prophet of an
evolutionary vision of the design of a society. Sir Francis
Galton, a contemporary, was interested in eugenics (scientific
human breeding to advance the race). It was in the interest
of eugenics that he made his tries at "anthropometry" that
were the beginning efforts at mental testing. But Herbert
Spencer preached a social eugenics, society governed by
fitness and rewarding and promoting fitness, and it was
probably he who provided the climate for the ultimate acceptance
of such testing. Hofstadter's <u>Social Darwinism in American
Thought</u>[11] traces the Spencerian embodiment of evolutionism
in social thinking. In the 1870s and 1880s Herbert Spencer's
writings were so dominant in discussions of society and politics
that they virtually sank into the unconscious of American
political deliberation, ceased to be an argument, became obvious,
and became common sense. They remain strong even today. They
form the core of the "market mentality" satirized in the recent
best-seller, <u>Nixon Agonistes</u>;[12] that is, the notion that the social
arena must been seen as a competitive arena where the strong
survive and the weak die. The spencerian philosophy formed a
scientific core for outlooks that we today characterize as
elitism, racism, and imperialism. Hofstadter's review emphasizes
the alignment of Social Darwinism with conservative political
forces in the nineteenth century, and this seems fair. Spencer
seems to have courted the wealthy. But there was much of the
evolutionary philosophy built into the liberal politics of the
time. Progressivism had its Social Darwinism, too.

People approached the social changes of the turn of the
century with their minds formed by Spencer and the advocates
of Social Darwinism. Before Binet, or Thorndike, or Cattell,
or even Galton, people had made up their minds about the
centrality of intelligence as the epitome of human merit.
When the tests came along, they were not required to prove
their way. The tests could not then -- and they cannot now --
prove their way. They were exemplifications, definitions,
and manifestations, of an entity whose scientific and social
sanctity was given.

I have very briefly rehearsed the ideology of the time.
Now consider the import of that ideology on the social business
of the turn of the century. American society was in the process
of constructing more egalitarian arrangements. The actors on the
American scene -- aristocrats, workers, anarchists, immigrants --
were in search of new rules and procedures for the allocation of
social benefits and social status. Without relinquishing their
belief in aristocracy -- that there are better men and worse men --
people sought to abolish favoritism based on inheritance, or
land, or property. They felt that the only right and fair
aristocracy should be one of merit. To a society concerned in
finding ways in which the best might rule, Social Darwinism
offered the extremely important definition of bestness. Bestness
was intelligence. Bestness was developed by education. Spencer
did not speak of intelligence as solely an innately fixed trait;
he saw schools, and more generally, cognitive development as
adding to and enlarging human intelligence. Thus, Spencer's

arguments were important factors in several of the trends that enhanced the place of education in the social scene at that time: 1) the coming of common schooling; 2) the elaboration of colleges into universities; 3) the general feeling that social science and social scientists must take a more central role in social governance. John Dewey, in his writings, expresses the almost mystical progressive feeling prevalent at that time: that science, education, good government, public morality, all interpenetrate; so that to foster one is to foster all the others.

The argument then is that the intelligence test exploded into public acceptability and public use not because of its merits, but because it could be seized on as part of a more fair and more just system of social contracts. The test could be used as part of the system for allocating social opportunity. Needless to say, the tests could not have been so accepted if the people in power at that time saw the tests as potentially destroying their children's power. But the IQ tests of that time had the rather happy property of being a conservative social innovation. They could be perceived as justifying the richness of the rich and the poverty of the poor; they legitimized the existing social order. At the same time, they played a slowly subversive role, so that some of the actors -- the Germans and the Irish and the Italian and the Jewish immigrants -- could see their second- and third-generation offspring move toward social status.

All this being true, if it is, how do we get out of the magic circle we have created? How do psychologists cease being priests

of the mysteries of intelligence, rationalizing a semimystical
system of social allocation whose present defects have begun
to seriously outweigh any benefits gained from previous use?
How do educators reduce ine incessant pressures to negotiate
and explain the gaps between the myths and the realities of
education? There are probably no absolute answers and no safe
way out I believe, however, it is now time for us to construct
some new testing to replace the traditional IQ and achievement
testing; and I also believe that everything -- new ideology,
new social contracts, new data -- is coming into place to permit
us to do this.

We are in an active period in rebuilding social contracts.
This, I believe, is the deeper meaning of the poverty programs
of the 1960s and the ferment that continues now concerning education,
health care, family assistance, day care, and so forth. In diverse
ways, we are seeking to redefine the rights and responsibilities
of children, parents, teachers, physicians, social workers, courts,
and governmental agencies.

As one might expect, this social change is accompanied by a
change in the mythic system -- in Malinowski's terms, a new
"dogmatic backbone." We are into the politics of pluralism. The
old mythic system held that humans were arranged in a linear
hierarchy of excellence, blending the ancient human format of an
aristocratic order with newer social provision for a competition
of merit. The pluralisms of early twentieth century America were
to be resolved by the melting pot; that is, all species of
Americans were resolved into one species. In this context, the

fair fight for social place could take place on universal
standards of IQ and the open competition of the schools.

There is much to be admired in this conception. It was
a vision of a socially fair system, within which the practice
of intelligence testing could take an honorable place. It was
not important to understand the tests, because they were so
reasonable in intent that one could only see them as a benign
"white magic." Furthermore, various intercorrelations among
IQ, school achievement, income, and socioeconomic status (SES)
always turned out positive -- a little loose, but positive --
thus mixing a little science with the magic.

We are now moving to relinquish this mythic structure and
to replace it with another. The fundamental move is to dis-
entangle excellence from chosenness. It is simply not true that
human beings manifest one kind of excellence, that society rests
on one order of human excellence, or that schools should be in
the business of promoting one kind of excellence. If we step
outside the magic circle for a few moments and look beyond the
sacred trinity of IQ, school achievement, and SES, we can recognize
the everyday, scientific realities on which a new and pluralistic
mythic structure might be based.

Our test data do not tell us that one order, one linear
arrangement of human ability prevails. Our test data tell us
that humans have diverse, correlationally distinct abilities.
Our data from cognitive development, from psychoneurology, from
human learning, and from memory studies tell us that humans have
multiple knowledge systems, multiple systems of representation,
multiple gnostic centers, multiple short-term and long-term

memories, and multiple laws of learning.

Our experience with society tells us that there is more than one way for a human to make a social contribution, and that there is more than one order of social status. Humans give and receive respect on diverse grounds. Status based on money is not exactly the same as status based on education, and neither begins to classify the diverse social hierarchies based on vocational and political competencies.

Our experience with schooling tells us that children show diverse patterns of giftedness and achievement. This is true within the simplest form of the elementary school as a place to foster reading, writing, and mathematics. The similarities and differences among children concerning these skills are only lightly portrayed by a linear arrangement of grade-point-equivalent scores on a standardized achievement test. If one's conception of an elementary school includes all those other diverse aspects of training that are or might be put into the curriculum, it seems obvious that sooner or later the outcomes sought will be beyond the capacity of a single ordinal number.

I believe that the pluralistic picture I have been sketching is quite obvious. Certainly, no one should be surprised by the idea that children have diverse abilities, that schools foster diverse achievements, or that society uses diverse competences. Furthermore, I doubt that many will have trouble with the idea that a single valued intelligence test is simplistic. So let me, finally, turn to the central question: can we reform intelligence testing? Yes, I believe we can. But only to some extent.

Considering all the problems with intelligence testing, it is tempting to argue that we ought to throw the tests out as illogical and mischievous. It seems possible to do that. The Soviet Union officially banned all intelligence testing in 1936, and, so far as I know, it has gotten along without it ever since. But we might have problems doing that. Intelligence tests moved into usage because of difficult and real problems that bureaucracies had in their basic business of categorizing people. Suppose we were to throw out the tests and put the decisions they serve entirely in the hands of human judgment and estimation? What problems would arise from human bias, carelessness, and incompetence? How intense and how hurtful would be the problems of conscience and politics that afflict the decision maker who holds the power to help or hurt a child by choosing whether the child will go to a special class, receive extra remedial help, or qualify for higher education or a job? These are the problems now eased by the science-plus-magic of intelligence testing. The problems attendant on categorizing people are endemic in bureaucracies. On the one hand, we have national commissions deploring and viewing with alarm the problems of labeling children; and on the other hand, we have commissions calling for more widespread diagnosis of early handicaps (as though we could find true positives without false positives, or as though we could diagnose without labeling).

I believe we must imagine that the reform of intelligence testing can best be accomplished by the widespread adoption of plural tests of human mental abilities. Those giving mental tests have for some time recognized that human test performance tends not to be uniform but, in part at least, seems to be broken up, so that clusters of items tend to go upward and downward together in groups, setting themselves apart as intercorrelating entities. This kind of observation has brought forth various proposals that a plurality of human mental abilities exist -- such things as verbal ability, spatial ability, reasoning, numerical ability, idea fluency, mechanical knowledge and skill, and so forth. Some relief might come from this body of pluralized mental testing.

One problem facing this kind of option, however, is that diverse testers do not agree on the number and kinds of diverse abilities humans have. A second problem, probably the source of the first problem, is that the conception of the human's competence as a profile on an n-ability set of scales is much too simple. But, despite such problems, the invention and use of such a system of characterizing differences among children would have considerable social benefits. It would provide a larger magic circle, encompassing significantly more of the reality one encounters in schools. It would also provide a considerably richer mixture of science in the midst of the magic.

We would, through use of such a system, recognize in some official sense that human excellence and human social utility come in diverse forms. We would encourage the diversification of the aims and goals of education -- a matter wll worth pursuing. And if we still argued about the hereditariness versus

environmentalness in our new multiple system -- the modern
counterpart of traditional disputation about predestination
versus good works -- we would at least see, within the argument,
the vision of multiple roads to salvation.

Human beings have trouble finding intellectual formats
within which to comprehend the variety of dimly perceived
similarities and differences that float by in experience.
The discovery or reception of promising formats is a good deal
of what cognitive development, education, and science are all
about. One of the simplest and easiest formats available to
humans is the simple, linear ordinal arrangement. It can be
used by seven-year-olds. It comes easily to the mind. There
has been a recurrent human tendency to picture the universe as
filled with creatures of all possible degrees of perfection.
Lovejoy in his The Great Chain of Being[13] traces this three-
thousand-year-old tradition and shows how, in the nineteenth
century, Darwinism simply brought about the transposition of
the format on an evolutionary and biological scale. Now we find
it applied to humans and social affairs. The fact that the format
is ancient may only mean that it is easy, not inexorable. Once
upon a time the fifteenth century alchemists, now knowing much
about matter, imagined all elements to exist on a linear order
of nobility -- gold and silver the most noble of all. They
saw their problems in terms of this format. For example, they
saw the problem of transmuting lead into gold as essentially the
problem of freeing lead from impurity and baseness.

In a strikingly similar fashion, today we envisage the
solution of many educational problems as simply a matter of

removing from some children their impurity or baseness --
elevating the IQ, removing deficits or disadvantages, closing
the gap, or accelerating their cognitive development. It is
my hope that we will come to accept the notion that people are
quite as complicated as chemical elements, that takes a multidimensional format to begin to comprehend their similarities and
differences. Seeing people in this way, we may come to think in
new and useful ways about what the possibilities of better
education might be.

FOOTNOTES

1. B. Tuchman, The Proud Tower (New York: Macmillan Co., 1966).

2. N. M. Butler, Across the Busy Years (New York: Charles Scribner's
    Sons, 1939).

3. R. H. Bremner, ed., Children and Youth in America: A Documentary
    History, vol. II (Cambridge, Mass.: Harvard University Press, 1971),
    p. 34.

4. S. H. White et al., Federal Programs for Young Children (Washington:
    U. S. Government Printing Office, 1973), chap. 2; S. H. White,
    "Socialization and Education -- For What and By What Means?" in
    Raising Children in Modern American, ed. N. B. Talbot (Boston:
    Little, Brown and Co., in press).

5. A. Binet and T. Simon, "The Development of the Binet-Simon Scale,"
    in Readings in the History of Psychology, ed. W. Dennis (New York:
    Appleton-Century-Crofts, 1948), p. 417.

6. C. Spearman, The Nature of "Intelligence" and the Principles of
    Cognition (London: Macmillan Co., 1923), p. 10.

7. E. L. Thorndike, et al., The Measurement of Intelligence (New York:
    Teachers College Bureau of Publications, 1927).

8. D. Wechsler, cited in R. D. Tuddenham, "The Nature and Measurement
    of Intelligence," in Psychology in the Making: Histories of Selected
    Research Problems, ed. L. Postman (New York: Knopf, 1962).

9. B. Malinowski, Magic, Science and Religion and Other Essays (Glencoe,
    Ill.: The Free Press, 1948), p. 12.

FOOTNOTES - (Cont.)

10. Ibid., p. 85.

11. R. Hofstadter, Social Darwinism in American Thought (Boston: Beacon Press, 1955).

12. G. Wills, Nixon Agonistes: The Crisis of the Self-made Man (New York: Houghton Mifflin, 1970).

13. A. O. Lovejoy, The Great Chain of Being: A Study of the History of an Idea (Cambridge, Mass.: Harvard University, 1936).

THE SCORE AGAINST IQ: A LOOK AT SOME TEST ITEMS

MANY of the articles in this issue are illustrated with actual items from the intelligence tests. Lest you be tempted to conclude that the authors have deliberately selected the most outrageous examples from the tests, we urge you to take the time to examine the major tests in their entirety. Even with a generous selection of items, it is almost impossible to convey just how inadequate the tests are. To see them whole is to feel the full impact of the foolishness of trying to measure anything as complex as "intelligence" with such instruments.

However, for those readers who may not have easy access to the tests (and it is often needlessly difficult), we are including some additional selections here, with comment, both to provide a greater range of items and to cite some deficiencies of the tests not always mentioned elsewhere in this issue. It may be necessary to add that these items are neither the worst nor the best examples of the tests, but generally—and unfortunately—typify some of the basic flaws of the so-called intelligence tests.

THE EDITORS

❧

Something you see in your sleep is a . . .
☐ dream   ☐ fairy   ☐ wish   ☐ dread

Iowa Tests of Basic Skills,
Primary Battery, Level 7, Form 5,
Vocabulary Subtest

Dr. Freud might answer *wish* or *dread,* and a kid who's lost a tooth and put it under the pillow might answer *fairy.* And anyway, *see* is a poor choice of verbs. Did *you* see a dream last night?

hand beater : electric mixer : :
A broom : vacuum cleaner
B flashlight : light bulb
C sink : dish washer
D wrench : vise

Cooperative School and College Ability
Tests, Series II, Form 3B, p. 3

If the relationship intended is that of a hand operated household item to an electrical household item that is used for the same purpose, then couldn't B and C also be acceptable answers?

You can't ____ him; he was just doing his job.
R annoy   S help   T blame
U find   V trust

Cognitive Abilities Test, Form 1
Levels A-H, Verbal Battery, p. (

The answer wanted is *blame,* an excuse made famous by legions of low-level Nazis during the Nuremberg trials. In a Watergate government, the answer *trust* might be equally appropriate.

How tall is the average American man?
Any answer from 5'7" to 5'11".
(Do *not* give credit for 5'6½" or 5'11½".)

WISC-R, Manual, p. 68

It's hard to see how this question measures intelligence—or even intelligent guessing, if an answer that is off by half an inch is unacceptable.

Birds can fly.
Bats can fly.
Therefore, [1] a bat is a bird. [2] a bat is a mammal. [3] animals other than birds can fly.

California Test of Mental Maturity,
1963 Revision, Level 2, Test 9, p. 15

None of the answers are correct: without the additional statement that a bat is an animal, we cannot *logically* conclude that animals other than birds can fly.

When a dove begins to associate with crows, its feathers remain ____, but its heart grows black.
F black   G white   H dirty
J spread   K good

Lorge-Thorndike, Multi-Level Edition,
Level 3, Verbal Battery, p. 3

Not only is the statement itself erroneous, but think of the emotional impact of an item like this on a black child. (And, incidentally, not all doves are white.)

How the _____ roses flush up in the cheeks!

  R white **S** pretty **T** small
  U yellow **V** red

Lorge-Thorndike, Multi-Level Edition, Level 3, Verbal Battery, p. 3

The "correct" answer is *red*—but only if the cheek in question is white. Note also the quaint phrasing.

Grey hair is a sign of age, not of _____.

  R color **S** youth **T** courage
  U despair **V** wisdom

Lorge-Thorndike, Level 4, Form A, Verbal Battery, p. 3

Youth and *wisdom* are equally valid answers for this ambiguous question.

Where there is _____, let me sow love.

  R suspicion **S** friendliness **T** hatred
  U love **V** hope

Cognitive Abilities Test, Form 1, Levels A-H, Verbal Battery, p. 11

Another ambiguous question. Either *suspicion* or *hatred* would do, and—for those who need encouragement—so would *friendliness*.

dollar peso mark lira

  F change **G** franc **H** foreign
  J purchase **K** bank

Lorge-Thorndike, Level 4, Form A, Verbal Battery, p. 6

This question might pose no difficulties for the well-traveled child, but it requires at least a smattering of global economics for the others.

kaiser emperor king czar

  R senator **S** governor **T** pope
  U sultan **V** general

Cognitive Abilities Test, Form 1, Levels A-H, Verbal Battery, p. 17

If you've studied the Renaissance but not the history of the Middle East, *pope* might seem to be as good an answer as *sultan*.

tie cravat stock neckcloth

  A bib **B** collar **C** scarf
  D kirtle **E** girdle

Lorge-Thorndike, Level 4, Form A, Verbal Battery, p. 7

A, B, or *C*—and what, by the way, is a *kirtle?*

Find the drawing at the right that goes with the third drawing in the same way that the second goes with the first.

Ethnic stereotyping at its most unattractive, and outdated at that.

Lorge-Thorndike, Multi-Level Edition, Level 3, Nonverbal Battery, p. 6

The pictures in the box go together in a certain way. We say: "Boy is to trousers as girl is to what?"

Most little girls wear blue jeans these days as often as they wear dresses.

Otis-Lennon, Elementary I, Form J, p. 5; Manual, p. 10

In each row there is one picture that shows something which is the opposite of the first picture. Find it and mark its number.

10

A "non-sense" question. What can the opposite of a pillow be, except a non-pillow? How can you tell from this drawing? What are 1 and 2? Is 4 a brick or a sponge?

California Test of Mental Maturity, 1963 Revision, Level 2, Test 1, p. 3

TESTS CITED

California Test of Mental Maturity, 1963 Revision, Level 2. Elizabeth T. Sullivan, Willis W. Clark, and Ernest W. Tiegs (Monterey, Cal.: CTB/McGraw-Hill, 1963).

Cognitive Abilities Test, Multi-Level Booklet, Form 1, Levels A-H. Robert L. Thorndike and Elizabeth Hagen (Boston: Houghton Mifflin Co., 1971-72).

Cooperative School and College Ability Tests, Series II, Forms 1A-4B (Princeton, N.J.: Educational Testing Service, Cooperative Test Division, 1955-73).

Iowa Tests of Basic Skills, Primary Battery, Levels 7-8, Form 5. E. F. Lindquist and A. N. Hieronymous (Boston: Houghton Mifflin Co., 1972).

Lorge-Thorndike Intelligence Tests, Multi-Level Edition. Irving Lorge, Robert L. Thorndike, and Elizabeth Hagen (Boston: Houghton Mifflin Co., 1954-66).

Lorge-Thorndike Intelligence Tests, Level 4, Form A. Irving Lorge and Robert L. Thorndike (Boston: Houghton Mifflin Co., 1954).

Otis-Lennon Mental Ability Test, Elementary I Level, and *Manual for Administration.* Arthur S. Otis and Roger T. Lennon (New York: Harcourt, Brace, and World, 1967).

Wechsler Intelligence Scale for Children (WISC), and *Manual.* David Wechsler (New York: Psychological Corporation, 1949; revised edition 1974).

ETHNIC MINORITIES AND IQ TESTS:

THE PROBLEM OF CULTURAL BIAS IN TESTS

Jeffrey M. Blum

At various times during the last forty years, instruments known as
"culture-fair" IQ tests have served as vehicles for the transmission of
pseudoscience. Although the tests show no real basis for using the culture-
fair label, and are less valid as predictors of scholastic performance than
conventional IQ tests, many people nevertheless persist in believing that
such tests can provide trustworthy comparisons of the basic aptitudes of
different races and ethnic groups. This is thought to be so because it is
believed that the test items contain subject matter sufficiently universal
that no ethnic or status group could have any special disadvantage attributable
to the particularities of its culture. The reasoning which underlies this belief is clearly fallacious and easy to refute. The interesting question is
why the belief has gained the degree of acceptance which it has.

The misunderstandings about culture-fair tests, like those about conventional IQ tests, have stemmed from a pretense of verification which is for the
most part hidden from public view. People do not know exactly how these tests
came to be called culture-fair. They merely read books and articles where the
tests are called such, and assume on the basis of the label that the tests are
indeed culture-fair. For the tests to have acquired the label to begin with,
the pretense had to be explicit and elaborate. Now, however, the common practice
is merely to use the label, avoiding any discussion of its origin, and relying
upon the label itself to convey the deception. So, for example, in discussions
of racial differences in IQ scores, one will sometimes find statements like the
following:

> So-called "culture-free" or "culture-fair" tests tend to give Negroes
> slightly lower scores, on the average, than more conventional IQ tests
> such as the Stanford-Binet and Wechsler scales....The majority of studies
> show that Negroes perform relatively better on verbal than on nonverbal
> intelligence tests.

The precise effect of such statements is difficult to measure, but un-

Reprinted from Pseudoscience and Mental Ability, 1978, p. 98-109.

doubtedly they encourage at least some readers to dismiss the issue of cultural bias in tests and to assume that the racial comparisons are valid. To comprehend the deception involved, we must first understand the importance and complexity of the culture-bias issue. This can be done by looking at the matter historically and then examining current arguements.

The Problem in Historical Perspective

As several writers have shown, the use of IQ tests to compare intelligence levels of ethnic groups has a sordid history. "Scientific racism," the attempt to prove nonwhite races genetically inferior, first became prominent in the United States during the mid-nineteenth century. As slavery was becoming a burning controversy, its proponents turned increasingly to biological and religious doctrines which posited a qualitative difference between blacks and whites. Thus, one popular idea of the time traced blacks' inferior social position to their imaginary descent from certain biblical ancestors. Fifty years after emancipation, when blacks had acquired a token freedom but still resided at the bottom of the wage-labor system, they were acknowledged as equals in principle, but were seen as quantitatively inferior to whites, by a measure of fifteen IQ points. Since then, the economic position of most blacks has not improved much; nor have the psychometricians credited them with increased intelligence.

The stigma of a low IQ score has by no means been reserved exclusively for nonwhites. In the early twentieth century, when masses of white immigrants were living in poverty, facing an alien culture, and struggling to unionize, they too had test results which showed most of them to be mentally defective. Although test performance undoubtedly depended upon familiarity with American language and culture, the dominant interpretation of the First World War army data stressed that recent immigrants from southern and Eastern Europe had performed poorly because they were members of inferior races - Jews, Alpines, and Slavs, as opposed to Nordics who were superior. The correlation between test scores and number of years lived in America was explained by the fact that most of the earlier immigrants were from northern Europe and Great Britain while most of the recent ones were not. Carl Brigham, the primary author of this interpretation, received acclaim in psychology journals, influenced congressional debates over immigration restriction, and later came to head the College Entrance Examination Board.

Of course, we now know better. During the 1930s opinion shifted. Even Brigham repudiated his interpretation. What had made this outlook possible was an extremely shallow and ethnocentric conception of culture, together with a willingness to interpret ambiguous data carelessly. In the meantime, however, studies like Brigham's had fanned racist sentiments and promoted the passage of explicitly racist legislation.

While the early mental testers could be accused of promoting nativism and racial bigotry, on the charge of fostering sexism they must stand acquitted. Lewis Terman and others who followed deliberately designed their tests to show no sex differences in average levels of general intelligence. Galton and Spencer both had maintained that women were naturally less intelligent than men, and apparently women had performed worse on Galton's anthropometric tests. Even after Binet-type IQ tests were introduced, there was still considerable opportunity to label women inferior. On the army alpha test, given to soldiers in the First World War, women everywhere scored around ten points lower than men. But Terman and other psychometricians were not satisfied with this result. They tried to maximize the number of test items which showed no difference in the performance of men and women, and to further balance the scores they chose equal numbers of items favoring each sex. So, on the Stanford-Binet test, as on subsequent IQ tests modeled after it, objective measures of ability attested to a full equality of the sexes. Exactly why this happened is unclear. Perhaps the test designers had to reckon with the fact that girls usually performed better than boys in elementary schools. Perhaps they were responding to pressure generated by the strong women's movement of the period. Perhaps the fact that many of Terman's coworkers were women had some impact. Whatever the causes, women were accorded equal intelligence whereas blacks were not.

Most likely the early psychometricians did not have to connive or scheme in order to produce lower scores for blacks and Chicanos. The test designers themselves were white, middle-class academicians who had little if any familiarity with the cultures of ethnic minorities. There were hardly any nonwhites in the original standardization samples, so the testers could es-cape awareness of the special problems involved in communicating with children of disadvantaged minorities. They could churn out tests referenced toward white middle-class culture - the only culture they themselves understood - and assume that these were objective tests of ability. When it came time to interpret the low scores of blacks and Chicanos, they could fall back upon their own racial prejudice to eradicate any doubt about the results. Consider the tone of Terman's conclusion:

> Do races differ in intelligence? A nation which draws its constitutents from all corners of the earth and prides itself on being the melting pot of peoples cannot safely ignore this question. It is axiomatic that what comes out of the melting pot depends on what goes into it. A decade ago the majority of anthropologists and psychologists flouted the idea that there are any considerable differences in the native mental capacities of races or nationality groups. Today we have over-whelming evidence that they were mistaken. Army mental tests have shown that not more than 15 percent of American negroes equal or exceed in intelligence the average of our white population, and the intelligence of the average negro is vastly inferior to that of the average white man. The available data indicate that the average mulatto occupies about a mid-position between pure negro and pure white. The intelligence of the American Indian has also been over-rated, for mental tests indicate that it is not greatly superior to that of the average negro. Our Mexican population, which is largely of Indian extraction, makes little if any better showing.

The charge of cultural bias could have been raised against IQ tests at any time since their inception. It did not become a major controversy, however, until after the Second World War. Several things had to happen first. One was an intellectual legitimization of the belief in racial equality. This was supplied by the growing influence of Franz Boas in anthropology. Another was the acknowledgement that experience and environment greatly affected performance on IQ tests. If the tests measured hereditary ability, then there could be no such thing as cultural bias. But if they measured learning in a particular cultural setting, then the charge could have credibility.

Most important was the national shift in attitudes toward racial segregation which occurred largely as a result of the war itself. War-induced labor shortages had enabled unprecedented numbers of blacks to get jobs in major industries. As Russell Marks points out, this helped business leaders "to realize the importance of fully utilizing Black labor," and therefore to see the advantages of integrating blacks into white society.

The demands of industrial efficiency and social control were the driving
forces that largely changed the liberals' and businessmen's attitude toward
the Black. Once the Black was recognized as a capable productive unit,
whose economic potential could only be realized through more fully integrating him into society, then prejudice and discrimination were wasteful.

After the war it became fashionable to reinterpret test results in ways less
conducive to theories of white racial superiority. At the University of
Chicago, Allison Davis brought together researchers from several departments
to investigate the matter of cultural bias in IQ tests. The issue gained a
respectability and an acknowledged importance which previously it had lacked.
Even Lewis Terman came to doubt his earlier conclusions about the racial inferiority of blacks and Chicanos.

Business support of racial integration created a favorable climate for
the growth of the civil rights movement. The movement in turn challenged
IQ tests for being discriminatory against minorities. A series of court
battles helped to make the cultural bias of tests into a burning issue. The
integration of universities meant growing numbers of black and Chicano
psychologists would constitute a supply of competent professionals willing and
able to challenge the tests. All these factors dictated that the issue of
cultural bias could no longer be ignored.

Current Status of the Problem

As long as prevailing opinion was sufficiently racist, reports of the
inferior intelligence of ethnic and racial minorities were likely to be
accepted uncritically. However, as overtly racist statements have become
less fashionable, the meaning of blacks' fifteen-point deficit in IQ scores
has become problematic. Several linguists have been influential in swaying
opinion. William Labov, for example, has noted that until fairly recently
many whites observing the language of black children have interpreted it as
a symptom of mental inferiority. These observers have used test results
glibly to promote concepts like "verbal deprivation," according to which,

black children in the urban ghettos receive little verbal stimulation, hear very little well-formed language, and as a result are impoverished in their means of verbal expression: they cannot speak complete sentences, they do not know the names of common objects, cannot form concepts or convey logical thoughts.

Some educational psychologists have used these ideas to argue that the vernacular of black children should be disregarded in the classroom, because it is a symptom of mental inferiority. However, competent linguists like Labov have shown this view to be largely a product of the ethnocentrism of observers who, because they are unfamiliar with the language of black children, assume it is illogical, ungrammatical, and conceptually deficient. More careful examination of the language shows most of the charges to be clearly unwarranted. Stigmatizing children's normal language certainly cannot help them to learn in school and probably makes matters considerably more difficult. Hence, Labov points out, linguists "are unanimous in condemning this view as bad observation, bad theory, and bad practice."

Others have stressed that differences in dialect may hinder a teacher's relationship with minority children even when the teacher intends to avoid all forms of bias. As Gumperz and Hernandez-Chavez conclude:

> culture plays a role in communication that is somewhat similar to the
> role of syntactic knowledge in the decoding of referential meanings.
> Cultural differences, in other words, affect judgment both above and
> below the level of consciousness. A person may have every intention
> of avoiding cultural bias, yet, by subconsciously superimposing his
> own interpretation on the verbal performance of others, he may neverthe-
> less bias his judgment of their general ability, efficiency, etc.

The accusation of cultural bias in IQ tests is part of a larger critique which says that racism is instiutionalized in the curricula, teaching methods, and evaluation procedure of public schools. According to the traditional view of psychometricians, schools and IQ tests both provide fair assessments of any minority group's mental abilities. Black and brown children perform worse in school than whites because they generally have lower aptitudes and tests measure their lower aptitudes. According to the critique, black and brown children perform poorly because numerous subtle and not-so-subtle forms of discrimination in schools discourage them from doing their best. Their lower scores on IQ tests can be attributed to cultural bias in three different senses:

(1) Test items are selected which require information generally more accessible to white, middle-class children than to nonwhite minorities.

(2) Performance on tests depends greatly upon learning in school, hence lower test scores are a direct reflection of the various forms of discrimination in schools.

(3) Because black and brown children frequently have hostile or indifferent relationships with teachers and school authorities, they are not likely to be highly motivated to do well on tests. Hence, tests measure their negative attitudes towards tests rather than their capacities for learning.

The accusation of cultural bias in tests has confronted psychometricians with a tricky problem. On the one hand, the charge clearly has at least some validity. On the other hand, it is very difficult to know how much validity, since performance in school, the normal criterion against which tests are validated, is itself suspect. To know whether the black-white education gap is caused by the lower intelligence of blacks or the institutional racism of schools would require, at the very least, much painstaking observation of interactional processes in the classroom, a mammoth task for which most mental testers have neither the training nor the inclination. Even after this was done it is likely that evidence could be marshalled for either viewpoint, and the decision would come down to a moral and political choice of whether to blame the ethnic and racial minorities or the school system.

The problem is further compounded by the ability of black psychologists to design IQ tests referenced toward black culture. Because such tests have an obvious bias in favor of those familiar with ghetto language, whites tend to perform poorly on them. On the Black Intelligence Test of Cultural Homogeneity (BITCH), for example, a sample of blacks produces an average score 36 points above that of the sample of whites. Clearly, valid comparisons of ethnic groups would require some objective standard of culture-fairness. But thus far no one has been able to devise such a standard.

Most contemporary psychometricians have disdained interest in the theoretical question of comparing minority groups' intelligence levels. They have chosen to ignore the larger issue of cultural bias in tests and schools, and instead have focused on the more limited question of <u>selection bias in the tests as they are used for job selection and admission to schools.</u> A number of statistical approaches to this problem have been designed, all of which presuppose that the criterion performance measure (for example, college grade point average) is fair by definition. Selection procedures using tests are seen as fair or biased depending upon how well the tests predict subsequent performance. One popular approach, for example, claims that a test is fair for selection purposes if it predicts grade point average as well for blacks as it does for whites. Another approach contends that selection is fair when the percentage of minority applicants admitted is the same as the percentage reaching some specified level of criterion performance.

While all the approaches address themselves to important issues of selection, none are of much use in answering the basic question: Are the lower scores of ethnic minorities attributable to culture-bias or do they reflect genuinely lower capacities? The eugenics paradigm has specified this as an important question, and for the investigators who continue to work within the paradigm, culture-fair IQ tests have seemed to furnish the best strategy for answering the question.

Deficiencies of Culture-Fair IQ Tests

Culture-fair tests have maintained a considerable mystique. It is not uncommon to hear that they measure basic capacities which are largely unaffected by culture and learning. On the other hand, examination of the pertinent evidence shows the tests to be seriously deficient in two respects: their predictive validity appears to be considerably lower than that of conventional IQ tests, and their pretense of being impervious to cultural variations is unsupported and most likely false. Briefly reviewing the two most popular of these tests will make the point.

The two most widely acclaimed culture-fair tests have been Raven's <u>Progressive Matrices</u> and Cattell's <u>Culture-Fair Tests of g</u>, originally designed in 1938 and 1940, respectively. These two have followed the dominant approach of "employing simple figural materials (and) requiring subjects to engage in reasoning, inference, generalization, and other basic mental processes in terms of relationships between geometric forms, patterns, etc." For example, the four subtests for young children considered fully culture-fair by Cattell involve copying symbols, classifying pictures, tracing paths through mazes, and identifying similar drawings. Older children and adults are required to complete sequences of drawings by selecting from among five options, to pick out the drawing which differs from the others in a series, and so forth. Raven's matrices consist of geometrical designs from which the subject chooses the alternative which properly completes the sequence.

While no IQ test has a predictive validity sufficiently broad to justify use of the general intelligence concept, some of the standard tests, like the Stanford-Binet and Wechsler scales, are at least moderately able to predict performance in school. This establishes a baseline for what constitutes a valid IQ test. Although Raven's and Cattell's tests have been in existence for over thirty years, there appears to be virtually no evidence that they attain even this baseline of predictive validity. Reviewers generally sympathetic to the tests have noted this deficiency. About Cattell's test, one states that, "the evidence on the validity of the tests in predicting scholastic achievement is not impressive," and then he mentions one study showing a low correlation with performance on the Stanford Achievement Test for a small sample of only twenty-eight children. He also notes that the most recent handbook of the test lacks evidence relating to the test's validity. The other reviewer states that he "would need to see some real longitudinal validity data," before he could endorse the test. The situation is basically similar for the Progressive Matrices test. One reviewer says that the literature dealing with test validity and reliability is "equivocal," and that the test's "relevance to intellectual functioning in general remains to be documented." Another proclaims that "no really satisfactory conclusions as to validity are possible," on the basis of data reported.

The author warns us against taking the test as one of "general intelligence," but has nevertheless himself proceeded on some such basis to draw what appear to be inappropriate conclusions about "The Development and Decline of Mental Ability" (reviewer's italics) and specifically

describes his five rough screening grades as "intellectually superior,"
....."definitely above average in intellectual capacity,"....."intellectually
average" and "definitely below average in intellectual ability,".....and
"intellectually defective."

Some effort is made to circumvent the question of predictive validity
by proposing as a substitute criterion the g-factor loading of the tests
(that is, the extent to which test items are similar to one another in what
they measure). Since the tests were designed deliberately to maximize this
loading by eliminating items and subtests not highly saturated with g, it
is to be expected that the g-factor loadings will be high for both tests.
But all this means is that the items on each test are similar to one another.
It says nothing about the tests as measures of mental capacity outside of an
IQ-type test situation. In short, there can be no substitute for evidence
of predictive validity, and on this criterion the leading culture-fair tests
appear to be quite weak.

Of course, it could be argued that the predictive validity of conventional IQ tests stems precisely from their cultural biases; that is, the fact
that they contain subject matter familiar in school curricula is what makes
them effective predictors of classroom performance. This line of reasoning
suggests that it would be very difficult to construct a valid IQ test which
was not obviously culture-bound. As Anne Anastasi has argued, "a test
constructed entirely from elements that are equally familiar in many cultures
might measure trivial functions and possess little theoretical or practical
validity in any culture."

The fact that Raven's and Cattell's tests use geometrical forms rather
than words makes them less obviously culture-bound than conventional tests,
since geometry is presumably universal to all cultures. Also, average scores
appear to be the same for a variety of cultures - French, Taiwanese, British,
and American whites, for example. But scores tend to be lower for many
nonwhite groups - people of India, Puerto Ricans, and American blacks. Some
investigators are tempted to conclude that these nonwhite groups have less
capacity to reason abstractly, but there is an obvious alternative explanation
which casts serious doubt upon any such conclusion. The lower scoring populations may simply be less oriented to solving geometrical design problems.

They may have grown up using different shaped blocks as toys less often than the higher-scoring populations. Or they may have less experience with the systematic exploration of two-dimensional surfaces, like the pages of a test booklet. Games with dominoes are sometimes used as culture-fair IQ tests. But little effort is made to see how much time children from different races and strata actually spend playing with dominoes. It could be that children from relatively affluent families spend more time playing solitary, indoor games which resemble IQ test items because they have their own rooms whereas lower class children usually do not have their own rooms. So the latter are more oriented to communal, outdoor games and do not do as well on geometrical tests.

These differences may be especially important because familiarity with test items can greatly affect scores. As one reviewer says about Raven's Progressive Matrices test:

> The graceful will o' the wisp of "innate capacity" is perhaps even more enticing in the geometrical jungle, but recently published results of the Heim's experiments in Cambridge and other evidence seems to suggest that considerable gain in scores may be expected in well motivated repeated testing in (the test's 1938 version) without any knowledge of results.

Nonverbal tests may contain tremendous cultural biases, but these are camouflaged by the fact that only a cumulative record of children's play habits could reveal their true extent. Needless to say, such records are not sought by the tests' proponents. In short, the fact that a given test is less obviously biased does not mean that it is less biased.

Quite apart from any questions of test content, the testing situation itself may discriminate against minority children. Frank Reissman points out that the low scores of many black children may be due to poor rapport with examiners, low motivation to perform on tests, and a lack of meaningful, directed practice in taking tests. When Ernest Haggard trained examiners to establish better rapport, offered special incentives for doing well, and gave disadvantaged children three hours of practice with tests, the result was a dramatic improvement in their average IQ.

Critically examining the arguments made in favor of culture-fair tests raises the question of why test proponents have relied upon this defective reasoning. Why, for example, have some been willing to conclude that a high g-factor loading is sufficient evidence of the test's validity? Why has the comparability of some ethnic or racial groups' scores been seen as showing that the tests provide fair comparisons for all minority groups? What justification has there been for deciding that performance on geometrical design problems is largely unaffected by learning; or alternatively, that the relevant sorts of learning are equally present in all cultures? To answer these questions we must recall the illusions under which proponents labored when the tests were created.

CONSEQUENCES OF ABILITY GROUPING
FOR BLACKS AND OTHER MINORITIES
Ronald Samuda

The cardinal and most salient point of this present section
is that ability grouping inevitably leads to ethnic and socioeconomic separation. The second point, which follows logically
from the first, flows from the unequivocal and clear demonstration
of research studies which indicate that socioeconomic status is
correlated positively with both the scores on intelligence tests
and the level of scholastic achievement. Third, since blacks
and other minorities are, as a whole, in the lower socioeconomic
bracket, then it follows that ability grouping will have its most
potent effect on the learning situations of minority children.

The consequences of ability grouping are not merely confined
to the cognitive domain. The most pernicious influence of such a
strategy is found in forming, reinforcing, and maintaining myths
and stereotypes which themselves become part of the value systems
of teachers and the public at large; thus the vicious cycle is
formed. Tests, especially standardized group tests of intellectual
ability, are used to "prove" the "inherent intellectual inferiority"
of blacks, which leads to stratification in terms of estimated
potential, which leads to lowered self-concept and the perceived
lowered expectations of teachers, which, in turn, leads to poor
learning conditions and, inevitably, to inferior performance on
tests of achievement. In other words, the application of

Reprinted from Psychological Testing of American Minorities: Issues
and Consequences, 1975, p. 107-115.

standardized tests and the general organization of classes in terms of ability groups (together with the assumed relationship of IQ scores with potential achievement level) subscribe to the celebrated predictive validity of the IQ and other tests of intellectual aptitude. In these circumstances it is not so much that x (IQ) is related positively to y (achievement), but that xz is related to yz where z (the moderator variable) produces the positive correlation between aptitude and achievement. This means simply that minorities, in particular, and poor people, generally, bear the brunt of those stereotypes and practices that assume the appearance of scientific objectivity but have dire consequences that are educationally unsound, socially divisive, dehumanizing for minorities, and politically indefensible within a democratic society.

The only proper responsible and valid reason for adopting any educational device or strategy should be that it serves to enhance the learning of students in general. In the following pages the consequences and empirical evidence concerning ability grouping will be examined in terms of (1) segregating of citizens ethnically and socioeconomically within school systems, (2) resegregating of students within schools, (3) mislabeling of minority children in classes for the mentally retarded, (4) perpetuating racial discrimination and unfair educational practices, and (5) denying minorities and the poor the right to equality of educational opportunity.

Racial Segregation

Racial segregation, until fairly recently, was an established and institutionalized fact in the social, political, and educational structure of the United States. The Court's decision in Plessy v. Ferguson (1896) formally and legally sanctioned the establishment of parallel systems of education and the separation of students in different schools. Segregation was enforced in the Southern states as a way of life while in the North the races intermingled to a slight degree in the schools of New York, Chicago, Detroit, and elsewhere.

But whether or not segregation existed by law, the clustering of whites in certain more affluent, and often exclusively white, neighborhoods tended to ensure de facto segregation. In reality, then, blacks were isolated by economic limitations and by residential restrictions. The consequences of both de jure and de facto segregation were that blacks were either isolated within low-income neighborhoods and excluded from white school districts or attended schools within mixed neighborhoods where the majority of students were black.

The principle of "separate but equal" facilities was challenged in the case of Brown v. Board of Education of Topeka (1954), when it became illegal to bar any student from attending a school on the basis of his ethnicity only. However, passing a law cannot guarantee changes in the ingrained attitudes and stereotypes born of centuries of racial discrimination. Nor did the militancy of the civil rights movement and the aggressive desegregationist postures of the Kennedy and Johnson administrations serve to eradicate, or even substantially reduce, the fact of segregation. For, as the U. S. Commission on Civil Rights (1967) reported, racial isolation in the schools was perpetuated and compounded by policies and practices within school districts, by the influx and concentration of blacks within urban centers of Northern cities, and by the exodus of whites to the suburban neighborhoods where the purchase of homes by even those few blacks who could afford them was made almost impossible by real-estate manipulation.

In 1965 it was reported that 75 percent of black students lived in areas where the elementary schools contained 90 percent or more black children; 83 percent of the white elementary school population was living in areas 91 percent or more white. One may well ask: Why should schools be integrated? What is the educational advantage ensuing from desegregation?

As we have seen in the earlier sections, it is a well-documented fact that lower socioeconomic classes and minority ethnic membership are highly correlated with lower levels of performance on tests of intellectual ability and achievement. Thus ability grouping, especially when practiced by whole educational systems, results in racial isolation. The deleterious effects of ethnic isolation and de facto socioeconomic separation operates to the detriment of children of black, Puerto Rican, Indian, and Mexican-American ethnicity, since they are denied the opportunity of an optimum learning situation. For whether isolation of ethnic minorities and lower socioeconomic groups is accomplished through overt or covert strategies of discrimination, or whether the separation of class and caste is the result of ability grouping, the effect is to isolate students of one level from those of another to the detriment of the ethnic minority individuals and the less fortunate white students. As Findley and Bryan put it, "the impact of school upon individual students is a function of peer interactions -- that is, students tend to learn as much from other students as they do from teachers" (1971, p. 45). Moreover, the basic issue and the consequences of segregation were nicely articulated in the judgment prepared and presented by the late Chief Justice Earl Warren on behalf of a unanimous court. The central theme of the judgment might very well apply equally to ability grouping as it does to the separation of the races and the concomitant isolation on the basis of ethnicity:

>Does segregation of children begin in public schools solely on the basis of race, even though the physical facilities and other "tangible" factors may be equal, deprive the children of the minority group of equal educational opportunities? We believe it does.
>
>. . . To separate children in grade and high schools from others of similar age and qualifications solely because of their race generates a feeling of inferiority as to their status in the community that may affect their hearts and minds in a way unlikely ever to be undone. The effect of this separation on their educational opportunities was well stated by a finding in the Kansas cases by a (lower) court which nevertheless felt compelled to rule against the Negro plantiffs.
>
>Segregation of white and colored children in public schools has a detrimental effect upon the colored children. The impact is greater when it has the sanction of the law; for the policy of separating the races is usually interpreted as denoting the inferiority of the Negro group. A sense of inferiority affects the motivation of a child to learn. Segregation with the sanction of law, therefore, has a tendency to retard the educational and mental development of Negro children and to deprive them of some of the benefits they would receive in a racial (ly) integrated school system.
>
>We conclude that in the field of public education the doctrine of "separate but equal" has no place. Separate educational facilities are inherently unequal . . . Such segregation is a denial of the equal protection of the laws (Brown v. Board of Education of Topeka, 347 U. S. 483, 1954).

The decision of the Supreme Court, aside from recognizing that racial segregation is incompatible with the basic tenets of democracy, also forced many teachers, social scientists, and the general public to reexamine their values. Though the "separate but equal" doctrine died legally on May 17, 1954, it triggered sociopolitical conflict that has not yet been resolved, for integration in education is part of the larger context of integration and equality of opportunity in employment, housing, and political representation. Until there exists unfettered participation in the political and economic areas, until there is the possibility for true social mobility with free access to residence, there can be no equality of educational opportunity.

Impact of the Exodus from the Cities

The judgment of the Warren Court outlawed overt segregation. However, the crucial issue of the 1970s is found in the more or less covert separation of the races in urban and suburban neighborhoods. It represents, indeed, de facto segregation, for although integration within the local political boundaries of the district may have been accomplished, the city-suburban boundary and the ability to purchase a home in a suburban neighborhood have now become the deciding factors of segregation and racial isolation. The special problems of urban areas, in particular, and the critical issues in American education, generally, find eloquent expression in Peter Schrag's (1967) words:

> In city after city the exodus continues. A few years ago urban planners spoke hopefully of the return to the center, of a migration back to the core city by people who had had enough of car pools and commuting, of mowing lawns and compulsory neighborliness. But although some came back -- most of them people whose children had grown and moved away -- the tide never turned. Nevertheless the planners continued to produce their schemes, each of them

calling for more ambitious programs in transportation, housing, and general redevelopment. Yet none ever focused on the single public service that must constitute the very essence of urban life and renewal -- public education . . .
. . . .The resources exist, but they still flow in overwhelming abundance to the private sector and to the communities that least need them. They flow to the suburbs and to the great establishments of private wealth; and every year, despite the apparently increasing programs of public welfare, the inequities become greater. If we really mean to have effective public education, then urban and suburban systems can no longer operate as independent enterprises each with its sepapate and unequal local financial capabilities, its own special, and often limited facilities, its own little circumscribed area of concern . . . There is, moreover, no academic rationale for the maintenance of clusters of hundreds of independent little school districts in a single metropolitan region; what they can do separately in integrating schools, and in financing them, in planning and operating programs, they can do far more effectively together. The only educational reason for their separation is the perpetuation of segregation and inequity (in Ehlers 1969, pp. 75-76).

The migration of white, middle- and upper-class citizens from the cities can only help to compound the problem inevitably making of the city a place for the very rich, the poor, the old, and the minorities. At the heart of the issue lies social injustice and racial prejudice. The differential migration of whites to the suburbs and blacks to the inner city can only ensure a return to separate, but unequal, facilities, for it is not possible to establish separate and equal facilities while this trend continues. Segregation stamps an inferior status on the persons who are barred from full participation in society -- with it go inescapable and concomitant feelings of rejection and lowered self-esteem, which in turn affect performance in school and elsewhere. As the president of Morgan State College, Martin Jenkins, has stated, "the best education for all students, from the elementary through the graduate level, can be achieved only under conditions of racial integration in our society" (in Wilcox 1971, p. 49).

Resegregation Through Ability Grouping

Ability grouping operates as a kind of fail-safe mechanism to ensure that when children of mixed ethnicity attend the same school, they are once more resegregated along essentially ethnic and socioeconomic lines under the guise of grouping by standardized objective-test results. As was stated previously, there is no lack of evidence to support the fact that black students score, on the average, one standard deviation below the level of white students on standardized tests of intellectual ability and also on standardized achievement measures (Shuey, 1966; Dreger and Miller, 1960; Heathers, 1969; Findley and Bryan, 1971).

Therefore, it stands to reason that placement into classes on the basis of standardized tests -- must result in a preponderance of minorities in those tracks comprising lower-achieving students. Ability grouping, it has been pointed out, results in socioeconomic and ethnic stratification and consequently, drastically affects the learning of the poor and minority students through the negative attitudes of teachers, the lowered expectations held by teachers and students themselves, the loss of self-esteem of the minority students, the watered-down curriculum within the class, the impediment to ego development for students labeled inferior, the feelings of rejection, and the overt and covert attitudes of superiority and dominance on the part of students in high-ability groups. When the facts of the student's color and ethnic origin are coupled with lowered performance, lowered self-concept, and, as is frequently the case, with the conditions of poverty and insufficient facilities within the home, the minority child sooner or later comes to accept his role and to act in accordance with the social stereotype. As Heathers (1969)

remarked: "Ability grouping may thus be, in effect, an agency
for maintaining and enhancing caste and class stratification in
a society."

The issues and consequences of ability grouping were
dramatically surveyed and presented in the critical court decision
of Hobson v. Hansen (1967). Once again, as in the Brown case
concerning racial segregation, it was the courts that determined
educational policy and pinpointed the injustice of ability
grouping as another form of racial isolation through resegregation
within the school itself. The case dealt with the use of
standardized tests to establish the tracking system of homogeneous
ability groups throughout the entire school system of Washington,
D. C. Both elementary and secondary school levels were stratified
on the basis of test results into homogeneous ability groups ranging
from "basic" for the lowest achievers to "honors" for gifted
students. The curricular content of each track, or ability level,
was geared accordingly. The elementary and junior secondary schools
were organized into three tracks: basic or special academic (for
"retarded" students), general (for the average or above-average
students), and honors (for gifted students). At the senior high
school level, a fourth track, called regular, was added for college
preparatory study for above-average students.

Data presented by the defendants clearly demonstrated that:
(1) track placement was directly and almost perfectly correlated with
income levels of the students' homes; (2) those schools within the
income bracket of $6,000 or below enrolled over 90 percent black
students; (3) the predominantly white high school served a
community of average income equivalent to $10,374 and had all but

8 percent of students enrolled in honors or regular tracks in 1964 and 1965; (4) while 16 percent of blacks in elementary and junior secondary schools were enrolled in honors programs in 1965, 70 percent of their white peers were enrolled in the advanced curriculum; (5) black students were substantially overrepresented in special academic tracks for the "retarded." Thus the court was compelled to recognize the separation of students along socioeconomic and, to a lesser degree, ethnic lines. As Judge Wright put it:

> The evidence shows that the method by which track assignments are made depends essentially on standardized aptitude tests which, although given on a system-wide basis are completely inappropriate for use with a large segment of the student body. Because the tests are primarily standardized on and are relevant to a white middle-class group of students, they produce inaccurate and misleading test scores when given to lower class and Negro students. As a result, rather than being classified according to ability to learn, these students are in reality being classified according to their socio-economic or racial status, or -- more precisely -- according to environmental and psychological factors which have nothing to do with innate ability.

Mislabeling of Minority Students

The overrepresentation of minority students in the lowest-ability classes of elementary and secondary schools is an observable and easily documented fact. The classes for slow learners, the educable mentally retarded (EMR), and the mentally retarded (MR), house significantly greater proportions of black and Hispanic students than white students. The study by Coleman et al. (1966) showed that at the elementary and secondary levels the school attended by the average black child contained a significantly greater

proportion of children in the lower tracks. Dunn (1968) noted
that at the national level, minorities comprised more than 50
percent of the mentally retarded. The figures issued by the
Bureau of Intergroup Relations of the State Department of Education
for the State of California in the fall of 1970 reveal that whereas
blacks, who represent 9.1 percent of the total student population
of the state, account for 27.5 percent of the educable mentally
retarded, they constitute only 2.5 percent of the mentally gifted.
Although these statistics have been publicly recorded and announced,
it took two major "studies" to point up in clear and dramatic
detail the pernicious effects of standardized tests of intelligence
and their use for mislabeling minority children. The first was a
study conducted over an eight year period by Jane Mercer, a
sociologist and researcher at the University of California at
Riverside; the second consisted of the presentations and judgment
of a case (supported by the ABP of the Bay Area) tried in the city
of San Francisco on behalf of black students against Wilson Riles,
the superintendent of education for the State of California.

Mercer's study (1971), since it was confined to the southern
region of California, is of particular significance for children
of Chicano Hispanic-American ethnicity, but it dealt also with
the mislabeling of black children and their placement in mentally
retarded classes on the basis of tests of intelligence. Her
contention is that so-called intelligence tests, as presently
used, are, to a large extent, "Anglocentric"; that is, they
mirror the standards, values, and experiences of the white,
Anglo-Saxon middle-class person. Inevitably, the results of such

tests affect, to a greater degree, persons from a different cultural background and those from lower socioeconomic status. The eight-year study documented the fact that public schools had been sending more children to MR classes than any of the 241 organizations contacted by Mercer and her co-workers (law enforcement agencies, private organizations for the MR, medical facilities, religious organizations, public welfare centers, and so on). Criteria for selection and placement in such classes were based on (1) the almost exclusive reliance on IQ test scores and the almost total absence of medical diagnosis; (2) the utilization of a high cutoff score (IQ of 79 or below as compared to a recommended IQ of 69 or below) in order to draw the border line between mental retardates and normal students; (3) the failure to take into account sociocultural factors when interpreting IQ test results. The study found that over four times as many Mexicans and twice as many blacks were enrolled in the classes for the mentally retarded, a disproportionate number for their population in the state. However, when a "two-dimensional" definition of mental retardation is used (a definition that not only takes into consideration intellectual performance but also assesses adaptive behavior) and when IQ scores are interpreted with the knowledge that sociocultural factors contaminate them, then, Mercer showed that racial imbalance in classes for the MR disappeared. Consequently, she argued, approximately 75 percent of the children enrolled in MR classes were mislabeled, incorrectly placed, and suffered from stigmatization and lowered self-esteem as well as a learning environment that was far from optimum.

In the Case of Larry P. et al. v. Wilson Riles et al. (1972),
the plaintiffs, six black San Francisco elementary schoolchildren,
charged the defendants namely, the California State Department of
Education and the San Francisco School District, with having placed
them in EMR classes on the basis of IQ tests alone. When the
plaintiffs were retested by certified black psychologists using
techniques that took account of the cultural and experiential
backgrounds of the students, all achieved scores above the cutoff
point of 75. Accordingly, the U. S. District Court judge Robert
Peckham ordered that:

> Defendants be restrained from placing black students in
> classes for the educable mentally retarded on the basis
> of criteria which place primary reliance on the results
> of IQ tests as they are currently administered, if the
> consequence of the use of such criteria is racial imbalance
> in the composition of such classes.

In an unprecedented decision, the court recognized the
pervading cultural bias of the present tests and the misplacement
of and ensuing harm done to black children when tested by such
measures. The court order was aimed at preventing future wrongful
placement of black children in special classes, but it did not
provide for the elimination of the effects of past discrimination,
nor did it rule that the use of intelligence tests be suspended
or that the EMR black children should be released and retested for
fairer placement. However, it cited the efforts of the New York
City school system, which banned group IQ tests, and the Massachusetts school system, which attempted to minimize the importance
of IQ tests, as alternative plans to be used pending the
development of appropriate tests.

Summary

In the studies and court judgments cited in this section on ability grouping, evidence has been brought to bear upon the harmful effects of the use of standardized tests to establish homogeneous ability groups in schools. As Mayeske (1970) in his interpretation of the Coleman Report has indicated, the environment of the school reflects, in large part, the underlying problems of American society -- that of racial prejudice and ethnic separation, which permeate almost all institutions. Standardized tests, inasmuch as they are used to rationalize such cleavages, are injurious to minorities and adversely affect the well-being of the entire nation.

Ability grouping seems to have no positive value for helping students in general. Its major and hence most undesirable effect is to isolate the poor and minority students in lower-achieving classes. As Findley and Bryan (1971) concluded, removal of ability grouping does not affect racial discrimination in areas where the exodus from the city has left the urban areas ethnically isolated. Finally, ability grouping per se without drastic changes in curriculum, teaching methods, and materials does more harm than good.

ELEMENTARY AND SECONDARY ACHIEVEMENT TESTS
George Weber

Most of the standardized tests that children take in school are achievement tests. While over the thirteen years of elementary and secondary school (counting kindergarten) a child may take several I. Q. tests, one reading readiness test, and several college admission tests (discussed in the next section), he will almost certainly take six or more achievement tests, and he may well take as many as eleven or twelve. Some school systems are now giving achievement tests in every grade, or in almost every grade. Six widely used achievement series are the SRA Assessment Survey and the Iowa Tests of Educational Development (published by Science Research Associates for grades 1 - 12); the Stanford Achievement Tests (Harcourt Brace Jovanovich, grades 1 - 9); the Cooperative Primary Tests (Educational Testing Service, grades 1 - 3); the Iowa Tests of Basic Skills (Houghton Mifflin, grades 1 - 9); the Metropolitan Achievement Tests (Harcourt, Brace, Jovanovich, grades 1 - 6), and the Sequential Tests of Educational Progress (Educational Testing Service, grades grades 3 - 14). What do such tests measure? How well do they do it? For what purposes are the results used?

All of the six test series named above purport to measure reading and mathematics achievement at every level. Beyond the primary grades some or all purport to measure, in addition, achievement in science, social science, punctuation, English expression, and study skills. While these are very important subjects, it should be borne in mind, in view of the tests' general names and the tendency to equate their scores with general academic achievement, that not one of these tests tries to measure directly either of two important skills: speaking and writing. Nor do they attempt to test many other things that many people believe are important outcomes of good schooling; for example, interest in learning, initiative, imagination, morality, self-discipline, knowledge and skills in the arts, ability in foreign

Reprinted from Uses and Abuses of Standardized Testing in the Schools, #22, 1977, p. 10-21.

languages, and physical development. Turning to the form of the tests, they are all multiple-choice tests. All except the Cooperative Primary Tests are timed; that is, they are given with specific time limits with the knowledge that many or even all of the students will fail to finish within the indicated periods. (The lowest level of the SRA, Primary I, is a partial exception since it has a time limit so generous, according to the publisher, that about 90 per cent of the pupils finish.) The series are arranged in different levels, each one designed for a different grade range. The content of each is supposedly related to the usual curriculum in those grades. The Stanford series, for example, has six levels, designed respectively for grades 1-2, 2-3, 3-4, 4-5, 5-6, and 7-9.

How well do these tests measure what they claim to? The answer depends upon the purposes for which the results are used, the level of the test, the subject matter involved, and the competence and integrity of their administration.

The purposes can be divided between those related to the scores for the individual students and those related to the scores for groups. The individual's scores are used to promote to the next grade, to assign to a class within a grade or to a group within a class, to assign to a special program (for example, for the retarded or the gifted), and to indicate the kind of courses he is permitted to take in junior high school and high school. They are also used, sometimes, to indicate the areas of his schooling that need greater attention. The individual's scores are also used in a counseling function, that is, in talking with the student and his parents in connection with choices in which they at least nominally take part: courses, programs, need for outside help, career plans, and so forth. Finally, and sometimes subtly, the individual's scores may well influence the teachers' expectations about the student.

Generally speaking, these purposes are somewhat better served by these tests the higher the grade level of the test and are more poorly served in reading than in other areas. Over-all, the tests provide less information about the student's achievements in the various fields than is already known to his teachers, assuming them to be even moderately competent. For example, the classroom elementary school teacher should know more about her pupils; individual reading and mathematical ability, either from their previous teachers or from her own experience, than the tests can tell her, but she has been told that her judgments are not as

dependable as scores on standardized tests. And when it comes to particular
skills within these areas, the tests are even less helpful. For example,
an arithmetic test may include a half-dozen multiple-choice questions on
long division. There is no way of knowing how may of these are answered
correctly by chance. A teacher can get a more reliable index of the child's
skill by giving him six problems to do in the usual way (no guessing possible).

Some Faults of Reading Tests

The tests in reading deserve special attention because they are usually
given the most weight in the various decisions listed above. One of the faults
of the reading tests at the lower levels is the frequency of inappropriate
vocabulary. The test makers say that the words used are from the children's
hearing and speaking vocabularies, but most second-graders do not know log,
chimney, tale, ribbon, village, polite, chatting, sapling, postage, baggage,
peak, and harvest. By using a number of words such as these, the test
makers have made a reading test dependent in part on breadth of vocabulary.
Breadth of vocabulary is one aspect of reading skill in the higher grades and
in high school, but in testing the mechanical skills of beginning reading it
penalizes the child with a small hearing vocabulary.

Another important fault of these tests is their cultural bias. All of
our children, including those from inner-city houses and from homes where
Spanish or some other foreign language is spoken, should try to determine
their ability to do so. But selection of vocabulary, pictures, and subject
matter should not bias the tests in favor of some groups of children, and in
some cases it does. Cutting the grass, raking leaves, going to the beach,
taking a vacation trip in a car, having a pet turtle, and celebrating
birthdays with a party for other children are more likely to be familiar to
some groups of children than to others. In the lower grades, the solution to
the vocabulary faults outlined above lies in using words that are familiar
to all English-speaking American children of the particular grade level.
For organizations as large and as talented as the big test makers, this should
present no difficulty, since the number of words understood by ear by all
these children in the lower grades runs into the thousands. Pictures and
subject matter present a somewhat more difficult problem, but a great deal
can be done to make the tests fairer in this regard. Incidentally, the newest

tests are less culturally biased than those of a decade or two ago, but much improvement remains to be accomplished.

Another fault of the reading tests lies in the structure of some of the reading comprehension questions. In theory, these questions test the child's ability to read a paragraph, but in fact some of the questions can be answered correctly without even reading the paragraph.[5] Moreover, a few questions cannot be answered correctly without information that the paragraph does not provide. In such case, the test is measuring the extent of general information known, not reading ability. Here is an example of a question that can be answered correctly without reading the accompanying paragraph: "At the museum there were ( ) paintings ( ) books ( ) dogs." And here is a question that requires information not provided in a paragraph about a boy who comes from a country where almost everyone speaks Spanish: "Juan might have come from ( ) Germany ( ) England ( ) Mexico ( ) France." The paragraph makes no mention of Mexico, and so the pupil has to know that Mexico is a Spanish-speaking country. These are faults that are easily remedied. In fact, most of the reading comprehension questions do require reading of the paragraph and can be answered correctly with the information it contains. There is no reason why they all could not meet these obvious requirements.

Still another fault of the reading tests (and one that applies to other tests as well) involves their time limits and their scoring. The scoring on all these tests is based on the number of items right, with no penalty for wrong answers. Since, with the exception of the Cooperative Primary Tests, these are all timed tests, some or even all of the students will fail to finish. Yet a pupil who gets 30 right and 10 wrong on a 40-item test gets exactly the same score as a pupil who does only 30 and gets all of them right! Obviously this gives an advantage to the pupil who works faster because of habit, coaching, or greater familiarity with this kind of test. This fault could, and should, be eliminated or reduced in significance. There is no reason whatsoever why the tests cannot be scored in a way that penalizes wrong answers. And the time factor could be either eliminated by allowing all children to finish (as in the case of the

Cooperative

[5]The frequency of this flaw is analyzed in "Determining the Passage Dependency of Comprehension Questions in 5 Major Tests" by J. Jaap Tuinman (Reading Research Quarterly, IX [1973, 1974], 20.

Cooperative Primary Tests) or greatly reduced in importance by extending the time allowed.

These faults greatly limit the value of individual scores, even for the teacher who is incompetent or lacks confidence in her own judgments of her pupils' abilities.

Interpreting the Scores

Beyond the tests themselves and the raw scores that result, there are weaknesses in the testing procedure that relate to the method of interpreting the scores. The raw scores are typically interpreted in terms of national norms, which are estimates of nation-wide performance. These national norms are usually recorded and reported as grade-equivalents. In other words, the student's score is recorded as 4.7 (fourth grade, seventh month) in reading, for example, or 8.6 (eighth grade, sixth month) in social studies. This method of interpreting the student's achievement is so important that it requires further explanation.

The national norms are derived from giving the test to what is supposed to be a representative sample of students. But since the samples are different and are taken at different times, the norms for different tests vary. As a result, the normed score for a student depends partly on which test he takes. Recognizing this fact, in 1971 the U. S. Office of Education granted some $700,000 to the Educational Testing Service for a project to develop conversion tables for the various national norms on the reading and vocabulary sections of seven tests widely given to grades four, five, and six.

The method of reporting national norms in terms of grade-equivalents is one which Dr. Henry S. Dyer, a former vice-president of Educational Testing Serivce, has called "absurd, wrong and misleading."[6] The grade-equivalent represents the estimated median score that pupils in that month of that grade would achieve on the test nation-wide. For example, a 3.8 in reading would mean the average score for a child in the eighth month of the third grade. One trouble with this procedure has already been referred to -- the fact that the grade-equivalent score for a given person varies from test to test. Moreover, on some tests, a few answers one way or the other can make as much as a whole year's difference in the grade-equivalent score. Obviously, the tests are not that accurate. Another problem lies in the frequent misconception that the score means that a child has mastered the standard curriculum up to that

---

[6]The New York Times, March 23, 1974.

point in schooling; that is, that the child with the 3.8 score has mastered reading through the material given in the eighth month of the third grade. The score has no such meaning. Even if the 3.8 grade-equivalent were always an accurate estimate of the average achievement for the child in the eighth month of the third grade, that average child has not mastered the reading curriculum to that point; he is merely at that point in his schooling.

Parents, and even teachers, usually do not understand this. If Susan, in the third grade, gets a 6.8 score on her reading test, her proud parents usually believe that she reads as well as typical children in the eighth month of the sixth grade. This is usually not the case. Even if the norming is accurate, it means that Susan, on a third-grade test, got a score equal to the average score that children in the eighth month of the sixth grade would get on that test. If Susan took a reading test intended for sixth-graders, with much more difficult vocabulary, syntax, and content, she probably would not receive a 6.8 on that test. It is important to understand the distortions at the other end as well. Johnny, a fourth-grader who takes the SRA reading comprehension test intended for fourth-graders and receives a 2.6 score, is, in all probability, not reading as well as the average pupil in the sixth month of the second grade in any useful sense. That score is the median chance score on that multiple-choice test if all questions are answered, and so Johnny, quite possibly, is not able to read at all! No wonder Dr. Dyer had such harsh words for grade-equivalent scores.

Fortunately, most tests offer national norm scores in other terms. (In fact, the Cooperative Primary and Sequential tests do not provide grade-equivalent tables.) A better way of interpreting the raw score is in terms of percentiles. In this method, a 35 means that the pupil's score is estimated to be better than 35 per cent of children at his stage of schooling. The weakness of this scoring system is that it conveys a false sense of accuracy. The child who scores 35 may well score 25 or 15 on another test or at another sitting. Because of this problem, some tests offer stanine or percentile-band scores. Without going into the details, it can be said that these scores indicate broad ranges of achievement. In the stanine system, the score ranges from 1 (very low) to 9 (very high). These rough-cut systems reflect the rough accuracy of the tests themselves and avoid the many problems of grade-equivalencies. They are adequate for reporting to parents and are less subject to misinterpretation by the teachers who want to use them.

Besides teachers and parents, others use the individual's scores
on the standardized achievement tests, notably counselors, principals,
and the system as an institution. The scores, rather than teacher judgments, are often used for the purposes listed earlier: promotion,
assignment, and counseling. If all our teachers were competent and
confident of their judgments, this would be unnecessary. But in the
real world, many teachers are incompetent or lack confidence in their
judgments, and the test scores seem to offer a disinterested measure of
the individual's achievements. As already mentioned, the measure is
actually a partial one and one that is deficient in other respects as well.
Nevertheless, if the scores form a consistent pattern over the years, they
may be of help to the principal or counselor in some situations, particularly
in placement of students coming in from other schools. In recent years,
authorities have used the scores in an attempt to change promotion changes.
In New York City, for example, the chancellor (superintendent) recently ordered
that a student would henceforth not be given an eighth-grade diploma if he
were more than a year behind in reading on the basis of the standardized test.
The student so behind will, however, be given a certificate that will enable
him to proceed to high school, or be "transferred" with neither diploma nor
certificate. This order tightened up an effort started several years ago to
eliminate the embarrassment of turning out high school graduates who are
functional illiterates. This shameful situation illustrates the occasional
usefulness of the standardized test scores in circumstances (by no means
confined to New York City) where existing school systems leave much to be
desired.

Uses of Group Scores

Group scores on achievement tests (scores for classes, other groups
of students, schools and whole school systems) serve purposes quite different
from those served by individual scores. Group scores are used by the teacher
to judge the progress of the class in the several skills, by various people to
assess curriculum, and to evaluate projects, teachers, schools, and the school
systems. Here again, the grade-equivalent national norms are usually used,
despite the shortcomings stated above.

For the first purpose, the teacher can rely on the class scores in the various skills and subjects with somewhat more validity than she can on the individual scores. The reason for this is statistical; while a given pupil's score on a few long division questions is subject to considerable chance, the combined score of 25 pupils is subject to a great deal less. The teacher can therefore use the relative scores to compare achievement in long division and, say, in multiplication. She might conclude that she needs to give more attention to the skill with the lower score. The same conclusion, however, can be reached by the competent teacher by other means, notably tests of her own making. The situation is similar when the test covers a number of other subjects. Results on the tests that cover several subjects may suggest that the class is doing relatively worse in science than in, say, reading, and the teacher can adjust her teaching accordingly.

The other purposes of group scores involve a fundamentally different situation that of scores being used by people outside the classroom. The principal and assistant principals of a school, particularly a small school, in appraising the pupils' collective achievements, the effectiveness of various materials and programs, and their teachers' competence, should be able to make better judgments than those based simply on the group scores of the various classes and grades. Yet the group scores may be of some value if the principal or assistant principal understands the tests and knows the background of the pupils. When it comes to people physically outside the school-- the researcher, central office administrators, the school board, parents, and the public--there is no convenient way to evaluate the students' collective achievements except by the group scores on the tests. In these cases, the tests, despite their shortcomings and abuses, provide the best information available. For reasons that will be outlined below, the scores must be interpreted with great care.

The fundamental weakness of the use of group scores lies in the fact that one cannot always count on honest and competent administration of the tests. Typically, the tests are given by teachers, but occasionally they are given by project directors or researchers. The accuracy of the scores depends on precise administration. It also depends on honest administration, and as more importance is being attached to the results, the temptations to cheat are becoming greater. It is well to remember that the tests are being administered in most cases, by persons who have, or think they have, something at stake in the outcome. A teacher wants to be judged successful; a project director is in the same position; and a firm with a performance contract has perhaps most of all at stake. The brief experience with performance contractors has already led to efforts to provide independent, outside auditors. Most teachers and administrators try to administer the tests honestly. But the possibility of cheating must always be borne in mind, particularly in the lower grades, where the nature of the tests makes cheating quite easy.

Most cheating takes the form of coaching (excessive preparation), but there are other, more flagrant types of misbehavior, such as teaching the particular words or items that appear on the test, practicing on the test itself, changing the answers before the tests are scored, giving pupils aid during the test, allowing additional time, and failing to test pupils who are expected to do poorly. Since the tests do not penalize wrong answers and most have time limits, even such apparently innocuous acts as urging the children to guess or urging them to work more rapidly can make a significant difference in the scores. It is no wonder that some schools have considerably higher test scores than their students' day-to-day achievement warrants.

The Value of Group Scores

Taking into account this problem of competent and honest administration, what can we say about the value of group scores for various purposes? They are sometimes of value in assessing curriculum. The state of California saw its elementary test scores in mathematical computation decline year after year for seven or eight years concident with the state's adoption and increased use of a "new math" series of textbooks. Although many of the teachers in the state were undoubtedly aware of the decline in computational skills in their own schools, the decline of the scores state-wide, at the same time as reading scores were not declining, was a fairly conclusive way of locating the difficulty. The same thing happened in the state of New York. Without widespread routine achievement testing there probably would have been great argument about whether computational skills were declining, and, if so, whether the "new math" programs were responsible.

The two cases point up a number of things. The routine administration of achievement tests provided data that could later be analyzed in various ways. If the tests had been administered on an ad hoc basis to determine the accuracy of suspicions about the impact of the "new math" on computation, the testing and investigation would have taken years, which would have delayed conclusions and remedies. Moreover, a special testing program would have been subject to great argument over the proper tests to give and the procedure, and perhaps even the integrity of the testing would have been jeopardized. The valuable data were available in a timely fashion because they resulted from a testing program that was routine and done without previous knowledge of the purpose to which it was to be put.

Similar applicatons of routine test results can be made in other fields. For example, a school system may find that its scores in English usage are far below those of other systems in similar localities, or far below their own scores in other subject areas. Such a finding can properly lead to an investigation of its curriculum. Note that I have mentioned two different kinds of analyses: one that compares test results over time and one that compares test results at a single point in time. Both can be useful.

Using test scores to evaluate a particular project, program, or experiment is difficult business. Even if the test is appropriate to the purposes of the particular project, the testers have a stake in the outcome; they are the people who have advocated the experiment or who publish the materials being tried out. An independent evaluation is necessary, but even that is not as easy to achieve as may first appear. If those who have a stake in the experiment know the test that will be used to evaluate it, it becomes possible to "teach to the test" and thereby improve the chances of a favorable evaluation. It is desirable to allow the independent evaluator to use any reasonable test he chooses, without informing interested parties of the choice in advance. Even that is not as sure a guarantee as it may seem because of the similarity among the various standardized achievement tests.

An additional safeguard for sound evaluation is to provide for an experimental period of at least three years. As Dr. Roger Lennon, executive vice-president of Harcourt Brace Jovanovich, has pointed out, the standardized achievement tests are not accurate enough to form the basis for judging experiments when the period is a year or less.[7] We must therefore question the marvelous success stories about programs that raised the score of the pupils so many months during an instructional period of so many months.

---

[7] "Accountability and Performance Contracting," an address to the American Educational Research Association. New York City, February 5, 1971.

On experimental programs, we must demand an independent evaluation that shows, over a period of three years or longer, a gain in achievement of a year or more over what could otherwise have been expected. There are such success stories, but they are few and far between.

The use of achievement test scores to evaluate the performance of teachers is theoretically possible, perhaps, but not now practical. One obvious flaw is that the teacher to be rated is giving the test herself! Another obvious difficulty lies in the fact that most teachers have their students only one year. When a fairly discrete subject is taught in one year, as say in the case of high school physics, the quality of the teaching might make a substantial difference in the year-end test scores. But in most subjects reading, mathematics, social studies -- the teacher of one year is building on what others have done, and the subjects are too extensive to be mastered in a year. Accordingly, a judgment as to what a teacher has achieved during the year should take into account not just the level of achievement at the year's end, but the level of achievement at the beginning of the year and the learning ability of the students she had to teach. A competent principal knows the ability of the teachers in his school, and this judgment depends only in part on the achievement test scores of the pupils.

For some years, almost all school systems have been compiling achievement test scores school by school. Beginning in 1966 with the publication of scores for the New York City schools, a small number of school systems have released these results to the public. Unfortunately, these scores cannot always be taken at face value. School personnel know that some schools have cheated on their tests, but the scores have to be published anyway. Even though perhaps 90 per cent of the schools have roughly accurate scores, there is usually no way for the outsider to know, short of conducting an independent evaluation, whether a given school's scores are sound. One can safely assume that where the scores reflect average or below-average performance in relation to the background of the students, the results are roughly accurate. It is where the school reports high scores in relation to the background of its students that skepticism is in order. But these scores do provide useful information to the central administration and the school board, and they give the general public a better picture of academic achievement than it would otherwise have.

The users of these figures should, however, bear in mind a number of things. The most important, perhaps, is that an average score means true accomplishment for a school where the background of the students is poor, whereas it means the opposite for a school where the background of the students is good. That is, the quality of the school's effort cannot be inferred simply from its test scores. Another fact is that the scores are usually reported only as a single-figure average, which does not show how many students score far above or far below that point. Another fact is that all of these scores are in terms of national average achievement, and there is no indication whether this is good, bad, or indifferent in terms of reasonable standards. It may seem strange, but the fact that a given school's third grade does as well on a given test as the national third grade average does not reveal how well the children can read. Since reading achievement in the primary grades is generally below what could reasonably be accomplished, reading scores suggest a better achievement than is in fact the case. For example, study the scores as long as you like and you will still not learn that from 10 to 15 per cent of our third graders, nationwide, cannot read at all.

A fair comparison of achievement scores between school systems is difficult and often impossible. One reason is that different school systems use different achievement tests, and the norms are not easily comparable. Another reason is that the students may not be similar. For example, if one wanted to compare achievement scores for Baltimore with those of Chicago, one would discover that Baltimore uses the Iowa Tests of Basic Skills and Chicago uses the Metropolitan. Besides, although Baltimore and Chicago may seem to have similar groups of students, one would have to go into this question carefully to determine if this were actually true.

While fine comparisons between school systems are very risky; gross comparisons are possible. If one system's sixth graders have an 8.4 median score in reading and another system's have a 6.4, one can safely assume that reading achievement at the sixth grade level in the first system is higher, even though different standardized tests were used. If the same test was used, a narrower difference will allow the same conclusion. It should be remembered, however, that these are single-figure averages. The highest individual scorers in the 6.4 system will be above the lowest scorers in the 8.4 system. Usually the highest scoring school in the 6.4 district will have a higher score than the lowest scoring school in the 8.4 district, though in a given case this may not be so because the 6.4 district may be a large city in which the children from the most favorable backgrounds in the metropolitan area are in the suburban districts and private schools and the 8.4 district may be a homogeneous suburb of families with highly favorable backgrounds. As a general rule, schools differ in achievement more than do school systems, and individual children differ most of all. In a study of inner-city schools that I made several years ago, the school with the lowest over-all reading achievement at the third grade level nevertheless had 19 per cent of its third graders scoring above the third grade level.

Summary

In summary, the standardized achievement tests given in the elementary and secondary schools are of little or no value to competent teachers in appraising the work of individual students. The individual scores are of value to people outside the classroom, such as counselors, when they form a regular pattern over a number of years, and in occasional other circumstances, such as attempts to raise standards of promotion. Group scores can be of value to teachers in studying the relative progress of a class. Group scores, if they are interpreted and used with care, can be of value to others (principals, researchers, central office administrators, school boards, and the public) in making judgments about curriculum, programs, and school systems.

COMPETENCY 6

Acquire a thorough knowledge of the philosophy and theory concerning bilingual education and its application.

RATIONALE:

Bilingual Education is a manifestation of a cultural-language conflict in schooling. It is important to recognize the significance one's language or dialect has in the learning process.

Instructional Objectives:

1. The learner will be able to define bilingual education and explain the historical perspective of its evolvement, including landmark judicial cases.

2. The learner will be able to describe various models of bilingual education and evaluate the strengths and weaknesses of each.

3. The learner will be able to formulate his/her own conceptualization of bilingual eduation and its purpose.

4. _____

    _____

    _____

Enabling Activities:

1.* Read: H. Prentice Baptiste, Jr. and Eileen Straus, "Historical Perspectives of Bilingual Education".

2.* Read: Dr. Philip Ortego y Gasca, "Sociopolitical Implications of Bilingual Education." Reprinted from Mano a Mano, February, 1976.

3. Examine the meaning of the "Lau v. Nichols" case and Title VII of Elementary and Secondary Education Act, and be able to relate these to education today in a class discussion.

4. Read: H. Prentice Baptiste, Jr., Multicultural Education: A Synopsis, Houston, Texas: University of Houston, 1976, pages 36-46.

5. Read: Thomas Carter, Mexican Americans in School: A History of Educational Neglect, New York: College Entrance Examination Board, 1970.

6. Read: "A Better Chance to Learn: Bilingual-Bicultural Education,"
    United States Commission on Civil Rights Clearinghouse Publication
    #51, May, 1975.

7. _____

    _____

    _____

Assessment of Competency:

Learners are expected to have a thorough understanding of bilingual education
and its relationship to multicultural education. In an essay, the learner
will trace the history of bilingual education, including landmark judicial
cases, and involvement on the local, state, and federal levels. The essay
is to include the learner's evaluation of the strengths and weaknesses of
each model and the learner's conceptualization of bilingual education and
its purpose in today's education.

Instructional Notes From Class Meetings:

Date Competency Achieved_____

HISTORICAL PERSPECTIVES OF BILINGUAL EDUCATION
H. Prentice Baptiste, Jr. and Eileen Straus

In the United States the concept of bilingual education is not a new and revolutionary idea. In private and parochial schools the use of the child's mother tongue, German in parts of the Midwest, French in Louisiana, and Spanish in New Mexico flourished during the nineteenth century.

In order to draw German children into the public schools, "the state of Ohio passed a law in 1840 that made it 'the duty of the Board of Trustees and Visitors of common schools to provide a number of German schools under some duly qualified teachers for the instruction of such youth as desire to learn the German language or the German and English languages together.' In this same year Cincinnati introduced instruction in the grades as an optional study and may thus be credited with having initiated bilingual schooling in the United States."[1] In the ensuing years from the fragmentary data available on similar bilingual programs, it has been conjectured that at least one million children received a part of their instruction in German.

However, with the great influx of immigrants and the advent of the melting pot ideology around 1920, bilingual schooling in the United States disappeared, and in the words of Ellwood P. Cubberly, it became the role of the school to:

> assimilate and amalgamate these people as part of our American race, and to implant in their children so far as can be done, the Anglo-Saxon conception of righteousness, law and order, and popular government, and to awaken in them a reverence for our democratic institutions and for those things in our national life which we as a people hold to be of abiding worth.[2]

Thus, it assumed the desirability of maintaining English institutions, the English language and English-oriented cultural patterns and made assimilation desirable only if the Anglo-Saxon cultural pattern was adopted as ideal. One of the chief proponents of this position was President Theodore Roosevelt who on several occasions delivered very assertive speeches stating, "...any man who comes here...must adopt the institutions of the United States, and therefore he must adopt the language.... It would be not merely a misfortune but a crime to perpetuate differences of language in this country...."[3]

The concern over the deficiency of some children in English and the attempt to insure they learn said language resulted in the use by some school

officials of rules against using a language other than English in schools.
Some of the more significant justifications for this included:

1. English is the standard language in the United States and all
    citizens must learn it.

2. The pupil's best interests are served if he speaks English well;
    English enhances his opportunity for education and employment
    while Spanish (or another language) is a handicap.

3. Proper English enables Mexican Americans (and other ethnic groups)
    to compete with Anglos.

4. Teachers and Anglo pupils do not speak Spanish (or another language);
    it is impolite to speak a language not understood by all.[4]

However, in their concern to Americanize everyone by requiring them to
learn and learn in English and by providing everyone with the same education
which was equated with equal educational opportunity, the affect on the students
and the effect on their cognitive skills were ignored.

The major turning point in the education of minority groups came on May 17,
1954, when the decision in the case Brown v. Board of Education was handed
down. Basically, the Supreme Court agreed with a statement made by a lower
Kansas court that:

> Segregation of white and colored children in public schools
> has a detrimental effect upon the colored children. The
> impact is greater when it has the sanction of the law for
> the policy of separating the races is usually interpreted as
> denoting the inferiority of the Negro group. A sense of
> inferiority affects the motivation of the child to learn.
> Segregation with the sanction of law, therefore, has a tendency
> to retard the educational and mental development of the Negro
> children and to deprive them of some of the benefits they
> would receive in a racial(ly) integrated school system.[5]

At the same time though, it reversed the decision of the lower court and stated,

> We conclude that in the field of public education the
> doctrine of "separate but equal" has no place. Separate
> educational facilities are inherently unequal. Therefore, we
> hold that the plaintiffs and others similarly situated for
> whom the actions have been brought are, by reason of the
> segregation complained of, deprived of the equal protection
> of the laws guaranteed by the Fourteenth Amendment.

After the Brown decision, only slight progress was made in the courts
until 1971, when a United States District Court handed down its decision in
the case United States v. Texas. Although the basis for the decision was

the court's prior determination that there had existed de jure segregation and its purpose, therefore, was to eliminate discrimination, the court did require "the development and submission to the Court of a comprehensive educational plan containing sufficient educational safeguards to insure that all students in the San Felipe Del Rio Consolidated Independent School District will be offered equal educational opportunities. By order of the Court, these safeguards were to 'include but...not necessarily be limited to bilingual and bicultural programs, faculty recruitment and training and curriculum design and content."[6] To avoid the creation of a stigma of inferiority in the Mexican American students, the Anglo students were required to learn to understand and appreciate their different linguistic and cultural attributes.

Taking this into consideration the plan for curriculum design was based on the following principles:

--that the cultural and linguistic pluralism of the San Felipe Del Rio Consolidated Independent School District student body necessitates the utilization of instructional approaches which reflect the learning styles, background and behavior of all segments of the student community...

--that the educational program of the district should incorporate, affirmatively recognize and value the cultural environment and language background of all its children...

--that language programs be implemented that introduce and develop language skills in a secondary language (English for many Mexican-American students, Spanish for Anglo students), while at the same time, reinforcing and developing language skills in the primary language, even though it will be called to the attention of the students that English is the basic language of the United States.[7]

The landmark case in the area of bilingual education is that of Lau v. Nichols. The court action was brought by thirteen non-English speaking students on behalf of approximately three thousand Chinese-speaking students in the San Francisco Unified School District. "These students alleged that they were being effectively denied an education because they could not comprehend the language in which they were being taught. It was further claimed that this deprivation of an education was 'dooming these children to become drop-outs and to join the rolls of the un-employed.' They argued that the failure to teach them bilingually should be prohibited on two legal grounds. First, that not to do so was a violation of their Constitutional right to 'equal protection under the law.' Second, that it was a violation of the Civil Rights Act of 1964."[8]

On the other hand, the San Francisco Unified School District, the defendant in the case, argued that "these students were not being discriminated against. The reasoning used was that they were being taught in the same facilities and by the same teachers at the same time as everyone else. Thus, since everything was the same for all students, there was no discrimination, and therefore, no violation of anyone's right to equal protection. In effect, their position was that the schools had no obligation to recognize and respond to the demonstrable communications difficulties encountered by those non-English-speaking students."[9]

After the District Court ruled in favor of the school district on the grounds that all that was required was equal access to facilities and not the opportunity to derive equal benefits, the students appealed their case to the U.S. Circuit Court of Appeals. At that time Judge Trask stated what he considered to be the underlying problem with the claim:

> Every student brings to the starting line of his educational career different advantages and disadvantages caused in part by social, economic and cultural background, created and continued completely apart from any contribution by the school system. That some of these may be impediments which can be overcome does not amount to a 'denial' by the Board of Educational Opportunities within the meaning of the Fourteenth Amendment should the Board fail to give them special attention, this even though they are characteristic of a particular ethnic group.

He further went on to state:

> Because we find that the language deficiency suffered by appellants was not caused directly or indirectly by any state action, we agree with the judgment of the district court... Under the facts of this case, appellees responsibility to appellants under the equal protection clause extends no further than to provide them with the same facilities, textbooks, teachers and curriculum as is provided to other children in the district.... The classification claimed invidious is not the result of deficiencies created by the appellants (children) themselves in failing to learn the English language.

On January 21, 1974, the Supreme Court of the United States, reversing the decision of the lower courts declared that:

> ...there is no equality of treatment merely by providing
> students with the same facilities, textbooks, teachers
> and curriculum; for students who do not understand English
> are effectively foreclosed from any meaningful education.
>   Basic English skills are at the very core of what these
> public schools teach. Imposition of a requirement that,
> before a child can effectively participate in the educational
> program, he must already have acquired those basic skills
> is a mockery of public education.

Their decision was based not on the Constitution but, since the San Francisco Unified School District was the recipient of federal funds, on S 601 of the Civil Rights Act of 1964, which states, "No person in the United States shall on the ground of race, color, or national origin, be excluded from participation, be the benefits of, or be subjected to discrimination under any program or activity receiving Federal financial assistance."

However, in reversing the decision of the lower courts, the Supreme Court did not grant the plaintiffs their request for bilingual education, thus not setting a precedent for mandating it in future cases. Instead it remanded the case to the District Court for it to establish "appropriate relief."

Likewise, the Supreme Court by choosing to base its decision on a statute instead of the Constitution has limited the extension of its decision, such that any school district not receiving federal funds could be exempt from providing "appropriate relief."

Lastly another limiting factor could be the separate but concurring opinion of Justice Blackmun in which he stated:

> that when, in another case, we are concerned with a very few
> youngsters, or with just a single child who speaks only
> German or Polish or Spanish or any language other than English,
> I would not regard today's decision or the separate concurrence,
> as conclusive upon the issue whether the statute and the guide-
> line require the funded school district to provide special
> instruction. For me numbers are the heart of this case and
> my concurrence is to be understood accordingly.

The impact of Lau v. Nichols was far-reaching but since the Supreme Court remanded the case to the District Court to prescribe a remedy, it is necessary to look to the lower court decisions to determine its implications.

The first of such cases was Serna v. Portales Municipal School District. While the plaintiffs recognized that discrimination exists throughout the Portales School system, the focal point of this case pivoted around the education provided at Lindsey School where the Spanish-surnamed children comprised a "called the 'Cardenas Plan' and was based on Jose Cardenas' concept of incompatibilities between traditional programs developed for a white, Anglo-Saxon, English-speaking middle class population and the characteristics and learning styles of minority children. The scope of the plan was comprehensive, including school district modifications in its philosophy, policy, rules and regulations, scope and sequence, curriculum materials and methodologies, staffing patterns and training, co-curricular activities, student personnel services, pupil non-instructional materials, community involvement and evaluation activities."[12]

However, on appeal to the Tenth Circuit Court the decision was again reversed since some of the schools in which the plan was to be pilot tested were not included in the desegregation pupil assignment plan. Furthermore the Court stated, "... the court's adoption of the Cardenas Plan, in our view, goes well beyond helping Hispano school children to reach the proficiency in English necessary to learn other basic subjects. Instead of merely removing obstacles to effective desegregation, the court's order would impose upon school authorities a pervasive and detailed system for the education of minority children. We believe this goes too far."

The case was again remanded to the lower court where hearings were being held for determination of a court order relating to bilingual/bicultural education.

Thus, the position of the court has been to allow two schools to remain predominantly Spanish-surname in composition for the purpose of implementing a program of bilingual education.

What are the implications of these decisions for the future?

First, schools are going to have to implement programs which will provide non-English-speaking children with a "meaningful education." Exactly how the Supreme Court defines the term meaningful education has not yet been clarified. However, the lower courts have concluded that some form of bilingual education is necessary.

Second, since the numerical requirement has never been judicially determined, there exists the possibility that the non-English-speaking population could be so small that its problems could be ignored. Presently, for the purpose of several states legally nineteen students are too few and can be ignored, but twenty becomes the magical number that cannot.[13] However, as the law provides that a special program be provided for one disabled or handicapped child, why not for one non-English-speaking child? Or in the future will the inability to speak English be construed as a language handicap?

large majority. The plaintiffs claimed that the discrimination was not due to an inferior program at Lindsey but due to an educational program designed to educate the middle class child from an English-speaking family without regard for the educational needs of the child from an environment where Spanish is the predominant language spoken.

In its ruling the Court recognized that the Portales School District was aware of these conditions, had taken steps to alleviate the problem and had made positive improvements. However, these procedures were not considered to be adequate and the District was ordered to:

1.   Reassess and enlarge its bilingual programs directed to the special needs of Latino students

2.   Expand bilingual/bicultural programs to all the other schools in its district having Spanish-speaking students

3.   Seek new funding sources to improve equality of education for Latino students

4.   Increase recruiting efforts of bilingual/bicultural teachers and/or obtain sufficient certification for Spanish-speaking teachers to allow them to teach in the district.[10]

Another case, Keyes v. School District No. 1, began as a desegregation case. However, it differed from the previous desegregation cases in that: 1) it was the first segregation case outside the South, and lacked the clear-cut dual system of education for Blacks and whites commonly found in southern states; 2) made fine distinction between de facto and de jure segregation; and 3) addressed itself to issues of equality of educational opportunities rather than limiting the integration effort to pupil assignment.[11]

The Court of Appeals, in its ruling, held that it could not be concluded that due to the single factor of segregation an inferior education was being received. It went on to say:

> ... even a completely integrated setting does not resolve these problems if the schooling is not directed to the specialized needs of children coming from low socio-economic and minority racial and ethnic backgrounds. Thus, it is not the proffered objective indicia of inferiority which causes the substandard academic performance of these children, but a curriculum which is allegedly not tailored to their educational and social needs.

After remand from the Supreme Court, the District Court requested assistance in the development of an instructional program designed to equalize school achievement. The program finally adopted by the District Court was

Third, the courts by basing their decision on Title VI of the Civil Rights Act of 1964 have provided only one method of enforcement, the withholding of federal funds. It is conceivable that a district which receives little or no federal funds, if the costs of complying are too great, could choose not to do so. If this were to happen, would the Court rule on the "equal protection" clause of the Fourteenth Amendment?

Issues in Bilingual Education

The solution being proposed to provide meaningful instruction for those of limited-English-speaking ability is bilingual education. However, the question of what kind of program can best meet the needs of these children still remains unanswered.

Presently, in the United States the most prevalent model and the one mandated by state legislation is transitional bilingual education, also called compensatory bilingual education because it views the limited-English-speaking child as linguistically and even culturally disadvantaged. It is defined[14] as:

> ... a full-program of instruction (1) in all those courses or subjects which a child is required by law to receive and which are required by the child's school district which shall be given in the native language of the children of limited English-speaking ability who are enrolled in the program and also in English, (2) in the reading and writing of the native language of the children of limited English-speaking ability who are enrolled in the program and in the oral comprehension, speaking, reading and writing of English, and (3) in the history and culture of the country, territory or geographic area which is the native land of the parents of children of limited English-speaking ability who are enrolled in the program and in the history and culture of the United States....[15]

Thus, the principal goal is to use the students' native language and culture to move to the English language and the mainstream culture of the school. Therefore, children are given instruction in two languages for a limited period of time and/or until the student is able to understand and communicate in English, usually defined as a period of three years.

Dr. Joshua Fishman foresees that even though transitional bilingual education attempts to provide "marked language children" with the opportunity to master the unmarked language of the school and society as quickly as possible and no matter how successful it may be linguistically, the following recurring problems will exist:

> First of all, it tends to weaken the marked language child's
> home and native community ties...weakening the two sources
> from which he might have drawn consolation and guidance.
> Secondly, compensatory/transitional education typically
> is 'granted' or 'imposed' by the unmarked language
> community and, as such, it does not seek nor attain the marked
> language community's involvement in, nor control over, the
> education of its own children.... Thirdly, the implied oppor-
> tunity for social mobility into the unmarked community which
> compensatory/transitional bilingual education dangles before
> the hearts and minds of the marked language pupils may actually
> turn out not to be feasible, or not to be feasible to the
> extent or at the rate implied.[16]

An alternative to the transitional model is maintenance bilingual education whose goals include:

1. the development and maintenance of the four basic language skills, speaking, understanding, reading and writing, in the first language or mother tongue,

2. the development of the four basic language skills in a second or target language (English, if it is not the child's mother tongue),

3. the improvement of the students' functional learning abilities and basic skills in all content areas through the use of both languages in the classroom,

4. the development of a positive self-concept in each student,

5. the development within the students of a feeling of pride in their native language and culture,

and most importantly it views the ability to communicate in a second language and to interact in the non-dominant culture as an asset.

A third and controversial model is immersion, also called the sink or swim technique. It represents "an attempt to use the second language as a medium of instruction, thereby shifting the emphasis from a linguistic focus to one where language is seen as a vehicle for developing competence in academic subject matter."[17]

The best known and most researched immersion program is the St. Lambert's Project in Quebec. English-speaking children in kindergarten were taught with French texts. English language arts was not introduced until the second grade. However, by the end of the fourth grade the children could read, write and speak English as well as their monolingual English peers who had attended traditional classes.

Likewise, the Spanish immersion program in the Culver City Unified School District in California, patterned after the St. Lambert Project, reported that "in the second grade, after introduction to reading in English, there is no difference between their reading skills and those of non-Spanish Immersion Program children. Except, that is, that they can also read and comprehend Spanish."[18]

In Quebec, English and French have been accorded equal status, and in the Culver City Program the children's native language was the unmarked or dominant one. However, in the United States since the melting pot era, as shown by statistics of attrition and level of education completed, immersion, as the basic method to educate children of a marked language has been proven to be inadequate.

Who should receive bilingual instruction? Should it be for the monolingual non-English-speaking, for the limited English-speaking, for those who are bilingual when they enter school or should it also include the Anglo and English-speaking minorities? The United States v. Texas decision said that to avoid the creation of a stigma of inferiority in the Mexican-American students, the Anglo students were required to be included in the program.

On the other hand the federal government in the Bilingual Education Act of 1968, also known as Title VII of the Elementary and Secondary Act of 1965, states:

> In recognition of the special educational needs of the large numbers of children of limited English-speaking ability in the United States, Congress hereby declares it to be the policy of the United States to provide financial assistance to local educational agencies to develop and carry out new and imaginative elementary and secondary school programs designed to meet these special educational needs. For the purposes of this title, "children of limited English-speaking ability" means children who come from environments where the dominant language is other than English.

Still another opinion is expressed Aspira of New York v. Board of Education of the City of New York, in which the decision, without discussing the merits of various tests, "did say that all students should be given a test to determine their proficiency in the use of the English language. Those students who fall below the twentieth percentile and who come from an Hispanic background should be given another test to determine their proficiency in Spanish.

If their percentile score in Spanish is higher than in English they should receive bilingual instruction."[19] In other words, according to the consent decree all students who score above the twentieth percentile are competent in English and need no special bilingual help and are not entitled to any.

Another debatable question is that of teacher certification. Due to the lack of foresight and planning after the passage of the Civil Rights Act of 1968 and the short span of time between the Lau v. Nichols decision and the implementation of "meaningful" instruction which has come to be defined as bilingual education there has existed an acute shortage of properly trained qualified teachers.

In an effort to aid the schools and to alleviate this shortage, some states established certification requirements of the ability to pass a language proficiency examination in the language of the target population. This falls far short of the Guideline for the Preparation and Certification of Teachers of Bilingual/Bicultural Education in the United States of America established by the Center for Applied Linguistics which state that teachers of bilingual/ bicultural education should have the following qualifications:

1. A thorough knowledge of the philosophy and theory concerning bilingual/bicultural education and its application.

2. A genuine and sincere interest in the education of children regardless of their linguistic and cultural background, and personal qualities which contribute to success as a classroom teacher.

3. A thorough knowledge and proficiency in the two languages involved and the ability to teach content through them equally well; an understanding of the nature of the language the child brings with him and the ability to utilize it as a positive tool in his teaching.

4. Cultural awareness and sensitivity and a thorough knowledge of the cultures reflected in the two languages involved.

5. The proper professional and academic preparation obtained from a well-designed teacher training program in bilingual/bicultural education.[20]

Thus, it must be concluded that important, significant differences within the field do exist, and the need for research is imperative.

FOOTNOTES

[1] Theodore Anderson, "Bilingual Education: The American Experience," Bilingual Schooling: Some Experiences in Canada and the United States, ed. Merrill Swain (Toronto: The Ontario Institute for Studies in Education, 1972), p. 56.

[2] Ellwood P. Cubberly, Changing Conception of Education, quoted by Mark Hansen, "Cultural Democracy, School Organization, and Educational Change," in The Mexican American, ed. by Alfredo Castaneda and others, (New York, Arno Press, 1974), p. 51.

[3] Theodore Roosevelt, "The Foes of our Household," quoted by Jesus M. Gonzales, in "Coming of Age in Bilingual-Bicultural Education: A Historical Perspective."

[4] U.S., Commission on Civil Rights, The Excluded Student: Educational Practices Affecting Mexican Americans in the Southwest, Report III: Mexican American Education Study, May, 1972 (Washington: Government Printing Office), cited from Stan Steiner, La Raza, The Mexican American, pp. 212-213.

[5] Stephen R. Goldstein, Law and Public Education, (Indianapolis, the Bobbs-Merrill Company, Inc., 1974), p. 551.

[6] Ibid., p. 700.

[7] Ibid., pp. 701-702.

[8] Joseph Grant, "Bilingual Education and the Law: An Overview," (Austin, Dissemination Center for Bilingual Bicultural Education, 1976).

[9] Ibid.

[10] Frank Aguila, "Laws Ruling Set Bases for Bilingual Programming," Kent State University, Ohio: Center for Educational Development and Strategic Services, 1975.

[11] Jose A. Cardenas, "Keyes v. Denver," ERIC Clearinghouse, May, 1976, p. 1.

[12] Ibid.

[13] For examples see the Bilingual Education Acts for the states of Illinois, Massachusetts and Texas. Also see the "Lau Remedies," guidelines for schools provided by HEW for compliance with the Lau v. Nichols decision.

[14] The Texas Bilingual Education Act defines it in the same manner except that it also includes oral comprehension and speaking of the native language.

[15] Illinois, Bilingual Education Act, 122 S 14C-2, 1973, and Massachusetts, Bilingual Education Act, C. 71A S 1, 1971.

[16]Joshua A. Fishman, "Bilingual Education for the Children of Migrant Workers: the Adaptation of General Models to a New Specific Challenge," Bilingual Education, ed. Hernan LaFontaine, et al., (Wayne: Avery Publishing Group Inc., 1978), pp. 204-205.

[17]Jeffrey L. Derevensky and Tima L. Petrushka, "French Immersion: An Attempt At Total Bilingualism," Bilingual Education, ed. Hernan La Fontaine, et al., (Wayne: Avery Publishing Group, Inc., 1978), p. 210.

[18]Karen Shender, "Bilingual Education: How Un-American Can You Get?," Bilingual Education, ed. Hernan La Fontaine, et al., (Wayne: Avery Publishing Group, Inc., 1978), p. 222.

[19]Grant.

[20]Center for Applied Linguistics, Guidelines for the Preparation and Certification of Teachers of Bilingual/Bicultural Education in the United States of America, (Arlington, 1974) cited by Anita Bradley Pfeiffer, "Designing a Bilingual Curriculum," Proceedings of the First Inter-American Conference on Bilingual Education, ed. Rudolph C. Troike and Nancy Modiano (Center for Applied Linguistics, 1975), p. 138.

BIBLIOGRAPHY

Aguila, Frank, "Laws, Ruling Set Base for Bilingual Programming," KEDS Annual Report, V. 2 n. 4, June, 1975.

Cardenas, Jose A., "Keyes v. Denver," ERIC Clearinghouse, May, 1976.

Castaneda, Alfredo, and others, ed., The Mexican American, New York: Arno Press, 1974.

Goldstein, Stephen R., Law and Public Education, Indianapolis, The Bobbs-Merrill Company, Inc., 1974.

Gonzalez, Jesus M., "Coming of Age in Bilingual/Bicultural Education: A Historical Perspective." Inequality in Education, XIX (February, 1975), 5-17.

Grant, Joseph, "Bilingual Education and the Law: An Overview," Dissemination Center for Bilingual Bicultural Education, 1976.

Kirp, David L., and Mark G. Yudof, Educational Policy and the Law, Berkley, McCutchan Publishing Corporation, 1974.

La Fontaine, Hernan, and others, ed., Bilingual Education, Wayne: Avery Publishing Group, Inc., 1978.

Swain, Merrill, ed. Bilingual Schooling: Some Experiences in Canada and the United States. Toronto: The Ontario Institute for Studies in Education, 1972.

Troike, Rudolph C., and Nancy Modiano, ed., Proceedings of the First Inter-American Conference on Bilingual Education, Arlington: Center for Applied Linguistics, 1975.

U.S., Commission on Civil Rights, The Excluded Student: Educational Practices Affecting Mexican Americans in the Southwest, Mexican American Study Report III, Washington: Government Printing Office, 1972.

U.S., Commission on Civil Rights, Una Mejor Oportunidad Para Aprender: La Educacion Bilingue Bicultural, Washington: Government Printing Office, 1975.

von Maltitz, Frances W., Living and Learning in Two Languages. New York: McGraw Hill, 1975, pp. 6-10.

SOCIOPOLITICAL IMPLICATIONS OF BILINGUAL EDUCATION
Dr. Philip Ortego y Gasca

As we approach the 21st century, we are faced in the United States at all levels of government, with the necessity of appropriating significantly more money for education. Yet, we are everywhere assailed by crises in the classrooms and the suggestion that American education has somehow become a colossal failure. How are we then to resolve this growing dilemma? On the one hand, champions of traditional education and its trappings exhort us to place more emphasis on the basic values of education (whatever that means) and to reaffirm the principles of neighborhood schools and local control. On the other hand, the most vocal critics of American education in its present form suggest radical transformation of our education concepts, even to the point of "de-schooling" American society, since the very concept of "school" in itself is part of the problem. The way out of this dilemma must be, of course, somewhere between these two positions, although my own proclivities tend toward the latter.[2] Nevertheless, whichever way we turn, the sociopolitical implications of our move will either precipitate applause or opprobrium. Add to the problem the growing demands of linguistically different Americans for equal education opportunities via bilingual education programs and this mess of educational porridge becomes a potent and volatile brew. For we add to the compass of social political implications a whole new set of tensions which place non-traditional stresses on an already beleaguered institution.[3]

To determine the sociopolitical implications of bilingual education, we ought first to consider the form and function of American education. In _form_, American education is still structured around the concept of the "common curriculum,"[4] a concept which in its incipiency assumed the existence of homogeneity among its people. And indeed, that assumption was not altogether amiss. For the common denominator in early American society was the European heritage of its individual members. Anomolous clusters of peoples of non-European stock were considered insignificant, and their assimilation into the Anglo-European cultural mainstream was quickly achieved despite their "outcast" heritage. However, the degree of assimilation of "outcast" groups depended upon their color and linguistic acceptability. Thus, non-whites early experienced

Reprinted from _Mano a Mano_, February, 1976.

cultural exclusion in America, although many--like the Blacks--became Anglos in all but physiognomy and color.

It is important to bear in mind that "the forms of education assumed by the first generation of settlers in America were a direct inheritance from the medieval past,"[5] as Bernard Bailyn points out, as well as a direct legacy from an England having only recently evolved a distinct national identity in the wake of Norman cultural ingress. The history of early American education was simply an extension of English education, though not as encompassing or efficient, given the non-contiguous character of that colonial enterprise. Still, early American education mirrored in little the goals and objectives of education in the homeland. The basis of education in England and the American colonies thus "lay secure within the continuing traditions of an integrated, unified culture."[6] And that continuity, however much it diminished in the 18th and 19th century, continued nevertheless to influence the evolving models of American education. Well into the 20th century, few American educators questioned the reality of that continuity, despite the visibly altered cultural and ethnic composition of the United States.[7] In fact, the fiction of that continuity grew stronger and more emphatic, institutionalizing unalterably the notions of the common curriculum. In brief, the common curriculum fostered the "come-and-get-it" philosophy of education.[8] That is, education--its goals and objectives clearly delineated and thriving hardily from its past successes-- was ready and waiting, available to one and all who wanted it. The chief motivation was desire. Little thought was given to refashioning education to keep apace with the times. For education, like the church, became an institution which had come to believe in its own infallibility. Bent thus on its own rituals, few of its priestly teachers and administrators were cognizant of the hardening arteries already afflicting the body education they had unknowingly stifled. Attempts to revivify the victim have included more of the same medicine which has only temporarily resparked a breath of life in the afflicted body. No systematic or long-range cure for the ills of education appears in the offing.[9] The symptoms continue to be treated with little respect for the malady.

Serious suggestions to attack the problems of education at their roots have met with guarded approval, for in essence most American educators and teachers believe fervidly in the efficacy of the tried and true methods of teaching and learning. And to suggest that the fault lies not with the students but with themselves and the institution is a monstrous heresy which must be immediately quelled. Half-heartedly, concessions to compensatory education have been made by educators on the chance that perhaps their efforts could be streng- thened by strengthening the deficiencies of those students who are ill-prepared for the common curriculum. Indeed, they reason, the problem lies with the students still, not the common curriculum, which was after all designed to produce "good" American men and women. Essentially this has been the form of American education.

Function of American Education

Let us turn now to the _function_ of American education. At heart American education differs little in function from education in other countries. For basically education is not just a formal pedagogy but the vital process "by which a culture transmits itself across the generations."[10] Only after the advent of democracy was public education regarded as "an instrument for dimin- ishing the degree of social stratification" in American society. Indeed, thirty or forty years ago most public school teachers really thought they were educating for democracy. This was before _Brown_ v. _Board_ _of_ _Education_ (1954). Still, other functions of American education were seen as utilitarian in purpose and to provide training for specific social roles. Eventually this function was broadened to include training for public and civic responsibility. An ancillary function was to train citizens in character and proper principles. At the heart of these functions, the teacher was seen as the guardian of educational tradition and the textbook writer as the high priest.[12] The textbook was supposed to be the repository of the highest values of the society. That these values have until recent times been a panorama of fantasy has upset few educa- tors let alone parents. After all, some arguments persist, we should teach our children not about the world as it is but as it should be. Textbooks have become fictitious models of life, models which have fostered the misconceptions and stereotypes of a bygone age. Schools and textbooks became, thus, instru- ments for national aggrandizement rather than tools for the liberation of the human spirit.

Having thus considered the _form_ and _function_ of American education, let me straightaway focus on the sociopolitical implications of bilingual education. To begin with, the most serious implication of bilingual education, as I see it, is the repudiation of the traditional form and function of American education.

For bilingual education must perforce challenge not only the assigned values
of the culture previously transmitted across the generations but the validity
of transmitting at all the culture embodied by the national language. Since
bilingual education asserts the primacy of the students' first language for
instructional purposes, that assertion encourages the use of cultural materials
and concepts inherent in the language of instruction.[13] At once we have bilingual education at odds with traditional American education which has consistently
sought to eliminate the "foreignness" in non-Anglo American students from the
very first day of school.[14] For one of the first chinks in the traditional
posture of the schools of the American southwest, for example, was the annulment
of prohibitions against Spanish being spoken on school grounds outside of Spanish
language classes. One of the repercussions of this apparent concession to a
foreign language has been polarization of communities along linguistic lines,
Anglo English speakers insisting doggedly, and petulantly at times, that this
being an English speaking country everyone ought to speak English. Those who
didn't think so could just as well go back to Mexico despite the fact that the
overwhelming majority of Spanish-speakers in question were born in the United
States.

Thus bilingual education is seen by Anglos as a diminution of their cultural-
linguistic superiority, threatening not only their linguistic identity but their
social identity as well. Little thought is given to the *eiconic damage visited
upon Spanish-speaking children subjected to the education of a thoroughly lexo-
centric society. Hence, from the other side of the coin, a significant sociopolitical implication of bilingual education is the eventual salvation of
hundreds of thousands of Spanish-speaking youngsters who will be spared the
linguistic traumas experienced by previous generations of Mexican Americans.
Indeed, concessions to bilingual education signal an end to the narrow linguistic insularity of the United States, an insularity which has led to a national
hauteur, toward the non-English language world and its linguistically different
experiences. Thus conditioned, Americans abroad have tended to depreciate other
linguistically different cultures solely on the basis of a criteria predicated
on their own linguistic insularity and reality.

Cultural Pluralism

In great part, the success of bilingual education will determine the success of cultural pluralism in this country, a notion now replacing the old and

equally fictitious "melting pot" theory of American society. Bilingual education derives its validity from the larger world model of society. Different
groups require differentiated curricula and teaching patterns, to say nothing
of the training of teachers for bilingual education.[15]

The long intoned te deum of "individual differences" of students will at
long last be more than just a chant to which we give only passing lip service.
For bilingual education focuses squarely on the individual differences of linguistically different children. In other words, we recognize that our students,
like our larger society, are the products of different cultures and languages
or dialects and cannot thus be treated educationally as if they were all culturally and linguistically homogeneous. Uniformity as an educational goal
must give way to cultural and linguistic relativity[16] just as the geo-centered
ptolemaic view of the universe gave way to the copernican view. Taxonomies of
education must be designed with such relativity in mind.

A remote sociopolitical implication of bilingual education may be the
displacement of the English language, but I doubt seriously that possibility,
though I am sure the Romans of Caesarian days doubted equally the linguistic
displacement of alteration of Latin in the Roman world. But more immediately,
bilingual education augers changes in social attitudes toward the culturally
and linguistically different. The changes also portend significant therapeutic
value for zenophobic Anglo Americans.

Given then the sociopolitical implications of bilingual education I have
discussed, one can readily see why bilingual education is such a hot potato
and why efforts at implementing it as an educational concept beyond the mere
token efforts undertaken thus far have been nominal. Moreover, given the
socialization and politization role of American education, one can also appre-
hend the growing reluctance and retrenchment on the part of the dominant
society in aiding and abetting an educational innovation that may carry with
it the seeds of powerful and irrevocable change. In short, bilingual education
is adjudged good or bad in terms of the Anglo perceived threats of its character. This is why predominantly Anglo school systems refuse to budge beyond
the model programs of bilingual education and why genuine efforts to make it a
working reality are not present. Few people care to walk willingly into what
they regard as a lion's den. So the lion must come to the fearful spectator.
Unfortunately, the lion is still a cub. But the day is coming![17]

REFERENCES

[1]See, for example, Charles E. Silberman, Crisis in the Classroom: The Remaking of American Education (New York, 1970).

[2]See Phillip D. Ortego, "Montezuma's Children", The Center Magazine (November-December, 1970), and "Schools for Mexican Americans: Between Two Cultures," Saturday Review (April 17, 1971).

[3]James B. Conant, Slums & Suburbs (New York, 1961).

[4]This assertion is more fully developed in Problems and Strategies in Teaching the Language Arts to Spanish-Speaking Mexican American Children, by Carl L. Rosen and Philip D. Ortego, U.S. Office of Education (ERIC/CRESS) and New Mexico State University (Las Cruces, New Mexico, 1969), and in "Language and Reading Problems of Spanish Speaking Children in the Southwest," by Carl L. Rosen and Philip D. Ortego, Journal of Reading Behavior (Winter, 1969).

[5]Bernard Bailyn, Education in the Forming of American Society (University of North Carolina Press, 1969), p. 15.

[6]Bailyn, p. 21.

[7]See, for example, Ruth Miller Elson, Guardians of Tradition: American Schoolbooks of the Nineteenth Century (University of Nebraska Press, 1964).

[8]Philip D. Ortego, "The Education of Mexican Americans," The New Mexico Review, Part I, September 1969; Part II, October 1969.

[9]Despite the testimony on equal educational opportunity before the Select Committee on Equal Educational Opportunity of the United States Senate, August 18-21, 1970, Washington D.C. See transcript of Hearings, Part 4 - Mexican American Education.

[10]Bailyn, p. 14.

[11]James Bryant Conant, Shaping Educational Policy (New York, 1964), p. 2.

[12]Elson, passim.

[13]See Philip D. Ortego, The Linguistic Imperative in Teaching English to Speakers of Other Languages, U.S. Office of Education (ERIC Clearinghouse for Linguistics) and the Center for Applied Linguistics (Washington D.C., 1970).

[14]See Philip D. Ortego, "Some Cultural Implications of a Mexican American Border Dialect of American English," Studies in Linguistics Vol. 21, 1969-70.

[15]See Philip D. Ortego, "English Teaching: Some Humanistic Goals and a Personal Credo," Proceedings of the NCTE Spring Institutes, (NCTE Publications, Champaign/Urbana, Ill., 1972).

[16]For a discussion of linguistic relativity see Edward Saper, <u>Culture</u>, <u>Language</u> <u>and</u> <u>Personality</u> (University of California Press, 1964).

[17]Alternatives are discussed in Philip D. Ortego, "Chicano Education: Status Quo? Reform? Revolution?" address to the AAUW Biannual Convention, Dallas, Texas, June 30, 1970, <u>AAUW</u> <u>Journal</u> (August, 1971).

* Theory of images. Eiconic psychology, for example, deals with the various dynamics of perception (internal and external), self-esteem, and in general with the development of one's image about oneself. See, for example, Kenneth E. Boulding's <u>The</u> <u>Image</u>: <u>Knowledge</u> <u>in</u> <u>Life</u> <u>and</u> <u>Society</u> (University of Michigan, 1956).

COMPETENCY 7

Acquire, evaluate, adapt, and develop materials appropriate to multicultural education.

RATIONALE:

The paucity of multicultural materials for the classroom makes it quite obvious that the teacher must be able to revise, modify, and supplement existing materials for use in the classroom.

Textbooks and other curriculum materials are still not devoid of racism and sexism. Most curriculum materials at best, are complacent in their treatment of minorities. It is quite apparent that publishing companies do not intend to cease publishing racist and cultural biased materials. Publishing companies are motivated by profits and are reactive to needs of the school populations when it is profitable.

Therefore, teachers must develop educational resources which are devoid of racism, sexism, ageism, and cultural bias. They must become engineers of multi-culturalism. As an engineer of multiculturalism, one must have the capability not only to design educational materials that are fair and characterized by cultural diversity, but also able to take monocultural and/or cultural biased materials and point out their deficiencies.

Instructional Objectives:

1. The learner will be able to demonstrate how a lesson can be modified using existing materials, to create a lesson devoid of racism, sexism, ageism, handicapism, and cultural bias.

2. The learner will be able to provide examples of supplementary materials that can be utilized to create a lesson devoid of racism, sexism, ageism, and cultural bias.

3. _____

_____

_____

Enabling Activities:

1. Do research and make a list of supplementary materials that can be used in your subject area or grade level, to help create lessons devoid of racism and sexism.

2. *Read: H. Prentice Baptiste, Jr. and Mira Baptiste, "Developing Multicultural
   Learning Activities" in Multicultural Education, Commitment, Issues and
   Applications, ASCD, 1977.

3. _____

    _____

    _____

Assessment of Competency:

Mastery of this competency requires the learner to demonstrate a lesson that
has been modified using existing materials to create a lesson devoid of racism,
sexism, ageism, handicappism, and cultural bias. The learner is expected to
design the lesson with supplementary materials being utilized. The lesson should
be characterized by fairness and cultural diversity.

Instructional Notes From Class Meetings:

Date Competency Achieved _____

DEVELOPING MULTICULTURAL LEARNING ACTIVITIES
H. Prentice Baptiste, Jr., and Mira Baptiste

During very recent years the relationship between cultural pluralism and multicultural education has been questioned by educators on numerous occasions. This is a very complex concept which raises difficult questions. The search for curriculum materials reflective of cultural pluralism is demanding. Establishing criteria for evaluation of curriculum materials, utilization of existing local resources, identification of subject integrating concepts, and formulation of guidelines for implementation of the multicultural processes are examples of this complex multifaceted problem.

Complexity of Multicultural Processes

Cultural pluralism has been defined from many vantage points that reflect various areas of concern, ranging, for example, from the national government to the smallest school district. Whatever the area of concern, underlying the definition of cultural pluralism is a philosophy that strongly recommends a particular set of beliefs, principles, and ideas that should govern the relationship of people of diverse cultures. The cornerstone principles of cultural pluralism are equality, mutual acceptance and understanding, and a sense of moral commitment. Equality in cultural pluralism does not mean the assignment of percentage and ratio opportunity chances for certain individuals or particular groups. Equality in the context of cultural pluralism is the antithesis of racism, prejudice, oppression, and assigned percentage opportunity of chances.

Another fundamental principle of cultural pluralism is the mutual acceptance and understanding of cultural diversity. Groups as well as individuals must learn that diversity, not uniformity or sameness, is the order of the day. As Carlos Cortés explains, knowledge is not equivalent to understanding.[1] Knowledge of cultural groups does not guarantee understanding. Subsequently, creative instructional strategies along with valid materials must be utilized to facilitate understanding.

Multicultural education is the process of institutionalizing the philosophy of cultural pluralism within education systems. This is not an easy process. As Tomás Arciniega has stated, "The issue of moving schools and universities toward a culturally pluralistic state may appear, to some, to be a simple matter. The fact is, however, that the thrust toward achieving cultural pluralism in educational form and practice is a complex and value-laden undertaking."[2]

[1] Carlos Cortés. "Understanding Not Tolerance." Portion of a videotape entitled: *Perspectives on Multicultural Education.* Developed by H. Prentice Baptiste, Jr., 1976.

[2] Tomás A. Arciniega. "The Thrust Toward Pluralism: What Progress?" *Educational Leadership* 33 (3): 163; December 1975.

Reprinted from Multicultural Education: Commitments, Issues, and Applications, 1977.

As one develops the multicultural processes within an elementary and secondary school, he/she is confronted with traditional obstacles like the monocultural process of the assimilation or the melting pot philosophy, unequal availability of educational opportunities, hostility or disregard for diversity, racism, and prejudice which mitigate against its implementation. However, proponents of multicultural processes must affirm the ethical commitment of schools to the aforementioned principles of cultural pluralism.

The multicultural process is not an add on to existing educational programs. It does not mean studying certain minority groups, for example, Native Americans, or Japanese Americans, from two o'clock to three o'clock on Mondays and Wednesdays. The studying of Mexican American literature in isolation from the American literature course implies a certain illegitimacy about Mexican American literature. Mexican American literature, as well as the literature of other ethnic groups, has a legitimate place in the regular American literature course. Bilingual programs which are based on a transitional model, that is, elimination of instruction in mother tongue as soon as second language acquisition occurs, are not representative of the multicultural process. Language curricular activities which neglect the cultural value systems of the languages are detrimental to formation of valid instructional activities. Educators who tend to utilize only special ethnic holidays, religious ceremonials, super-heroes, and foods to culturalize their instruction are being dreadfully shortsighted. Furthermore, they are miseducating our youth to the real values of various cultural and ethnic groups.

The Quest for Materials

Numerous instructional materials contain subtleties of velvet racism, sexism, and stereotypes, and are supportive of the assimilationist philosophy. As Banks has indicated, most materials are insensitive, inaccurate, and written from an Anglo-Saxon perspective.[3] Several guidelines have been suggested elsewhere which provide criteria to facilitate selection of good materials.[4] However, many teachers must face the reality that they will have to utilize available materials and resources from their school district to supplement their instructional strategies. Nevertheless, inaccurate, insensitive, stereotypic materials need not provide an impassable obstacle to knowledgeable multicultural-oriented teachers. Especially is this credible if one believes the teacher is the curriculum.[5]

[3]James A. Banks. "Evaluating and Selecting Ethnic Studies Materials." *Educational Leadership* 33 (7): 593; April 1974.

[4]"The ABC's of Freeing Day Care From Racism, Sexism." *Interracial Books for Children Bulletin.* Vol. 6, Nos. 5 & 6. New York, N.Y.: Council on Interracial Books for Children; Gloria Grant. "Criteria for Cultural Pluralism in the Classroom." *Educational Leadership* 32 (3): December 1974; Task Force on Racism and Bias in the Teaching of English. "Criteria for Teaching Materials in Reading and Literature." Urbana, Illinois: National Council of Teachers of English; Max Rosenberg. "Evaluate Your Textbooks for Racism, Sexism!" *Educational Leadership* 31 (2): 108-109; November 1973; Maxine Dunfee. "Curriculum Materials for Celebrating the Bicentennial." *Educational Leadership* 33 (4): 267-72; January 1976.

[5]Milo Kalectaca, Gerald Knowles, and Robin Butterfield. "To Help — Not To Homogenize Native American Children." *Educational Leadership* 31 (7): 592; April 1974.

The quest for multicultural materials often leads one to commercial materials; but it appears that the companies which produce educational materials do not believe a market exists for such. On the other hand, some companies do believe a market exists, but are reluctant to develop materials because of the complex nature of such a national endeavor. Companies prepare educational materials for national markets and are not responsive to local concerns. The market has been flooded with numerous ethnic materials which usually have as their focus a specific ethnic group; but the need exists for materials which include a diversity of ethnic groups.

The feasibility of producing materials representative of all ethnic groups may not be resolved. The Institute of Texas Cultures in its attempt to produce materials about all groups who settled Texas is working on its 26th group.[6] In Pennsylvania, an agency has been formed at Bloomsburg State College to identify the various ethnic groups in that state.[7] This agency is also charged with identification, location, and development of instructional materials on ethnic groups within the state of Pennsylvania. Frequently, the catalyst for the development of clearinghouses on ethnic materials has been provided by federal funds. Efforts have centered on the identification of ethnic groups within a specific geographic region or unit such as a state. This has led to an identification of additional resources and the development of instructional materials. Productions of this sort are limited by several specifics: namely, geographic area involved, peoples contributing to this area, and available historical background information. Monies received by states for desegregation purposes have produced agencies such as The Center for Public School Ethnic Studies in Texas.[8]

The zealous effort to produce numerous ethnic materials is not totally good for culturally pluralizing educational programs. In many instances the quality of numerous ethnic materials tends to perpetuate or create erroneous myths, stereotypes, and pseudo super-heroes. No controls exist to ensure the purchaser/user of the authenticity of these materials. The user tends to overindulge in another myth by seeking a member of the group under study to verify the authenticity of the materials.

Ethnic materials per se tend to create a monoethnic or mono approach. Although it is understood that ethnic materials as well as certain ethnic experiences must be viewed in a multicultural program, nonetheless instruction must not end at this point. The teacher must bring about the multicultural processes via instructional strategies. He/she must serve as a cultural engineer to effectively utilize monoethnic materials.

[6]*People* 5; September-October 1975. Published by Institute of Texan Cultures, San Antonio, Texas.

[7]Pennsylvania Ethnic Heritage Studies Dissemination Project, Bloomsburg State College, Bloomsburg, Pennsylvania.

[8]Center for Public School Ethnic Studies, Extension Building, The University of Texas, Austin, Texas.

As one utilizes ethnic materials, he/she must be aware that some of these materials may contain examples of velvet racism and stereotypes. Another problem with some ethnic materials is the creation of new unfounded myths. Apparently the heroic nature of our "common culture" is encouraging the creation of numerous ethnic super-heroes. Many of these super-heroes are crumbling because there is little or no substantial evidence except mythology to support their deeds. Conflicting information characterizes too much of this material. Several materials relating the same event may contain not only opposing views, but also conflicting facts. Granted, some conflict is expected between interethnic materials; but the conflict referred to here is that produced by shoddy research regarding the event, the place, and/or the group of people.

Efforts To Provide Materials

Through the efforts of HEW's Ethnic Heritage Studies, ESEA and ESAA ethnic material resources on a national level are being identified, developed, and evaluated. AACTE has established a clearinghouse for the collection and evaluation of multicultural materials. Teacher Corps projects have for several years been involved in the development of multicultural materials.

Several states are facilitating, through coordination and provision of funds, the development, location, and dissemination of materials for multicultural education. As mentioned earlier, some states are specifically coordinating the identification, development, and dissemination of materials about cultural/ethnic groups within their borders. Interested educators can contact their state education agency for information in regard to the efforts of their state in this endeavor.

Teachers are usually quite surprised when referred to local resources for materials that will facilitate the multicultural processes. The local community is often a rich reservoir of materials. Historical information about the contributions of various cultural/ethnic groups within a community are usually available. Other primary resources within a community are the people themselves, business and industry, professions, and local education agencies.

Special interest groups or agencies within a community have ethnic/cultural and/or multicultural materials. These groups, for example, the Anti-Defamation League, American Red Cross, and French Speaking Union, will make available to teachers ethnic and also multicultural materials. In the latter category, the American Red Cross has a film — "Blood Is Life, Pass It On" — which is an excellent example of a good multicultural film. Usually, materials from community special interest groups are free or available at a nominal cost. Special interest groups tend to disseminate materials that are culturally and ethnically diverse in addition to promoting a culturally pluralistic philosophy.

The local library quite often is disregarded by teachers in their quest for materials, yet one may be surprised at the abundance of materials available for use. In some local communities, libraries are developing annotated bibliographies on available racial, ethnic, and multicultural materials according to grade levels, reading levels, and subject areas. It would be advisable for a teacher interested in "multiculturalizing" classroom instruction to visit the local library. One will also find, for the most part, that these libraries are becoming very sensitive to acquiring materials, that is, books, magazines, films, tapes, which reflect the ethnic/cultural makeup of the local population.

Most school districts have established departments of human relations, ethnic studies, or minority studies, which have as one of their responsibilities the collection, development, dissemination, and evaluation of ethnic/cultural and multicultural materials. In many instances, the staff of these departments, when invited, will come to schools and demonstrate the use of their materials.

Evaluating and Implementing

Knowing and being able to obtain ethnic/cultural or multicultural materials is only part of the solution. The other part is being able to evaluate the worth of these materials for instructional purposes. Evaluation of existing materials by teachers is of paramount importance. Several guidelines have been published which address only certain facets of multicultural materials. As an example, *Educational Leadership* published a set of guidelines to evaluate the inclusion of treatment of minorities in books and other curriculum materials.[9] Other guidelines have appeared which focus on racism or sexism.[10] Common attributes of most guidelines are an overall negativism and narrowness, which prevent their application to several facets of multicultural materials.

The furore created by community reaction to certain library books and textbooks has moved many school districts to formulate guidelines for instructional materials. The Council on Interracial Books has moved ahead in supplying leadership for groups which need guidelines.

There is no easy way to begin implementation of multicultural learning activities, nor is there a step by step approach. The subject-integrating concept will be used as the first example. The teacher decides upon a concept that may move across subject matter lines, but it must be readily adaptable to the philosophy of cultural pluralism. The teacher may or may not possess adequate knowledge about the concept. The activities and materials must work together. Selection of materials may dictate activities, and implementation of activities could depend heavily upon available materials.

[9]Max Rosenberg, "Evaluate Your Textbooks for Racism, Sexism," *op. cit.*
[10]See n. 4.

Slavery is a subject-integrating concept which cuts across time lines and cultural/ethnic groups. The phenomenon of slavery is introduced to every school child. Mistakenly, it is usually given as the cause of the Civil War, and most unfortunately it is *the* concept to unveil Afro-Americans. Thus, in the minds of many school children, slavery is linked with Afro-Americans.

Historically, numerous groups of people at one time or another have been slaves or enslavers. Ancient history or modern times offer starting points for this concept. The multicultural process is reflected in an exploration of the slaves and enslavers. A more valid conception of the term can be realized when students are given the opportunity to study slavery from a comparative perspective, which uses the underlying economic structure, religious beliefs, cultural values, and geographic environments.

Teachers have found literature to be a pliable content area, rich in materials and resources. Folktales which include contributions from several groups can be expanded to other subject areas such as music, art, or social studies. Content areas pose very few problems. A creative, sensitive teacher with good competencies in teaching strategies and a working philosophy of cultural pluralism can "multiculturalize" physical education, mathematics, science, art, music, language arts, reading, and even vocational arts. The key question the teacher must answer is "How do I include all peoples who have a rightful place in this lesson?" The teacher is the wheel that turns. The degree of each turn depends upon the teacher's understanding of different ethnic cultures, upon his/her attitudes toward differences in ethnic backgrounds, and upon his/her ability to develop teaching strategies appropriate for the philosophy of cultural pluralism.

Are learning activities in a curriculum reflective of cultural pluralism different from those in a traditional approach? Yes and no. Sound teaching strategies will always involve the students in the process; but multicultural education processes require the materials to illustrate all groups of people as equal, worthy of being, and having dignity. Exclusion is powerful. The absence of peoples, along with the unspoken words, leads students to acquire erroneous information. The teacher faces a double-edged responsibility when materials are chosen. The materials must promote a sense of unity within diversity. Teaching strategies go beyond the memorization of facts to focus on higher levels of knowledge, value analysis, and decision making. The teaching strategies used with the materials can communicate quite effectively the message of cultural pluralism.

The multicultural process includes diversifying the subject matter content as well as humanizing teaching strategies. The teacher should make a constant conscientious effort to create a teaching/learning environment reflective of power sharing, equality, and decision making. It is important for the teacher to realize that shared power and decision making flow in two directions between teacher and students. Designing learning activities which will enable the student to explore his/her self concept is often the beginning stage for the multicultural processes. Self-esteem and worthiness are undeniably linked to the feeling of having some control over one's environment. A real voice in decision making is fundamental for the student to acquire a positive self-esteem. Many subject areas such as art, drama, music, language, social studies, and sociology can be used by teachers to facilitate the positive growth of the students' self-esteem. Content areas are used as exemplars of cultural diversity actualized.

There are no curriculum guides, no material kits, no pre- or post-tests, no objectives, and no teacher editions available for one to plug into the existing courses for "Bingo! Multicultural Education." First and foremost, the teacher must evolve a cultural pluralistic philosophy which emerges as a multicultural experience. The true measure of multicultural education is vested in the behaviors, attitudes, and beliefs of the students. The consequent objective for material effectiveness is evaluated by the teacher not only in terms of students' gains in understandings and knowledge of other people, but in the reduction and resolution of conflicts.

COMPETENCY 8

Critique an educational environment to the extent of the measurable evidence of the environment representing a multicultural approach to education.

RATIONALE:

The educational environment (i.e., physical facilities, personnel policies and practices) is characterized by racism, cultural ethnocentrism, etc. Examination of an educational environment will enlighten one as to what should be changed or improved.

Instructional Objectives:

1. The learner will be able to evaluate his/her school/district for racism, sexism, cultural ethnocentrism, etc.

2. The learner will be able to assess the situation regarding racism, sexism, ageism and cultural ethnocentrism in his/her school/district and make suggestions for eliminating same in the school/district.

3. _____

    _____

    _____

Enabling Activities:

1. Read: National Council for the Social Studies, Curriculum Guidelines for Multiethnic Education, Arlington, Virginia: National Council for the Social Studies, 1976, pages 42-48.

2. View: Slide tapes "Different But the Same" and "Thinking About People" about the Multi-Culture Institute, giving an example of a multicultural model and how it was implemented, and discuss its success with the class.

3. View: Filmstrip on "Understanding Institutionalized Racism", an explanation of why practices and policies of institutions are the main factors behind racism.

4.* Complete the "Rate Your School for Racism and Sexism" Checklist and evaluate your school.

5. Attend and participate in a class seminar on various models on Multicultural Education. Focus on "Unified Science and Math for the Elementary School (USMES).

6. _____

_____

_____

7. _____

_____

_____

Assessment of Competency:

In order to demonstrate mastery of this competency, the learner must be able to identify examples of racism, sexism, ageism, and cultural ethnocentrism in the educational environment. Racism and sexism can be overtly and covertly illustrated in the school, district, or community, and the teacher must become aware of this. In a written evaluation, the learner will identify areas of racism and sexism, and will name five suggestions for eliminating racism and sexism from the chosen school/district. A checklist or chart may be used.

Instructional Notes From Class Meetings:

Date Competency Achieved _____

SCHOOL CHECKLIST FOR RACISM AND SEXISM

I *OBJECTIVE*
For participants to increase their awareness of the many forms of racism and sexism in education.

II *RATIONALE*
Since no school operating within a racist and sexist society can be free of these manifestations, examining one's own school can help each participant clarify what s/he would like to help change or improve.

III *TIME ALLOTMENT*
Variable. From two to ten class periods, plus advance information-gathering. Time depends on amount of discussion trainer wishes to encourage.

IV *MATERIALS*
Paper and pencil for participants and enclosed trainer's materials.

V *ACTIVITY*
1. Trainer reads enclosed materials.

2. Trainer, or assigned participants, gather statistics in advance for the information sheet (enclosed).

3. Trainer presents the information gathered to class. (National statistics in FACT SHEETS ON INSTITUTIONAL RACISM and ON INSTITUTIONAL SEXISM can be used as comparison.)

4. Vocabulary and definitions on the glossary sheet can be discussed in advance, or as questions arise, depending on the age and sophistication of the class or the group.

5a. Trainer introduces CHECKLIST and tells participants to listen to each numbered question read, and then write next to each number:

A—meaning, "Yes, always."	C—meaning, "Rarely."
B—meaning, "Sometimes."	D—meaning, "No, never."

Answers are to reflect each participant's own assessment of his or her school.

Or

5b. Participants may be divided into small groups to answer questions jointly.

6. When all questions have been answered—with or without discussion after each one—every participant tallies the number of A's, B's, C's and D's. If all participants are from the *same* school, trainer should see if there is any great divergence in tallies and—if so—allow discussion of differences. If participants represent *many* schools, then any wide divergence in school ratings should provoke discussion of what factors caused better scores at one school than at another.

7. If time is set aside to discuss change strategies, trainer should see that participants start with an analysis of the existing *power* set-up, existing *control of resources* and existing *decision-making* in their schools. After such an analysis, change should be structured around practical ways to achieve more equitable sharing of power and resources and more equitable decision-making for minorities and females.

VI *CAUTION*
If participants wish to work for change, stress the need to arrange for third world and feminist participation on goals and methods. It is also important that change be based upon *realistic* assessments of what can be tackled first, what support can be mustered, etc. Step-by-step organization for the goal decided upon is *at least* as important as a change agent's good intentions.

This SCHOOL CHECKLIST owes much to previous checklists produced by (1) the Civil Rights Commission (unpublished); (2) Integrated Education Associates; (3) the United Church Press; and (4) a very thorough checklist prepared by Dr. Claire Halverson for the EEO Center of the National College of Education.

Reprinted from Council on Interracial Books for Children, Inc.

CHECKLIST ON RACISM

COMMUNITY

	Yes, always	Sometimes	Rarely	No, never
1. Are parent meetings held at suitable times for working parents to attend?	A	B	C	D
2. Is language used at meetings understandable to all parents or translated as necessary for some?	A	B	C	D
3. Are all parents made to feel welcome and comfortable when they visit a school?	A	B	C	D
4. Are parents of all racial groups encouraged to participate and contribute to school programs and learnings?	A	B	C	D
5. Are third world and poor parents represented as advisors to school board? To administrators of each school? To curriculum committee?	A	B	C	D

SCHOOL BOARD

	Yes, always	Sometimes	Rarely	No, never
6. Does the school board reflect the racial and economic make-up of the community?	A	B	C	D
7. a. If board members are selected, are various racial and economic viewpoints involved in the selection process?	A	B	C	D
or b. If board members are elected, is it on a district basis that reflects the racial/ethnic and socioeconomic levels of the community, rather than on a city-wide basis in which a white, middle-class majority can predominate?	A	B	C	D
8. Does the school board encourage and facilitate meaningful participation of students and parents from all racial/ethnic and socioeconomic groups in decision-making?	A	B	C	D
9. Does school board get involved in community affairs related to housing, jobs, police and other matters directly tied to schools and racism?	A	B	C	D
10. Are the age, quality, facilities and maintenance of the school buildings which are attended by the greater proportion of third world students as good as those which are attended by a lesser proportion of third world students?	A	B	C	D
11. Is the per pupil expenditure the same for students from all racial/ethnic groups in all districts in your community? (This does not include ESEA Title I federal money.)	A	B	C	D
12. If not, do the schools that expend more money per student have a higher percentage of minority groups?	A	B	C	D
13. In negotiating contracts, is past discrimination against third world people recognized and compensated for in considerations of promotion or layoffs, rather than using seniority which results in "last hired, first fired" and counteracts affirmative action and equal employment efforts?	A	B	C	D
14. Does a good share of the school system's business contracts go to third world contractors and to contractors whose hiring and personnel policies encourage racial/ethnic and sexual equity?	A	B	C	D

ADMINISTRATION

	Yes, always	Sometimes	Rarely	No, never
15. Is racial make-up of administrative and guidance staff similar to racial make-up of student body? If student body is mainly white, does administrative staff represent racial diversity of this nation?	A	B	C	D
16. Do third world administrators hold positions of general authority rather than mainly positions relating more specifically to special federal programs, minority concerns or minority relations?	A	B	C	D
17. Are administrators and teachers encouraged to live or participate in the community where they teach?	A	B	C	D
18. When new administrators are hired, is their ability to relate to the community one important qualification?	A	B	C	D
19. Do administrators place high priority on creating and enforcing policies and practices which are aimed at achieving cultural pluralism?	A	B	C	D

	Yes, always	Sometimes	Rarely	No, never

20. Does the administration make decisions based on input from all students, parent and teacher viewpoints? — A B C D

21. Are good academic grades for third world students a topic of serious concern? — A B C D

22. Are school songs, symbols, decorations and holidays chosen to reflect all cultures and viewpoints? — A B C D

23. Are school announcements sent in the language which parents can understand? Are parent meetings conducted or translated so parents can understand? — A B C D

24. If busing is practiced for desegregation, are white students bused in equal numbers to blacks? — A B C D

TEACHERS

25. Is racial make-up of teaching staff similar to racial make-up of student body? If student body is mainly white, does racial make-up of teaching body reflect racial diversity of this nation? — A B C D

26. When new teachers are hired, is strenuous effort made to find members of all racial minorities? — A B C D

27. When teachers are interviewed for hiring, is it policy that the personnel committee contain third world staff and parents? — A B C D

28. Are in-service courses required of entire teaching staff to enable them to increase their awareness of racism in our society, to acquaint them with the culture, history and viewpoints of racial minority groups? Is this true even if school is predominantly white? — A B C D

29. Are teachers encouraged to learn to understand the language spoken by their students? — A B C D

30. Do teachers clearly demonstrate that their behavioral and academic expectations are high for all students? — A B C D

31. Do teachers routinely assign third world publications and authors for reading homework to all pupils? — A B C D

32. Do teachers encourage diversity of values, styles and viewpoints, even when these run counter to teacher's own preferences? — A B C D

33. Do teachers make special help accessible and comfortable for all students? — A B C D

34. Do teachers encourage full participation in all classes and extra-curricular programs by third world students? — A B C D

35. Do teachers contact administrators, school board and publishers to complain about stereotypes, bias and omission in materials and lack of multicultural materials? — A B C D

36. Do teachers confront statements made by white students and other teachers that are racially or culturally biased or prejudiced? — A B C D

GUIDANCE

37. Are third world groups represented on the counseling staff in proportion to their representation in the student body, or, in predominantly white schools, in relation to their proportion in U.S. society? — A B C D

38. Are guidance counselors required to attend in-service courses to enable them to increase their awareness of racism in our society, and to reexamine their views of racial/ethnic and culturally different students, including expected behavior traits, social mores, achievement potential, etc.? Is this true even if school is predominantly white? — A B C D

39. Are students assigned guidance counselors who can communicate with students and parents in the language used at home? — A B C D

40. Do guidance counselors arrange night hours to meet with working parents? — A B C D

41. Do guidance counselors encourage high academic goals for students from all racial and income groups? — A B C D

	Yes, always	Sometimes	Rarely	No, never
	A	B	C	D

42. Do guidance counselors provide those students who have decided to enter the work force after high school with effective career options rather than channeling them into low-paying service jobs?   **A B C D**

STUDENTS

43. Do students from all racial/ethnic groups have equal access to the school of their choice?   **A B C D**

44. If IQ and/or standardized achievement tests are used, are they offered in the language in which each student is most proficient?   **A B C D**

45. Are teachers, parents and students given a clear-cut explanation of the cultural and class bias inevitably built into all such tests?   **A B C D**

46. Are student performance and interest given equal or greater emphasis than test scores in decisions to track students?   **A B C D**

47. Are discussions with medical and psychiatric professionals, as well as with a child's parents, given equal or greater weight than IQ test scores in decisions to place students into EMR (mentally retarded) classes0   **A B C D**

48. If your school maintains tracked classes, does the racial breakdown in each class roughly reflect the racial breakdown of the school student body?   **A B C D**

49. Are students regularly moved from track to track, rather than frozen into the same track for most of their school life?   **A B C D**

50. Is the proportion of third world students in both college-bound and vocational/commercial courses equal to the proportion of third world students in the school (or system)?   **A B C D**

51. Are students in non-college courses provided counseling, training and worthwhile options that reflect changing economic and technical patterns in our society and lead to well-paying careers with good advancement potential?   **A B C D**

52. Are students encouraged to learn to understand and respect each other's language, dialect or expressions?   **A B C D**

53. Is bilingual, bicultural education available to all students who request it?   **A B C D**

54. Do students feel that all discipline rules are fairly and equally applied?   **A B C D**

55. Have third world students had input into creating discipline policies?   **A B C D**

56. Is there a grievance procedure in which students feel free to bring complaints about racial matters to those having authority, whether they be student government, teachers or administrators?   **A B C D**

57. Does the racial breakdown of students expelled or suspended reflect the racial proportions of the student body?   **A B C D**

58. Are students encouraged to discuss school events and current events which relate to race?   **A B C D**

59. Are they made to feel that their cultural group's dress and speech styles are as acceptable as are white middle-class styles?   **A B C D**

60. Does food served in cafeteria reflect the tastes of all racial and ethnic groups?   **A B C D**

61. Is care taken that students receiving free lunches are not made to feel self-conscious in any way?   **A B C D**

62. Do poor students get some funds to participate in extra-curricular activities?   **A B C D**

63. Does the school recognize the need for and facilitate the arrangement of self-segregation among students at times in the classrooms, extra-curricular activities and leisure periods?   **A B C D**

64. Are all students encouraged to participate in extra-curricular activities such as drama, arts and crafts, musical groups, dance groups, athletics, and student government?   **A B C D**

65. Do school groups and clubs include activities representing the diversity of racial and ethnic cultural contributions, to provide positive experiences for all students?   **A B C D**

	Yes, always	Sometimes	Rarely	No, never

CURRICULUM

66. Are instructional materials as anti-racist as possible? — A B C D

67. Does a curriculum committee, composed of school professionals, parent representatives, local minority and feminist group representatives, and student representatives (age permitting), screen all instructional materials prior to purchase? — A B C D

68. When ideal materials cannot be found, are teachers trained to detect—and to guide their students to detect—both overt and subtle manifestations of racism? (and sexism?) — A B C D

69. If materials aren't representative of our multi-racial, multi-cultural society, do teachers supplement them with materials that are? — A B C D

70. Do materials, resources and media available in the library, media center and guidance offices reflect the racial and ethnic diversity of the nation, the contributions and achievements of third world people and project anti-racist images and concepts? — A B C D

71. Do materials on classroom walls depict the racial diversity of this nation? — A B C D

72. Is it a requirement that curriculum for all students present the true nature of both historical and present-day racism? — A B C D

73. Is it a requirement that curriculum for all students include the culture, contributions and history of all racial groups? (and of women?) — A B C D

74. Does the curriculum make room for open discussion of racial conflicts in the larger society, the community and the school? — A B C D

75. Does the curriculum teach how minority values differ from dominant white values in our society? Are all values presented as equally valid? — A B C D

76. Are students encouraged to mold their future by becoming active participants in working for social justice in the school and community? — A B C D

CHECKLIST ON SEXISM

COMMUNITY

1. Are parents' meetings held at suitable times for working parents? — A B C D

2. Are feminist groups in the community encouraged to assist the schools in combatting sexist practices? — A B C D

3. Are poor and/or third world parents made to feel welcome to visit? — A B C D

4. Do schools perceive both mothers and fathers as equally concerned and responsible for children, and communicate with both in notices, in requesting parent-teacher meetings, in encouraging parental involvement in school related affairs? — A B C D

5. Do fathers participate equally in PTA activities such as organizing, planning events, record keeping, baking, etc.? — A B C D

	Yes, always	Sometimes	Rarely	No, never

SCHOOL BOARD

6. Are half the members of Board female?

7. Do they represent all classes and races in the community?

8. When drawing up contracts, is past discrimination against women administrators recognized and compensated for in considerations of promotion or layoffs, rather than using seniority which results in "last hired first fired" and counteracts affirmative action and equal employment efforts?

9. Are fringe benefits such as retirement plans, maternity and/or family leave, insurance benefits, and sabbatical and training opportunities equal for females and males?

10. Does the school system attempt to direct its business contracts to female contractors and to contractors whose hiring and personnel policies encourage sexual equity?

11. Are all specialized, technical and academic schools in the district open to both females and males equally?

12. Are community feminist groups encouraged to present their concerns to the Board?

13. Has Board hired as many female as male Superintendents?

ADMINISTRATION

14. Are women equally represented in the administrative positions of decision making and high salary in both the central administration and the individual schools (i.e., Assistant Superintendents, principals, assistant principals, etc.)?

15. Is input on feminist issues encouraged from students, teachers and parents?

16. Do administrators place high priority on creating and enforcing policies and practices which are aimed at achieving sexual equity and anti-sexist education?

17. Do school songs, holidays, symbols reflect anti-sexist concerns?

18. Are women invited to address assembly and graduation ceremonies?

19. Are curriculum materials in use carefully screened and teachers made aware of their sexism?

TEACHERS

20. Are male teachers as numerous as female teachers in the primary and elementary grades?

21. Are female teachers employed in equal number to male teachers in high schools?

22. Are females "heads of departments" as often as are males?

23. Are in-service courses required of entire teaching staff to increase their awareness of sexism in our society, and to re-examine their views of behavior traits, role expectations, achievement potential, etc. in regard to female and male students?

24. Are the average salaries of female and male teachers the same?

25. Do teachers contact administrators, school board and publishers to complain about sex role stereotypes and bias in materials, and the lack of materials by and about women's significant role in our society?

26. Do teachers confront statements made by students and other teachers that are sexist or reflect stereotypes about females?

27. Do teachers discuss the implication of—and avoid using—terms like "man" or "mankind" to refer to people or humankind; "he" or "him" when referring to an unknown individual; "chairman" or "congressman" when referring to a chairperson or congressperson, etc.?

28. Do teachers avoid imposing such sex-role expectations of femininity and masculinity on children as "girls love reading and hate math and science," "boys shouldn't cry," or that boys can be loud and noisy while girls must learn to control themselves?

	Yes, always	Sometimes	Rarely	No, never
	A	B	C	D

29. Do teachers avoid separating females and males when forming class into lines, asking for student assistance in classroom duties?

GUIDANCE

30. Are female counselors employed in equal numbers to male counselors?   A B C D

31. Are counselors informed on the realities of sex discrimination in employment and in turn do they provide such information to all students?   A B C D

32. Do counselors encourage and counsel female students to strive for skills and training that will equip them to compete for well-paying careers in *any* field, rather than assume that "most girls get married" after high school and don't join the work force?   A B C D

33. Do guidance staff avoid sex role stereotyping in all advice given?   A B C D

STUDENTS

34. Are females encouraged in math, science, sports and industrial arts, and males in home economics and commercial classes?   A B C D

35. Is similar behavior encouraged from girls as from boys?   A B C D

36. Are females who are pregnant or unwed mothers encouraged to continue schooling?   A B C D

37. Can girls and boys wear any comfortable, clean clothing they desire?   A B C D

38. Are females and males equally encouraged to participate and equally represented in extra-curricular activities such as drama, arts and crafts, musical groups, dance groups, athletics and student government?   A B C D

39. Do females have equal access—in terms of times available and equipment—to all athletic facilities in the school?   A B C D

40. Does the school encourage athletic programs which are most conducive to co-educational practices?   A B C D

41. Are equal amounts of money expended on boys' and girls' athletics?   A B C D

CURRICULUM

42. Are instructional materials as anti-sexist as possible?   A B C D

43. When ideal materials cannot be found, are teachers trained to detect—and to guide their students to detect—both overt and subtle manifestations of sexism?   A B C D

44. Does a curriculum committee, composed of school professionals, parent representatives (including minority and feminist groups) and student representatives (age permitting), screen all instructional materials prior to purchase for sexist stereotyping, omissions and distortions?   A B C D

45. If materials omit the contributions and struggles of women in our society, does the teacher supplement them with materials that provide this information?   A B C D

46. Is literature by women authors, literature about women, and literature with women as central characters in nonstereotyped roles equally represented in the curriculum?   A B C D

47. Do materials on classroom walls depict males and females in nontraditional non-stereotyped roles?   A B C D

48. Is a conscious effort made to bring in outside people—of all races—who counteract traditional sex roles? Female scientists, engineers, dentists and plumbers or male nurses, secretaries and house-husbands?   A B C D

49. Does your library avoid special sections listed "especially for girls" or "especially for boys"?   A B C D

50. Are new library purchases routinely screened for sexism?   A B C D

COMPETENCY 9

Acquire the skills for effective participation and utilization of the community.

RATIONALE:

The role of the community can be a positive force in the school's instructional process. Teachers must realize that possession of knowledge of basic community parameters and their cultural milieu will facilitate the design and delivery of instruction to the members of that community.

Instructional Objectives:

1. The learner will be able to analyze the school community using basic ethnographic techniques.

2. The learner will be able to identify community agencies, their functions, and their relationship to the school.

3. The learner will be able to formulate strategies for involving parents/guardians/caretakers in the educational process.

4. _____

    _____

    _____

Enabling Activities:

1.* Do: Community Analysis Field Study, formerly called "The Princeton Game", in Teaching in a Multicultural Society, University of Houston, 1977, pages 1-5.

2. Read: Carl Grant's Community Participation in Education, Allyn and Bacon, Inc., 1979, 262 pages.

Assessment of Competency:

In order to demonstrate mastery of this competency the learner must present an ethnographic analysis of a designated school community. The learner must demonstrate a knowledge of various strategies for effective involvement of various communities in the educational process.

Instructional Notes From Class Meetings:

Date Competency Achieved _____

I.   TITLE: Community Analysis Field Study
               (Formerly called "The Princeton Game")
               James Anderson

II.   PROSPECTUS:

      A. Rational Purpose

              There is widespread agreement among educators that
          the use of diagnostic instruments like sociometric games
          and tests, personal inventories and self-concept scales
          are indeed helpful and meaningful in enabling teachers
          to gain deeper insight and understanding of their students.

              Although much has been done and interest is continu-
          ously being generated regarding viewing the child in the
          school environment, comparatively little emphasis has
          been directed toward the home and community from where
          children come, which have similar implications for a more
          in-depth look and appraisal of the child. The instrument,
          community analysis field study, is a device used to assit
          teachers in obtaining a proper exposure to the community
          which is served by its schools.

              Too often a school and its staff constitute an island
          which is physically within, but spiritually and culturally
          removed from the surrounding environment. The need is for
          direct experiences which give the teacher a better
          knowledge and understanding for the problems and the
          strengths of the people in the kind of community in which
          he teaches. It is hoped that through this exercise
          teachers will be assisted in developing skills in inter-
          personal communication as well as obtaining certain basic
          information about their students and their community.

      B. Pre-requistes: None

      C. Approximate time: Term Project - Exact time to be assigned
                                    by instructor

      D. Objectives:

          1. The student will engage in and identify various
              forms of community field research.

          2. The student will be able to describe in writing,
              many of the various forces operating in a school-
              community which affect the way students learn or
              fail to learn in the school environment.

Reprinted from Teaching in a Multicultural Society, 1977.

III. PRE-ASSESSMENT:

Pre-assessment will consist of individual class or group conferences if needed with students to assess the degree of understanding of the instructions, for the community field study.

IV. ENABLING AND INSTRUCTIONAL ACTIVITIES

Activity 1

A. You will be given the name of a Houston area school, _____. Your task will be to study the community that school serves. The given school will serve as the center focus for the study and you will place it in the center location of your map that you will create yourself for the study.

Activity 2

A. Your next task will be to fill in your own constructed map of the assigned school community with the desired kinds of information including the names of the streets in the community. Use the following color and number code to fill in the map. Place the appropriate color dots or marks in the correct location on your grid map.

   Black, for any schools in the area (names and numbers)

   Orange, for any public community service agencies (names and numbers)

   Green, for any religious or political organization (names and numbers)

   Yellow, for any substandard housing

   Blue, for any places where children and teenagers play

   Purple, for any places where unemployed men gather (names and numbers)

   Brown, for any major industries (names and numbers)

   Red, for any condemned buildings or areas

B. (Where the word "names and numbers" appears attached to a category attach a numbered list to your map that gives the names and corresponding map numbers of those places or structures etc.

Activity 3

A. As you examine and study your designated school community, you will begin to collect various kinds of data concerning the area, as this happens, you must answer, completely, the following community analysis questionnaire. (If enough space is not provided on the questionnaire you may type out longer answers and attach them to the map.)

Activity 4

A. During the study and also after the study has been completed, you will have had numerous experiences many of which will make impressions on you. On the appropriate attached pages in your study, record your impressions. It is likely that some will be humorous, some unexplainable, some shocking, some even uncomfortable, some even very revealing to your-self and some very informative. These impressions may come as you are walking through the community or sitting at home relaxing etc., whenever and whereever, please record them on your "impressions log."

Activity 5

A. At the completion of this module, the student will type his complete study and turn it in to the instructor at the appropiate date. When the module has been completed you should be prepared to orally discuss your study with other students as well as with the instructor in class.

IMPORTANT INSTRUCTIONS' FOR THE MODULE

A very important and critical part of this study is to discover the most efficient ways to gather the necessary information or answers for the completion of the questionnaire. This is why there are pur-posely, only a limited number of specific directions as to how to gather your information, or where to gather it, or what kinds of people to talk with. This module is designed to examine and expand your resourcefulness and throughness in culturally diverse communities and to help prepare you for teaching in a multicultural society.

(Feedback will be sought at various times throughout the module)

V. POST-ASSESSMENT:

The completion of the entire study with all of the objectives met will constitute post-assessment for this module.

1. Development of The Community Analysis Project will be evaluated by the instructor using the following criteria. Descriptive Map - with proper colors and proper identification of structures and areas.

2. Completion of questionnaire for community analysis keeping in mind the thoroughness, depth of perception, and insight as illustrated by complete answers and the citing of the sources from which you gathered the data for the answer to each question.

3. The thoroughness of the recordings in the impression log again keeping in mind depth of perception and insight indicated in the recorded impression.

4. Added features, which provided extra dimensions and insights into the study, pictures, tapes, articles, clippings, literature, brochures, reports, etc.

5. Completion of assignment on time.

Community Analysis Field Study Questionnaire

1. Your Name_____ Name of School_____
   Address of School_____
   Section of City_____

2. What is the average rent for a four-room apartment in this area?_____

3. In what condition is the typical apartment renting for in this school community.

4. What attitudes do the designated school's students you interviewed in the area really hold toward the school and school teachers of their school? Interview at least three students and report their interviews separately.

5. Where do residents of the area buy most of their food?

6. How much do typical food staples cost in this area? (You may provide a sample listing if you would like)

7. How does the cost of those staples compare with costs in stores you usually shop in? (You may provide comparative listings if you would like.)

8. How does the quality of the meats, fruits, milk, and vegetables compare ?

9. What are the outstanding physical problems like garbage disposal, drainage, street cleaning and lighting in this area?

10. What if anything, is being done about these problems, and by whom? Make specific reference to each of the problems identified above.

11. What attitudes do the mothers or fathers of children who attend the school in the area express toward this school? Interview at least three parents and report each interview separately.

12. What are the major social problems of this area?

13. What if anything, is being done about these problems, and by whom?

14. Who owns most of the property in this section?

15. How good are the municipal services in this section?

16. What were the principal methods you used to get the answers to the above questions?

17. What is the racial or ethnic composite of the designated school community?

18. What is the racial or ethnic composite that attends the identified school?

19. What is the average family income in the area?

20. What is the cost range of the average home in the area?

IMPRESSIONS LOG (NOTE)

Do not forget to attach your impressions log to your study. See instructor for specific instruction.

COMPETENCY 10

Design, develop and implement an instructional module using strategies and materials which will produce a module/unit that is multicultural, multiracial, and/or multiethnic in character.

RATIONALE:

The paucity of multicultural curriculum instructional units implies that teachers will have to produce their own culturally diverse resources. The large amount of available monoracial, monoethnic, and monocultural resources can be effectively integrated in multicultural, multiracial, and multiethnic modules or units by a teacher skilled in multiculturalism.

Attainment of this competency demonstrates a very sophisticated level of multiculturalism, perhaps equivalent to Bloom's evaluation level or Krathwohl's value complex level of the taxonomy of educational objectives.

Instructional Objectives:

1. The learner will be able to design a module/unit that is reflective of cultural diversity, and be able to implement the module/unit in an instructional setting with learners.

2. The learner will be able to evaluate the module/unit using the criteria of increased awareness of the value of cultural diversity for a group of learners in an instructional setting.

3. _____

   _____

   _____

Enabling Activities:

1. Read: H. Prentice Baptiste, Jr., and Mira Baptiste, "Developing Multicultural Learning Activities", Multicultural Education: Commitments, Issues, and Applications, Washington, D.C.: Association of Supervision and Curriculum Development, 1977, pages 105-112.

2.* Read: H. Prentice Baptiste, Jr., and Mira Baptiste, "Multicultural Education: Knowing Me and You", Educational Perspectives, December, 1977, pages 23-25.

3.* Read: Geneva Gay, "Organizing and Designing Culturally Pluralistic Curriculum", Educational Leadership, December, 1975, pages 176-183.

4. Read: Mildred Dickeman, "Teaching Cultural Pluralism", in Teaching Ethnic Studies, James Banks, ed., 43rd Yearbook, Washington, D.C.: National Council for the Social Studies, 1973, pages 5-25.

5. Read: James A. Banks, Part I, "Goals, Concepts, and Instructional Organization", in Teaching Strategies for Ethnic Studies, Boston: Allyn and Bacon, Inc., 1979, pages 1-133.

6.* Examine the following examples of Multicultural Modules:

    a) "Who Am I?" by Barbara Sherman
    b) "Now You Can Give" by Mirabelle Baptiste
    c) "The Afton Falls Case" by William W. Witcher
    d) "The Comic Imagination" by Thelma Cobb
    e) "Interrelating Cultural Pluralism Through a Language-Experience Approach to Reading" by Loretta Walton

7. _____

    _____

    _____

8. _____

    _____

    _____

Assessment of Competency:

The major emphasis of this competency is having the learner demonstrate mastery of designing, developing, and implementing an instructional strategy (module/unit) that is multicultural, multiethnic and/or multiracial. The competency brings together most of the previous competencies which have helped the learner develop the ability to become a teacher in a cultural pluralistic society. To fulfill the expectations of this competency the module/unit must be a legitimate part of the learners' regular curriculum. The strategies and materials used must facilitate a culturally diverse approach to the subject matter. The implementation must take place in an instructional setting using at least ten to fifteen or more learners. The implementation period must be at least three or more instructional time periods.

A complete copy of the module/unit is to be prepared and presented to the instructor. A prospectus of one or two pages which is summative is required for distribution for each member of the class. An oral report of the module/unit is to be made to the class in which the objectives are stated, examples of learners' work is examined, the evaluation process is explained, and how this module/unit increased awareness of cultural diversity in the learners is illustrated. Examples of instructional materials, resources used, and audio-visual materials utilized are to be presented as a display for the presentation.

Instructional Notes From Class Meetings:

Date Competency Achieved _____

Guidelines for Multicultural Module Development
Implementation and Presentation
Competency 10

The teacher for Multicultural Education should demonstrate the ability to:

> develop and implement an instructional module using strategies
> and materials that are multicultural/multiethnic/multiracial
> in character.

To fulfill the expectations of this competency you should:

1. Select a topic(s), concept(s) or generalization(s) that is a legitimate part of your student's regular curriculum.

   -strategies and materials that will facilitate a culturally diverse approach must be utilized.

   -a module or unit or several related lessons must be evolved from the utilized strategies and materials.

2. The module (unit or related lessons) must be completely implemented within your classroom.

   -a valid implementation will necessitate several days in which different parts of the module are implemented. (Sufficient implementation cannot occur during two or three days.)

   -Unless other circumstances warrant, at least 10-15 students should be involved in the instruction.

   - multimedia materials and techniques should be incorporated in your strategies.

3. You will give an oral report (10 minutes) to your peers in which

   -you will distribute a one-two page abstract (prospectus) of your module.

   -you will have available samples of the instructional materials utilized in the module implementation.

   -samples of students' work should be presented.

   -you will include in your oral presentation a statement of objectives, and how they were evaluated.

   -you will turn in a complete copy of your developed module.

MULTICULTURAL EDUCATION: KNOWING ME AND YOU
Hansom Prentice Baptiste, Jr., Mirabelle Baptiste

The three major functions of our educational system are: (1) socialization, (2) cultural transmission, and (3) the development of self-identity.[1] The respective purveyors and objects of these functions are teachers and students. Educators and parents, for the most part, are in agreement on these functions. Disagreement lies in the contextual embodiment of these functions. We submit that the embodiment of these functions must be in a context of multicultural education.

Multicultural processes should be an intimate part of the teacher's instructional activities. One must eschew monocultural processes which foster the development of cultural alienation and self-degradation in most students. In its stead, teachers should strive for their students to acquire a respect for diversity — which is a basic principle of multicultural education. Instruction which has, as an objective, a respect for diversity, should begin with activities which focus on self-enhancement or self-concept. It should be apparent that students must feel good about themselves (i.e., family, community, cultural heritage) before they can relate positively (i.e., accept, respect and trust others) to other cultural groups.

Designing learning activities which will enable students to explore their self-concepts is often the beginning stage for multicultural processes. The enhancement of self-concept is undeniably related to the belief of having some control over one's environment. Subsequently, teachers should make a constant and conscientious effort to create instructional environments reflective of power-sharing, equality and decisionmaking, but being mindful that shared power and decisionmaking must flow in two directions — between teacher and students.

The classroom setting mirrors a small society which is much closer to the society of adults than it is to that of the family. Students and teachers are not brought together by personal feelings or preference, but for altogether general and abstract reasons. In a social system as tightly organized as that of most classrooms, the position and activities of any role depend upon those of its role-mates. In this sense, the student is dependent on the teacher. Being a student is a role-playing activity, with students developing strategies to cope with the "institutionalized dominance and subordination" built into the classroom-role structure. The teacher is in control of most of the action and does most of the talking. The conventional classroom situation allows academic success through a very limited range of intellectual approaches or styles. Most curricula and teachers reward skills in role-learning and a cognitive style characterized by analytical, abstract modes of thinking.

The two most critical roles in the classroom are those of the teacher and the student, with the quality of life in the classroom largely based upon the interaction between them. Age and status differences, as well as discrepancies in goals, contribute to disequilibrium in the teacher-student relationship; but another factor, the teacher's socio-economic background may contribute significantly to this disequilibrium. The teacher, like the student, comes to the school with a socio-economic history which affects his attitudes toward and interaction with students and other persons in the school.

More often than not, parts of what the student brings to the school have been ignored or even suppressed to the point the student is forced to lose self-esteem. Teachers usually bring to the classroom one set of values and beliefs and assume that these are the values and beliefs of the students in that classroom. Development of respect for diversity should become a part of the teacher's behavior and the school's curriculum. How a person develops this respect for diversity is one of the most important jobs that teachers and schools must assume. The acknowledgement of the uniqueness of each student in the classroom requires a knowledge of his cultural heritage.

In the past, the failure of the school system to recognize the cultural heritage of each student has promoted such labels as culturally-disadvantaged and culturally-deprived, even though the student's membership in a culture was providing him with all the attributes of a culture. The student, along with his culture, was existing in a hostile environment which was detrimental to his well-being.

This hostility, in part, develops from what is commonly found in the schools — a monocultural approach to education. The school or school system values only one culture and this culture is reinforced by teachers who for the most part espouse a middle-class philosophy. The

Reprinted from Educational Perspectives, December, 1977.

values and cultural beliefs that students bring to the classroom are largely ignored and the person believes his values and culture are not worthwhile. A tenet of multicultural education is to help students believe that *who they are* is important and *what they value* is worthwhile. Multicultural education deals with all aspects of the human being: his uniqueness, his differences, and his racial, ethnic and cultural heritage. A cultural-pluralistic philosophy demonstrates that a student is not only a part of a cultural and/or family group, but that he is born with characteristics which are unique and belong to no other person. The total society does not always recognized that we live in an *ethnics* society made up of many culturally-different groups.

Socio-economic status, race, ethnic group membership, religion and family attributes relate strongly to a student's school career. All affect academic success, both directly and indirectly, through their interaction and through their effects on other variables related to achievement. Individuals are born into families. The family in which the child is born is one of the major determinants of his subsequent success in school. Two kinds of family effects are important. First, the family has certain characteristics, including socio-economic status, race and religion which are attributed to the child simply by virtue of his family membership. The second set of variables has to do with the way the family is structured and the attributes and behavior of the members with respect to one another. No other characteristics besides family and race, which the child acquires at birth, have been the subject of more educational argument, analysis and soul searching.

It has been argued that the basic needs of people are the need for love and the need for self-worth. The schools are much more directly concerned with the second basic need, the need to feel worthwhile. Love and self-worth are so intertwined that they may properly be related through the use of the term *identity*. Thus, it may be said that the single basic need that people have is the requirement for an identity: the belief that we are someone in distinction to others, and that the someone is important and worthwhile. For most people of school age, only two places exist where they can gain a successful identity and learn to follow the essential pathways of social responsibility and self-worth. These places are the home and the school.

Inability to gain a successful identity does not mean that a person will have no identity. Each student comes to school with feelings about self and his self-worth. Very few people lead a life with no real knowledge of who they are. What happens in school interactions can strengthen or

weaken these concepts.

Inherent within multicultural education are the following basic principles: (1) recognition of all cultural, ethnic and racial groups within the total society, (2) development of respect for diversity, and (3) acknowledgement of each human being as a unique individual as well as a member of a cultural, ethnic and/or racial group.

Instructional activities designed by the teacher to include the abovenamed basic principals will include introducing the students to the fact that every person needs a feeling of security, recognition and self-worth. "Knowing Me and You"[1] is an example of a series of such activities. This example included the objectives designed by the teacher and students, namely: (1) the student will be able to describe himself in terms of self-pride and self-identity, (2) the student will recognize that every other student/teacher has some worth and dignity regardless of his ethnic, racial, cultural or economic classification, (3) each student will show, at the conclusion of the activities/experiences, some type of improvement on an undesirable self-trait that he had previously identified and chosen for self-improvement, and (4) the student will be able to appreciate and respect others, to some degree, for their right to be unique individuals and not necessarily like him.

The teacher's role in self-esteem and interpersonal activities is very crucial because these activities usually focus on the following categorizing factors — socio-economic status, age, religion, race, sex and culture. The teacher must demonstrate a positive attitude toward diversity in these categories. Students will quickly detect, within the teacher or any other authority figure, negativism toward difference. Students expect the teacher to be honest about himself, to be knowledgeable about individual differences, to be willing to share his values, opinions and beliefs, and to be trustworthy. Most importantly, the teacher must be able to communicate to the students that he, too, is in the process of knowing who he is. This tends to put the student and teacher on an equal, self-actualizing basis within the school environment.

There is some reason to believe that students learn better when their teachers know about them as individuals. Students' school records yield basic data, but how the student perceives himself as an individual cannot be gathered from these records. Any other information noted on the records is usually written as a result of some interaction between the student and teacher.

"Knowing Me and You" is an example of a series of

activities which promote interaction between student and teacher and among students. Activities such as: (1) self-portrait, (2) games designed to show social responsibility, body language and sharing with others, (3) collages to abstractly depict the person — within and without — and (4) journals about self, friends, desires, et cetera, build on personal and interpersonal relationships within the classroom setting. It is hoped the students who, at the beginning of these activities, are shy and insecure about their lives, or have negative feelings toward self will begin to feel better about themselves. Success in school is very basic to the individual, and building self-worth cannot be ignored.

Teachers must realize that the degree of effectiveness of self-concept units/activities is determined by the extent of their own involvement. Teachers who maintain an aloof attitude with their students tend to depersonalize the self-concept activities and dehumanize the students. An unwillingness to share yourself through participation in the self-concept activities can adversely affect the interactive sharing activities; thus producing a mechanistic atmosphere instead of the appropriate humanistic activities which should characterize self-concept activities.

Designing learning activities which will enable the student to explore his self-concept is often the beginning stage for multicultural education. The undeniable link of self-esteem and worthiness to the feeling of one having some control over his environment dictates flexible activities which will allow student input. One must remember that before a person can begin to accept others, he must feel good about himself.

Revealing one's self indicates a very significant step in the process of becoming. "Knowing Me and You" contains activities which allow the student to draw the boundaries himself. The journals kept by one set of students who were involved in this unit serve as examples of this activity. Topics such as, The Inner Me, The Outer Me, and Why I'm Proud To Be A Chicano were used as titles by the students, and with their permission, they are being reproduced.

THE OUTER ME

I'm 4'9½" tall,
My hair is brown
and I have brown eyes.
I have fair complexion.
That is what I look like.
                    T.G.

THE INNER ME

The inner me is
beautiful. Then
sometimes I feel
sad and sometimes
people make me
happy again.
The inner me is
sometimes I feel
mad to.
                    T.G.

WHY I'M PROUD TO BE A CHICANO

I am proud to be a Chicano
because when people go to the beach
they don't go to swim. They
go to get a suntan, well at least
most of them. The other reason is I
can Speak a different language.
                    M.G.

Footnotes

¹Thomas F. Green. *Work, Leisure and The American School,* New York: Random House, 1968.
²Hansom Prentice Baptiste, Jr., Mirabelle Baptiste and Barbara Sherman. "Knowing Me and You," *A Self Awareness Module Series,* University of Houston: Professional Development Center, 1974.

ORGANIZING AND DESIGNING
CULTURALLY PLURALISTIC CURRICULUM
Geneva Gay

Ethnically pluralistic curriculum content has the potential of producing
fundamental changes in the total school climate, and also of reforming the
entire nature of American education. For this potential to be realized
information about ethnic, racial, and cultural diversity in curriculum designs
must be handled carefully and conscientiously.

Fragmented and isolated units, courses, and bits of information about
ethnic groups interspersed sporadically into school curriculum and instructional
programs will not do the job. Nor will additive approaches, wherein school
curricula remain basically the same, and ethnic content becomes an appendage to
these curricula. Rather, in designing curriculum, well-conceived, systemagic,
organizational plans must be employed that allow for ethnically specific content
to become integral parts of all aspects of the school's educational programs.
Otherwise, our experiements with education for ethnic and cultural diversity are
likely to prove to be of no avail; or they may even prove to be counterproductive.

Curriculum Characteristics

Regardless of the subject matter or course which serves to introduce ethnically
pluralistic content into the curricula, there are some common design criteria
that must be observed to achieve optimum effectiveness. Curriculum designs must
reflect a real sense of purpose, and a clearly articulated philosophy. They
must be organized around clearly discernible objectives which can easily be
translated into instructional plans. Materials, activities, and experiences that
are authentic, interdisciplinary, multidimensional, comprehensive, integrative,
and that employ both cognitive and affective skills should be used to help students
understand ethnic differences and cultural diversity.

Multicultural curricula are obligated to address the many different dimensions
of the lives of ethnic group members. These include their cultural characteristics,
intra-group variations, their present status in society, conditions of their
political, economic, and social existence in historical perspective, and their
contributions to the development of American culture and the advancement of
humankind.

Reprinted from Educational Leadership, December, 1975.

Multiethnic curriculum should also be broadly conceptualized to include the experiences of all ethnic groups, both majority and minority, in American society. Specifically, this means including Blacks, Latinos, Asian Americans, Native Americans, as well as white ethnic groups, such as Anglo Americans, Polish Americans, Jews, Irish Americans, and Italian Americans. This suggestions does not mean that students need to memorize a barrage of factual information about each of these ethnic groups. Nor does it mean giving equal instructional time and curriculum space to all ethnic groups.

Factual information is important but the curriculum should process it through emphases on concepts and generalizations about ethnic groups; recurrent psycho-social themes and eco-political issues applicable to all groups; and using comparative ethnic perspectives in examining social, political, and economic issues and ideas pertinent to various ethnic groups. Ethnic content should be an integral part of all fundamental educational experiences, and a regular feature of the daily curriculum, instead of being reserved for special units, courses, and occasions. Thus, ethnic content affects all students in many different ways.

Global Objectives

While it is true that specific objectives of particular culturally pluralistic curricula will be determined by the needs of the populations to be served, there are some global objectives that are, and ought to be, applicable to all situations, and equally as appropriate for all students. These include helping students to develop skills in ethnic knowledge comprehension, reflective self-analysis, clarification of racial attitudes and values, comparative analyses of ethnic and cultural phenomena, and eliminating the ethnic isolation and psychological captivity resulting from distorted attitudes about ethnicity.

Most Americans know very little about their own ethnicity, and even less about ethnic groups other than their own. This lack of knowledge often leads to inter-ethnic group hostilities and misunderstandings. School experiences designed to develop pride on one's own ethnic and cultural heritages, expose students to alternative life styles and cultural options, and develop understanding of and appreciation for the validity of others' ethnicity, help to fill the educational voids most students have concerning racial, cultural, and ethnic diversity. Thus, they merit high priority in delineating multicultural curriculum.

Culturally pluralistic curriculum should also seek to elminate ethnic illiteracy, make students capable of functioning well in different ethnic settings, politically efficacious, and socially activist. It should increase their cognitive knowledge bases about ethnicity, their empathetic capabilities, and their experiential contacts with regard to ethnic groups and their existence in American society, history, and culture.

Design Strategies

The potential of education to help students develop understanding of and acceptance for the vitality of cultural pluralism and ethnic diversity in American life will not be realized unless some well-defined, systematic appraoches are employed to revise school curricula so that they will be pluralistic. Curriculum reforms cannot be left to happenstance; nor to the whims of individuals within school systems. They must be carefully conceptualized and instituted on a systemwide basis. Otherwise, attempts at culturally pluralistic curriculum reforms are likely to result in fragmented, poorly organized, and ineffective programs similar to those of the early days of minority studies. Without well conceived organizational plans it will be impossible for curriculum developers and classroom teachers to structure the mass of data about ethnic, racial and cultural diversity in ways that are manageable for students, and to achieve the objectives necessary for living effectively in a culturally pluralistic society.

Several different design strategies offer promising possibilities for making school curricula more ethnically diversified and culturally pluralistic. Probably the most popular approach is to integrate ethnic content into existing curricula and pluralize curriculum materials, particularly elementary basal readers, and secondary social studies and language arts. Other curriculum reform strategies include using a modified basic skills approach, a thematic approach, a conceptual approach, a cultural domponents approach, and a branching design.

Each of these design strategies has the capability of giving needed structure and direction to the process of incorporating ethnic content into school curricula. Each is inclusive in that it is not limited to any one subject area or grade level. They can all be adapted for use in most subjects for all grade levels, kindergarten through college.

Modifying Basic Skills Approach

This design strategy is based on the premise that ethnic and cultural diversity should permate all aspects of education. Therefore, ethnic materials should be used to teach such fundamental skills as reading, writing, calculating,

and reasoning. Students can learn reading skills using materials written by
and about Blacks, Mexican Americans, Italian Americans, and Jewish Americans
as well as they can from reading "Dick and Jane." Ethnic literature is as well
endowed with examples of "quality" and with literary techniques as is literature
written by Anglo Americans. Such literature can be used to teach plot, climax,
metaphor, grammatical structure, and symbolism as well as anything written by
Anglo Americans. Biology, chemistry, mathematics, and the other sciences can
be made more personal, interesting, and comprehensible by including individuals
from different ethnic groups who have contributed to the advancement of these
fields of knowledge.

Modifying basic skills teaching also argues for the inclusion of ethnic
literacy, reflective self-anaysis, decision making, and social activism among
the basic skills all students should master. These are as essential for living
effectively in a culturally and ethnically pluralistic society and world as
are knowing how to read and having a salable skill.

By using differnt kinds of ethnic content which has experiential meaning
and psycho-cultural significance to members of different ethnic groups to teach
fundamental skills, several other objectives can be achieved simultaneously.
Students' ethnic identity is enhanced; individual students receive new knowledge
about different ethnic heritages and are forced to confront their ethnic
stereotypes and racial attitudes; the use of ethnically diversified and culturally
pluralistic materials becomes routine in teaching and learning; and students
become aware of multiethnic perspectives regarding value systems, social
behaviors, and learning styles. Ethnic content interwoven into the study of
basic skills can function as a motivational device for ethnically different
youth. It increases the relevance of their classroom activities by making these
more compatible with their home experiences. Ethnic content also serves the
purpose of brining academic tasks from the realm of the alien and the abstract
into the experiential frames of reference of ethnically different youth,
through media which are meaningful to them.

Conceptual Approach

There is a complex, multidimensional body of knowledge about ethnic and
racial groups which students need to comprehend if they are to develop positive
attitudes and accepting behaviors toward cultural pluralism. Mere mastery of
factual information and memory of chronological events are insufficient. A
more useful technique is to design multiethnic curriculum around a series of

concepts selected from multiple disciplines, which are applicable to all ethnic group experiences. These might include such generic concepts as identity, power, survival, culture, communication, socialization, racism, location, acculturation and enculturation, change, and ethnicity. Additional concepts can be selected from such disciplines as demography, cultural geography, anthropology, sociology, psychology, sociolinguistics, economics, and political science.

Since these concepts are chosen from different subject matter disciplines and are inherent to the human condition - both individually and collectively - they lend themselves readily to multidimensional and interdisciplinary analyses, using comparative and multiethnic perspectives. The concepts of identity is as much a biological, sociological, and historical issue as it is a psychological one. Studying the concept of power means analyzing it from historical and contemporary political, sociological, and economic perspectives.

Culture as an anthropological concept has implications for analysis for the social sciences, the natural sciences, the fine arts, communications, the language arts, and interpersonal interactions. Therefore, all dimensions of the school's instructional programs can be made to accommodate ethnically significant concepts.

The curriculum development process should include selecting key concepts and supportive concepts from the various disciplines; identifying major and minor generalizations emanating from the concepts; delineating appropriate objectives; selecting and organizing curriculum materials, learning experiences, and instructional strategies to teach the concepts; assigning responsibilities to various school department accountable for implementing the different parts of the curriculum designs; and making plans for maintaining cohesiveness in the processes of implementation and evaluation.

Thematic Approach

There are many recurrent themes which characterize the human condition, the social realities, and cultural experiences of ethnic groups in American society. These are persistent and pervasive in that they are significant to all ethnic groups, and permeate the entire spectrum of their historical development. Ways in which ethnic groups and the society-at-large have responded to these themes have had a determining influence in shaping the life styles of different groups and individuals. Illustrative of these recurrent themes or concerns are a search for ethnic identity, or "ethnicity"; protest against injustices and inequities; the fight against dehumanization and depersonalization; the struggle for freedom; and the ever-present influence of ethnic groups on the American scene.

In a curriculum design that uses these themes as the organizing principles, the focus of attention is on the themes as opposed to the ethnic groups. Interdisciplinary techniques are used to examine the themes to determine how they relate to different ethnic group experiences. Thus, comparative, multi-ethnic perspectives are as applicable here as in using conceptual curriculum design strategies. It is equally as appropriate to examine Afro-American, Anglo American, Asian American, and Latino philosophies and literatures in studying their search for identity as it is to examine their music, their sociology, their psychology, and their history. Analyzing ethnic groups' struggles against injustices and inequities requires as much attention to their psychology and geography as it does to their political and social activism, their consumer habits, and their artistic and aesthetic expressions.

A multiethnic curriculum of this magnitude would consistently ask of students: How do the circumstances, causes, and responses of one ethnic group to a particular issue compare with those of other ethnic groups? Are these concerns inherent in the human condition? Are there conditions peculiar to the American setting that spawn these activities? These questions allow students to extend their analyses of recurrent themes significant to ethnic groups to a multinational level. This approach to curriculum design offers a novel, exciting way of studying different ethnic groups and their cultures, both within the United States and in other parts of the world.

Cultural Components Approach

This approach to curriculum reform focuses on those characteristics of different ethnic groups that combine to form unique cultural traditions. It is somewhat less comprehensive than the conceptual or the theatic approach. Whereas the former design strategies concentrate on achieving a holistic or total view of ethnic groups and their lives, the cultural components approach focuses only on the culture of ethnic groups. Primary emphasis is placed on extricating from among the generic cultural components of Americans those that are unique to specific ethnic groups. Ethnic perceptions, expectations, behavioral patterns, communications systems, socialization processes, value systems, and the styles of interpersonal interactions form the core of the curriculum. Materials necessary for examining these are selected from ethnic groups' literatures, histories, customs, traditions, folklores, religions, philosophies, cultural anthropologies, and family structures.

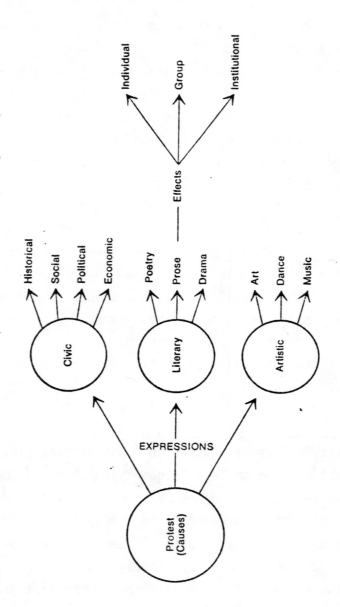

Figure 1. A Branching Design for Developing Culturally Pluralistic Curriculum

Branching Designs

The branching design to multiethnic curriculum reform is not so much a set of guidelines as to which ethnic content should be selected for use in the curriculum as it is an organizational technique for making ethnic content more comprehensible, cohesive, and pervasive throughout the school's total instructional programs. It suggests that students have a better chance of comprehending the complexities of ethnic groups' life styles, their cultural heritages, and their existential conditions in society if contact with ethnic content extends beyond a single course, or a single period of the school day. This can be achieved by taking an idea, issue, concept, or problem pertinent to ethnic groups that is being studied in one subject, extend it to another subject area, and add the perspectives of that particular discipline to the analyses of the topic under examination.

A branching design using "protest" as an illustrative example is depicted visually in Figure 1. It indicates that protest is a phenomenon familiar to all ethnic groups, and that it is multidimensional. These dimensional analyses of protest must include, for example, civic, literary, and artistic protest, and the various sub-categories within each of these. Any study of ethnic protest in whatever subject area would also want to explore the causes, the expressions or forms, and the effects of protest.

The branching approach to designing culturally pluralistic curriculum gives students the opportunity to examine a given ethnic issue in depth, to become involved with the issue to a degree greater than superficiality, and in ways that they begin to immerse themselves totally in the experiences instead of merely dealing with ethnic issues on an academic level only. It also allows teachers the security of working within the framework of their disciplines. Traditional lines of division among subject areas need not be abandoned, but teachers do need to work cooperatively to build complementary instructional programs on similar ethnic issues.

In summary, the strategies offered here for organizing and designing culturally pluralistic curriculum are no panacea. They do, however, have the optential for providing some needed structure and focus on efforts to incorporate content about ethnic, cultural, and racial diversity into school curricula.

Perhaps some will consider these strategies quite ambitious and beyond the present capabilities of many school systems. These approaches, however, can be adapted to accommodate local situations, and can be used as a means of reforming the entire curriculum development process. They provide ways of better managing the mass of data about ethnicity and ethnic groups that teachers and students must process if they are to develop authentic knowledge of and real appreciation for these vital features of American society. Their effective implementation depends upon serious commitment to the ideas and principles of cultural pluralism and multiethnic education, the resources school systems are willing to invest in the pursuit of quality education that is ethnically and culturally pluralistic, and the capabilities of the school personnel who are assigned the tasks of designing multiethnic curriculum and implementing it in the classroom. However great the potentials of curriculum design strategies may be, in actuality they are only as good as those who legislate, design, and implement them.

A CURRICULUM REFLECTING

CULTURAL PLURALISM

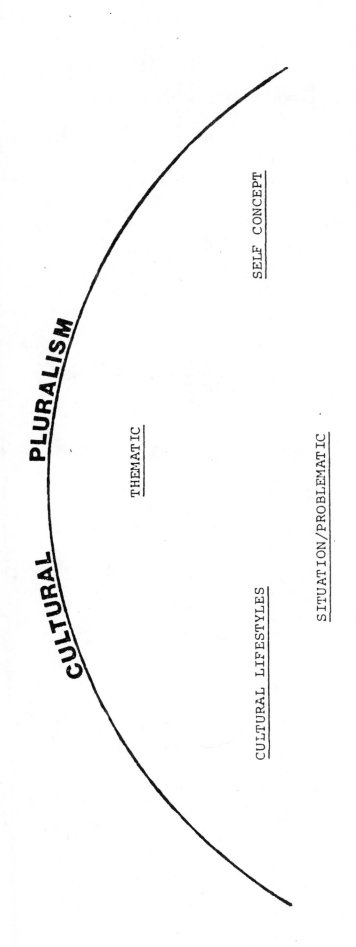

THEMATIC

SELF CONCEPT

BILINGUAL EDUCATION

CULTURAL LIFESTYLES

SITUATION/PROBLEMATIC

CULTURAL AWARENESS

ETHNIC CONTRIBUTIONS

*Representative of module prospectuses
on pages 231-252.

ESSENTIAL COMPONENTS OF MODULE

   I.   PROSPECTUS OR RATIONALE

  II.   FLOW CHART

 III.   PRE-TEST

  IV.   COMPETENCIES OR OBJECTIVES
        (Terminal & Sub)

   V.   **ACTIVITIES**

  VI.   POST-TEST

 VII.   EVALUATION OF MODULE

A SELF AWARENESS MODULE
Barbara Sherman

The possibilities for a child to develop a positive self-concept are extremely limited unless teachers and other authority figures perceive the child as a significant individual. Children, and adults, for that matter, will, for the most part never rise to levels of accomplishments beyond their own images of themselves. If the aim of education is as Carl Rogers suggests, the "Facilitation of Learning," the total process of evaluation can be justified only on the basis of improving learning experiences for children. A safe learning climate is needed for children to develop a positive self-concept.

Children have a need to learn more about their self-identity in order to aspire toward a fuller personal development. This module is concerned with the teacher who is participating in the development of individuals who have positive self-concepts, who function effectively, and who will serve as a model for positive behavior and attitudes. The major duty of the teacher is to create a climate of acceptance, understanding, and encouragement in the classroom.

Terminal Objective

.   The students will be able to identify and describe themselves in terms of self-pride. The students will recognize the worth and dignity of each other. Each student should be able to appreciate and respect, to some degree, others for their right to be unique individuals. It is anticipated each student will show some type of improvement on a self-trait he had previously chosen as not so desirable. Open-ended activities will facilitate the process and allow for a visible product of the student's progress.

---

*Complete version of modules presented in companion publication - Modules for Multiculturalizing Classroom Instruction.

WHAT IS BLACK?

Black is the night
When there isn't a star
And you can't tell by looking
Where you are.
Black is a pail of paving tar.
Black is jet
And things you'd like to forget.
Black is a smokestack
Black is a cat,
A leopard, a raven,
A high silk hat.
The sound of black is
"Boom! Boom! Boom!
Echoing in
An empty room.
Black is kind——
It covers up
The run-down street,
The broken cup.
Black is charcoal
And patio grill,
The soot spots on
The window sill.
Black is a feeling
Hard to explain
Like suffering but
Without the pain.
Black is licorice
And patent leather shoes
Black is the print
In the news.
Black is beauty
In its deepest form,
The darkest cloud
In a thunderstorm.
Think of what starlight
And lamplight would lack
Diamonds and fireflies
If they couldn't lean against
Black....

Reprinted from Hailstones and Halibut Bones by Mary O'Neill.

WHAT IS WHITE?

White is a dove
And lily of the valley
And a puddle of milk
Spilled in an alley——
A ship's sail
A kite's tail
A wedding veil
Hailstones and
Halibut bones
And some people's
Telephones.
The hottest and most blinding light
Is white.
And breath is white
When you blow it out on a frosty night.
White is the shining absence of all color
Then absence is white
Out of touch
Out of sight.
White is marshmallow
And vanilla ice cream
And the part you can't remember
In a dream.
White is the sound
Of a light foot walking
White is a pair of
Whispers talking.
White is the beautiful
Broken lace
Of snowflakes falling
On your face.
You can smell white
In a country room
Toward the end of May
In the cherry bloom.

Reprinted from Hailstones and Halibut Bones by Mary O'Neill.

WHAT IS BROWN?

Brown is the color of a country road
Back of a turtle
Back of a toad.
Brown is cinnamon
And morning toast
And the good smell of
The Sunday roast.
Brown is the color of work
And the sound of a river,
Brown is bronze and a bow
And a quiver.
Brown is the house
On the edge of town
Where wind is tearing
The shingles down.
Brown is a feckle
Brown is a mole
Brown is the earth
When you dig a hole.
Brown is the hair
On many a head
Brown is chocolate
And gingerbread.
Brown is a feeling
You get inside
When wondering makes
Your mind grow wide.
Brown is a leather shoe
And a good glove———
Brown is as comfortable
As love.

Reprinted from Hailstones and Halibut Bones by Mary O'Neill.

WHAT IS RED?

Red is a sunset
Blazy and bright.
Red is feeling brave
With all your might.
Red is a sunburn
Spot on your nose,
Sometimes red
Is a red, red rose.
Red squiggles out
When you cut your hand.
Red is a brick and
A rubber band.
Red is a hotness
You get inside
When you're embarrassed
And want to hide.
Fire-cracker, fire-engine
Fire-flicker red_____ .
And when you're angry
Red runs through your head.
Red is an Indian,
A Valentine heart,
The trimming on
A circus cart.
Red is a lipstick,
Red is a shout,
Red is a signal
That says: "Watch out!"
Red is a great big
Rubber ball.
Red is the giant-est
Color of all.
Red is a show-off
No doubt about it_____
But can you imagine
Living without it?

Reprinted from Hailstones and Halibut Bones by Mary O'Neill.

NOW YOU CAN GIVE

Mira Baptiste

Grade Level: These lessons are designed to be taught with upper elementary, junior high, and high school students. The time for teaching this unit will vary with the age/grade level of the students. It is anticipated that these activities could be accomplished within

    (a) 8-11 time periods for upper elementary students,
    (b) 4-8 time periods for junior high students, and
    (c) 3-5 time periods for senior high school students.

The time period depends upon the approach used by the teacher. If presented as a science unit the time will be shorter in contrast to the presentation of the unit within a multi-dimensional curriculum approach. The activities are designed to be used in various instructional settings and the activities include a multi-media base as well as utilization fo community resources. The teacher functions as the facilitator of learning.

Performance Objectives:

1. The student will be able to describe Charles Drew's contribution, its effect upon the life of man, and his technique of preserving plasma. The student will exercise his option in the method to describe the above.

2. Given access to materials that can be utilized to construct a model of a transfusion apparatus, the student will construct the model and demonstrate the mechanics involved in a blood transfusion.

3. The student will be able to state orally or in writing the social problems encountered by Dr. Drew as he perfected the techniques of preserving plasma an established blood banks.

4. Given acess to a diagram of the heart, and a heart model, the student will be able to label the four chambers of the heart and trace the flow of blood through the heart. Minimum acceptable performance will be the correct labelling of three of the heart chambers and correctly tracing the flow of blood through the heart.

5. Given access to a microscope, slides of blood cells, descriptive materials of blood, the student will be able to identify and describe blood cells in writing accompanied with diagrams of the cells.

Rationale: In the 1930's a great medical discovery was made. Blood could be drawn from a donor and preserved for a period of twenty-one days. Though many people were responsible for this medical discovery, the brilliant research of one man in particular, Dr. Charles R. Drew, made the preservation of drawn bolld possible. As Director of the first American Red Cross blood bank he overcame many technical problems which saved many thousands of lives during World War II. These lessons/activities have been designed to enable the student to formulate a conceptual framework which will explain the magnitude of this scientist's accomplishments.

<u>Initiating Activities:</u> The instructional setting can vary; but three small groups can work simultaneously together on the three activities. Another variation is to utilize the large group setting for all of the activities.

A. Group I

Materials: Tape recorder, listening post and audio tape on **Dr. Charles Drew** (Black Heritage series by Imperial International Learning, 1969), strips of tag board, magic markers.

Lesson:

    1. Student are instructed to listen to audio tape describing the life of Dr. Drew.

    2. After listening to the tape, each student is to write three words that can be used to tell the story of Dr. Drew and his accomplishment. Word strips are to be used for bulletin board.

    3. Teacher asks students to orally describe
        (a) Drew's accomplishment
        (b) social problems encountered by him
        (c) his childhood experiences

B. Group II

Materials: Film entitled "Circulation of The Boood" from **American Heart Association.**

Lesson:

    1. Students are to view film for purpose of obtaining a pictorical representation of the circulatory system and the blood cells' movement through the capillaries.

    2. Students are to formulate two questions they can answer about the circulatory system. These questions are to be used later in a sharing session with the large group.

C. Group III

Instructional Setting: Children may be arranged in a semi-circle to facilitate their seeing of models and posters.

Materials: Heart models, wall posters of heart and circulatory system, indicidual heart diagrams, and <u>About</u> <u>Your</u> <u>Heart</u> <u>and</u> <u>Your</u> <u>Bloodstream</u> (pamphlet, American Heart Association and Red Cross).

Lesson:

    1. Teacher asks students to read pages two and three of booklet. (allow 3-5 minutes) The instructor may begin the activity by asking the following questions:
        (a) How are cells able to receive food and get rid of wastes?
        (b) What provides the force for moving the blood through the body?
        (c) How would describe the heart?

After the students have described t and discussed the heart, then proceed to using the heart models and diagrams for tracing the blood flow through the heart. Allow the students to observe the heart chambers, valves, and major vessels and orally describe these to you. The students will freely provide observations about what they see. Utilize questions to focus their attention on certain parts of the heart, ex.: How do you think the blood gets from one chamber to another? How are the chambers different? What do you think the function of those strings (fibers attached to valves) is? Following the observation of the heart and an oral description of blood flowing through the heart, each child was given a heart diagram and asked to trace the flow of blood and label the parts of the heart.

Developmental Activities:
     Group I
        1. One group of students can construct the transfusion apparatus.
      Materials - two empty plastic hand-lotion or liquid soap con-
      tainers, twelve to eighteen inch piece of plastic tubing, electri-
      cian's tape, large paper clip, scissors.
      Directions - Cut the top from a plastic bottle. Insert a piece
      of plastic tubing into the top. Wrap electrician's tape around
      the top and the tube. Run the tube into another empty plastic
      container. Pour water into a small opening in the former container.
      Use a paper clip to show how the flow of liquid is controlled.
        2. Students may wish to work in pairs. Each team will explain
      the process to a member of another group of students.
     Group II
      The students may work in groups of twos. For each group a micro-
      scope should be set up with a blood smear slide (use oil immer-
      sion). At each microscope should be The Story of Blood
      (American Red Cross) pamphlet. (The student should be given
      specific instructions on how to use the microscope. With certain
      microscopes you may not want them to do the focusing.) Each stu-
      dent should be allowed to construct diagrams of the blood cells and
      describes them in writing or orally. The student may be asked the
      following questions: Do all blood cells look alike? Why are some
      cells different? Describe the shapes of the red and white blood
      cells. Following these questions, the students may be required to
      discuss their descriptions of blood cells.
    Group I and Group II combine to view the film, Blood Is Life Pass It
    On. This film is available from the American National Red Cross.
    This film will motivate the students to inquire about their values
    and opinions regarding the giving of blood. The teacher can serve
    as a discussion leader.

Culminating Activities:
    1. Divide the class into small groups and have each group plan a short
       dramatic skit portraying one of the following parts of Dr. Drew's life:
       (a) early years
       (b) success at Amherst
       (c) applying for medical school
       (d) laboratory work on blood plasma
       (e) the Red Cross project and controversy
       (f) return to Howard University
       (g) receiving the Spingarn Medal
       (h) the fatal accident
    2. A committee of students can write a letter or resignation from Dr. Drew
       to the Red Cross. His personal reasons for resigning and his feelings
       about the Army directive should both be included in the letter.
    3. Three other Black doctors have made significant contributions to the
       world of medicine: Dr. Daniel Hale Williams, a pioneer in open-heart
       surgery; Dr. Leonidas H. Berry, the developer of a gastro-biopsy
       instrument; and Dr. Samuel L. Kountz, one of the first to work with
       kidney transplants. Students may obtain information about each of
       these doctors and report their findings to the class in a sharing
       session.

4. Newspaper articles can be collected that relate to the use of
    blood, storage of blood, need for blood, etc. This can be used
    for a scrapbook or as part of the bulletin board display.
5. Sites for field trips could include
    (1) community Blood Bank
    (2) American National Red Cross
    (3) American Heart Association
    (4) Blood Bank Mobile Unit
    (5) Blood Bank of a large hospital

NOW YOU CAN GIVE

Resource Materials

American Heart Association, 44 East 23rd Street, New York, New York, 10010.
    Local: Consult your local branch office.

American National Red Cross, Midwestern Area, 4050 Lindall Blvd., St. Louis,
    Missouri, 63108.

Drew, Charles (tape) Black Heritage, Imperial International Learning,
    Kankakee, Illinois, 1970.

Haber, Louis. Black Pioneers of Science & Invention. Harcourt, Brace and
    World, Inc., New York, 1970.

Sterne, Emma G. Blood Brothers: Four Man of Science. Harcourt, Brace and
    Work, Inc., New York, 1970.

NOW YOU CAN GIVE

Performance Objectives

1. The student will be able to describe Charles Drew's contribution, its effect upon the life of man, and his technique of preserving plasma. The student will excercise his option in the method to describe this objective.

   #### Enabling Activities

   A. View filmstrip and listen to tape.
   B. Listen to tape.
   C. Read about his life (several books available).
   D. Read brochures from blood bank, American Red Cross, American Heart Association.
   E. Read appropriate newspaper articles.

****

2. Given access to materials that can be utilized to construct a model of a transfusion apparatus, the student will construct the model and demonstrate the mechanics involved in a blood transfusion.

   #### Enabling Activities

   A. Using index in science books, locate material that would be appropriate to read and view.
   B. Use the reference books.
   C. Use brochures from blood bank, American Red Cross, Etc.
   D. Remember what you have seen in a hospital or on T.V.
   E. Use newspaper pictures showing a transfusion apparatus to determine if yours is a workable model.

****

3. The student will be able to state orally or in writing the social problems encountered by Dr. Drew as he perfected the techniques of preserving plasms and establishing blood banks.

   #### Enabling Activities

   A. Complete objective 1.
   B. Locate in history book the period of time during which Dr. Drew lived. Look for a description of society and its attitudes toward Blacks at this time.
   C. Listen to tape by Dick Gregory.

4. Given access to a diagram of the heart, and a heart model, the student will be able to label the four chambers of the heart and trace the flow of blood through the heart. Minimum acceptable performance will be the correct labeling of three of the heart chambers and correctly tracing the flow of blood through the heart.

Enabling Activities

A. Locate a heart diagram in your textbook.
B. Locate a heart diagram in other science textbooks.
C. Do the Heart Puzzle.

****

5. Given access to a microscope, slides of blood cells, descriptive materials of blood, the student will be able to identify and describe blood cells in a written form accompanied by diagrams of the cells.

Enabling Activities

A. View blood cells through the microscope.
B. View pictures in the science textbooks.

****

Expectations

1. You are to keep all of your written work in your folder.

2. You will be able to work by yourself with only guidance from your instructor.

3. You will be able to plan your work in order to accomplish all of the stated objectives.

4. You will be able to achieve one objective which you will state and your instructor will approve.

5. You will be able to work independently and also within a group.

6. You are to become knowledgable about blood banks, current federal legislation regarding blood program/ services, individuals engaged in blood programs/services and skills/training required for employment within this area of health services. The daily newspaper offers you current factual information.

INTERRELATING CULTURAL PLURALISM THROUGH A LANGUAGE-EXPERIENCE APPROACH TO READING

Loretta Walton

PROSPECTUS

A language-experience approach to reading is one that interrelates the development of reading skills with the development of listening, speaking, spelling, and writing skills. This interrelation provides an opportunity for children to utilize their own thinking and background experiences as an aid for improving their reading skills. Since the concept of cultural pluralism involves providing an awareness, acceptance, and appreciation of various cultural backgrounds, then a language-experience approach appears to offer many advantages for teaching reading to children from varied ethnic backgrounds. Listening and speaking skills both play a very important part in the development of basic reading skills. Therefore, participation in the language-experience approach to reading will provide children of diverse cultural backgrounds the opportunity, not only to improve their reading skill development, but to gain a greater insight and appreciation for other cultures.

The language-experience approach is an effective technique for improving reading skills for some students, whereas other students may require other techniques or an eclectic approach. Therefore, the teacher should be flexible in determining what method or methods will be used. However, a language experience appears to offer many advantages, especially in teaching reading

to children whose language patterns tend to deviate from
printed textbook materials.

TERMINAL OBJECTIVE

Given a variety of materials, games, and activities, the
students will apply language skills to express themselves orally
and in writing by using their creative imagination. As a result,
the students will create their own stories and poems. They will
also become more aware of themselves as a unique individual
and learn to appreciate the cultures of other ethnic groups
and their contributions to society.

PERFORMANCE OBJECTIVES

1. Through the reading of short stories and poems, by the
teacher, the students will use their imagination to construct
stories and poems of their own.

2. Given pictures, drawings and art work from magazines,
and teacher made objects, the students will express in writing their
impressions and feelings.

3. Given games and activities that will enhance students'
creativity in thinking, the students will illustrate and write
their ideas.

4. Through the use of the student's stories, poems, etc., the
students will acquire increased language skills.

5. Given the opportunity to share their stories, orally
and in writing, students will become aware of other cultures
different from their own. As a result, they will appreciate

and respect the culture of themselves and others.

    6. Given story starters, students will write short creative stories of their own.

CULTURAL PLURALISM IN LITERATURE:
THE COMIC IMAGINATION*
Thelma M. Cobb

PROSPECTUS

A people's literature is the repository of its cultural
heritage. Imaginative literature is, possibly, the most
accurate and revealing picture of a people. To discover
similarities and differences in how people of different cultures
view a common human experience is to discover the richness of
the human experience and to affirm oneself in the process of
becoming human.

The study of literature is a process of probing for new
ways to widen and deepen one's perception of the human condition.
To study comedy is to discover one of the best insights into
the human condition. It makes us laugh at ourselves and at
the weaknesses, situations, and human institutions we encounter
in everyday life. Learning to laugh at ourselves and the world,
we learn a healthier way of living. To examine how writers of
our own and other cultures use the comic imagination to
illuminate human failings is to discover the bonds of commonality
we share as human beings.

Terminal Objective

Having read comic selections by Anglo-American, Afro-American,
and Mexican American writers, the student will be able to identify,

---

*The module was designed as a supplement to a thematic unit "The
Comic Imagination," prescribed for an eleventh grade English class.
The basic text included only one comic piece--a four line stanza
by Langston Hughes--among selections "representative of the comic
imagination in American Literature.

orally or in writing, at least two writers from each cultural group and tell how the writers use the comic imagination to create characters and situations that reveal an understanding and a greater awareness of themselves and of others who are both alike and different.

Performance Objectives

I. Using his/her own experiences as a frame of reference, the student will formulate, orally or in writing, a definition of comedy.

II. Given access to basic background materials, the student will demonstrate a knowledge of concepts relevant to an understanding of comedy by making functional use of the concepts in oral and written assignments.

III. Given selected background readings, the student will demonstrate an awareness of cultures other than his own by making cultural contrasts and comparisons in oral or written presentations based on the background readings.

IV. Having read comparative selections, the student will be able to identify and discuss, orally and in writing, the development of the comic character and situation and to recognize the nuances of cultural diversity.

V. Having done independent research, the student will be able to identify at least two writers of comedy from each cultural group and to discuss the type of comedy used and the target of the comedy. The method of presentation may be written, oral, or graphic.

ALL IN FUN! Try your hand with some of the items from the assessment inventory.

1. The real purpose of comedy is to (a) ridicule, (b) correct, (c) exaggerate.

2. Ogden Nash, Langston Hughes, and Javier Arechiga have all written (a) TV scripts, (b) Light verse, (c) melodrama.

3. Ethnic humor usually includes (a) put downs, (b) in group humor, (c) alienation.

4. Stock characters in the comedy of this group are the lover, the revolutionary, and the miser. (a) Black, (b) White, (c) Mexican American.

5. A theme common to Black and Mexican American comedy is the myth of the (a) Bean pot, (b) Melting pot, (c) Salad bowl.

7. That most popular comic strips and cartoons have been into several languages indicates that (a) humans have common frailties, (b) publishers are greedy, (c) American humorists are best.

8. A current stereotype of the Black American comic character is (a) minstrel, (b) Uncle Tom, (c) Superfly.

9. Stock characters form the bais for continuing (a) humor, (b) respect, (c) stereotypes.

AFTON FALLS CASE

William W. Witcher

PROSPECTUS

To clear the way for effective multicultural education, one of the most important steps is the elimination of prejudicial attitudes among different cultural groups. These attitudes are deeply engrained in individuals and have existed and been nourished for most of their lives. Developing a new attitude of understanding, respect, and tolerance of other groups is a long process. The eradication of such innate philosophies is therefore a task of monumental proportion, but nevertheless of critical importance.

Although time is perhaps the most crucial ingredient, one positive step is the awakening in individuals, whether or not they possess negative attitudes toward peoples of other ethnic and cultural groups, of the nature of prejudice and its interaction with forces at work in the American society. This module is a simulation exercise, an attempt to create a lifelike situation in which participants gain this insight through the role-playing technique.

Role-playing can be used effectively with most age levels and provides the active involvement necessary to achieve desired outcomes. This presentation has been designed as a flexible model.

The original development and implementation was with college students, but it is suitable for secondary school students with some minor adjustments. Elementary school students will react favorably to simulation exercises.

The key features of this module are its design in assigning roles and the unique situation in which the roles are joined and pitted against each other in resolving the question posed by the simulation. Participants are assigned roles different from philosophies they show on the pre-assessment test, and in researching and defending these roles, they begin to understand the essence of philosophy underlying their roles. During the actual role-playing, participants join others with different philosophies to work for a common goal and then oppose others who might have the same philosophy as theirs but who support a different goal.

Analysis of their behavior and of the arguments they must use in playing their roles during the simulation exercise affords the participants the opportunity to put their assigned and own real philosophies into proper perspective as a beginning step in the discovery of the nature of racism and prejudice.

UNIFIED SCIENCE AND MATHEMATICS FOR
THE ELEMENTARY SCHOOL (USMES):
THE JANOWSKI ELEMENTARY SCHOOL MODEL

Mira Baptiste

USMES is a project, a program, and a philosophy of education. It's Unified Science and Mathematics for Elementary
Schools developed by Education Development Center. The central idea is real problem solving. Solving real problems
entail using skills, concepts, and progress from social
science and language arts as well as math and science.

USMES is a program which involves students in the investigation and solution of real problems from their school community environment. Real problems are a dangerous cross-
walk near the school, classroom furniture that doesn't fit
the students in the class AND school supplies.

USMES is a philosophy which holds that children can themselves design and carry out the investigations and activities
needed to solve a problem. The philosophy also says the
students learn better when they see their work can lead to
useful accomplishment.

Each USMES unit is based on a real problem or "challenge."
The problems are "Real" in that they 1) have immediate,
practical effects on students' lives, 2) can lead to some
improvement by students, 3) have neither known "right" solutions nor clear boundaries, 4) require students to use their
own ideas for solving the problem, and 5) are big enough to

require many phases of class activity for any effective solution.

The Janowski Elementary School resource team has put into operation the implementation of several USMES units. Mrs. O'Neal's fourth grade class is implementing the unit on Traffic Flow. The USMES traffic control kids have recommended a new system for rerouting in one-way traffic lanes to improve the heavy traffic flow. One way and stop signs were posted to prevent interferences. Traffic Cop badges were issued to each homeroom to help control and catch the violators.

Mrs. Harris' sixth grade class was concerned with the cleanliness of the school. There isn't an USMES challenge entitled Clean Schools, but following the USMES format the class went to work to resolve a problem related to School cleanliness. The Clean Kids try and answer all requests from the principal for necessary repairs in and around the school building and on various other problems.

The Playground Design, Mrs. Burse's sixth grade class, undertook the USMES challenge of placing new playground equipment and prepared the site. The sixth graders worked in teams. They determined where the equipment should be placed and prepared the site, A safety committee was deemed necessary. These students demonstrated the skill of good decision making in determining the best location for the new pieces.

The Lunch Lines challenge better known at Janowski as
the Lunch Bunch wanted to improve behaviors in the school
cafeteria. Groups were formed to carry out plans for better
cafeteria behavior. A play dramatizing the cafeteria problems and a film capturing the Janowski students lunchroom
behavior serve as visual evidence of group work. These
students rearranged the seating in the lunchroom and found
it to be a most effective procedure.

Perhaps if anyone wanted to learn more about USMES,
the Janowski scond graders will be glad to tell you how to
"Get There". Janowski Elementary School is one place where
USMES will be a part of the school life. To solve a problem
both the teachers and students feel USMES is a successful
approach.

MULTICULTURALISM

Competency 11. Develop a rationale/model for the development and implementation of a curriculum reflective of cultural pluralism
(i.e., multicultural), within the K-12 school and be able
to defend it on a psychological, sociological, and cultural
basis.

COMPETENCY 11

Develop a rational/model for the development and implementation of a
curriculum reflective of cultural pluralism (i. e. multicultural), within
the K-12 school and be able to defend it on a psychological, sociological,
and cultural basis.

RATIONALE:

An educator should know why all education must be multicultural. One must
be able to cite sound reasons in support of multiculturalism which can be
coalesced into his or her own model for guidance and direction in the design
and development of one's own curriculum or curriculum support systems. Multicultural educators must not be guilty of a mindless direction in their
education activities. They must be able to argue the merits of their rationale
and/or model from a psychological, sociological, and cultural basis.

The major purpose of this competency is to aid the teacher in establishing
a philosophy for multicultural education.

Instructional Objectives:

1. The learner will be able to develop a rationale for multicultural education
    and defend it on a psychological, sociological, and cultural basis.

2. _____

    _____

    _____

Enabling Activities:

1. * Read: "Multiculturalizing Classroom Instruction," H. Prentice Baptiste and
   Mira Baptiste.

2. View: Film "Tapestry" to be shown in class and followed by a class
    discussion. Produced in El Paso, Texas, El Paso Independent School District.

3. Read: Geneva Gay, "Racism in America: Imperatives for Teaching Ethnic
    Studies," in Teaching Ethnic Studies, James A. Banks, ed., 43rd Yearbook,
    Washington, D. C.: National Council for the Social Studies, 1973, pages
    27-49.

4. Read: James A. Banks, Multiethnic Education: Practices and Promises,
    Fastback 87, Phi Delta Kappa Educational Foundation, 1977, pages 1-34.

5. Association for Supervision and Curriculum Development Multicultural
    Education Commission, "Encouraging Multicultural Education", Multicultural
    Education: Commitments, Issues, and Applications, Washington, D. C.:
    Association for Supervision and Curriculum Development, 1977, pages 1-5.

6. Harry N. Rivlin, and Milton J. Gold, <u>Teachers for Multicultural Education</u>, New York: Fordham University Teachers Corps, 1975, pages 1-12.

7. _____

_____

_____

8. _____

_____

_____

Assessment of Competency:

The learner is expected to demonstrate mastery of this competency by developing a rationale or model for multicultural education. Upon completion of Competencies One through Ten, the student is prepared to implement multicultural education, but must have an understanding of why. The learner will prepare a statement (five pages) explaining why the development and implementation of a curriculum reflective of cultural pluralism within the K-12 school is essential to the future of education. The learner will be able to defend it on a psychological, sociological, and cultural basis. The learner may choose to demonstrate this competency by constructing a model illustrating a lesson using the concept of multicultural education and videotaping the lesson in order to make a presentation to the class.

Instructional Notes From Class Meetings:

Date Competency Achieved _____

MULTICULTURALIZING CLASSROOM INSTRUCTION
H. Prentice Baptiste, Jr. and Mira Baptiste

One of the challenges of the 1970's in education has
been the development and implementation of classroom
instruction that is multicultural. Unfortunately, to many
teachers the concept of multicultural education is unfamiliar,
while to others it is still a rather hazy idea. The need for
multicultural education is based on the premise that the
United States is a nation composed of cultural pluralistic
groups. Acceptance of the concept of cultural pluralism
in America has outdistanced its implementation in American
education. One of the major purposes of multicultural
education is to make classroom instruction reflective of
the cultural pluralistic realities of this society.

The philosophy which must permeate education emanates
from an acceptance and belief in the values of cultural
diversity and a belief in a solid knowledge base of ethnic
and cultural information for all preservice and inservice
teachers. The unique field experiences offered by teacher
training institutions of higher education serve as experiential
training in cultural pluralistic environments where teachers

are required to demonstrate generic multicultural competencies
by: 1) effectively relating and creating instructional
strategies which meet the needs of a cultural pluralistic
population, 2) utilizing effective multicultural processes
for revising existing monocultural curricular, instructional
resources, course outlines, etc., 3) demonstrating a knowledge
of evaluative criteria and application for selection and
development of multicultural materials, and 4) responding
positively to the diversity of behavior involved in cross-
cultural environments.

The AACTE statement "No One Model American" serves
as a guiding principle for operationalizing multicultural
educational processes reflective of a cultural pluralistic
philosophy. The classroom instruction offered in today's
schools must operationalize the following quoted excerpts
from "No One Model American":

> . . . Multicultural education recognizes
> cultural diversity as a fact of life in
> American Society, and it affirms that
> this cultural diversity is a valuable
> resource that should be preserved and
> extended. It affirms that major education
> institutions should strive to preserve
> and enhance cultural pluralism.
>
> Multicultural education programs for
> teachers are more than special courses
> or special learning experiences grafted
> onto the standard program. The commit-
> ment to cultural pluralism must permeate
> all areas of the educational experience
> provided for perspective teachers.[1] . . .

During very recent years the relationship between cultural pluralism and multicultural education has been questioned repeatedly by educators on numerous occasions. This is a complex concept which raises difficult questions. Cultural pluralism has been defined from many vantage points that reflect various areas of concern, ranging, for example, from the national government to the small school district. Whatever the area of concern, underlying the definition of cultural pluralism is a philosophy that strongly recommends a particular set of beliefs, principles, and ideas that should govern the relationship of people of diverse cultures. The cornerstone principles of cultural pluralism are equality, mutual acceptance and understanding, and a sense of moral commitment.

Multicultural education is the process of institutionalizing the philosophy of cultural pluralism within the educational systems. This is not an easy process. As Tomas A. Arciniega stated in Educational Leadership, "The issue of moving schools and universities toward a culturally pluralistic state may appear, to some, to be a simple matter. The fact is, however, that the thrust toward achieving cultural pluralism in educational form and practice is a complex and value laden undertaking."[2]

As one develops the multicultural process within an educational setting, one is confronted with traditional obstacles like the monocultural process of the assimilation or the melting pot philosophy, unequal availability of educational opportunities, hostility, or disregard for diversity, racism, and prejudice which militates against its implementation. However, proponents of the multicultural process must affirm the ethical commitment of institutions to the aforementioned principles of cultural pluralism.

The multicultural process is not an add on to existing programs. Bilingual programs which are based on a traditional model, i. e., elimination of instruction in the mother tongue as soon as second language acquisition occurs - are not representative of the multicultural process. Language curricular activities which neglect the cultural value systems of the languages are detrimental to formation of valid instructional activities. Educators who tend to utilize only special ethnic holidays, religious ceremonials, super-heroes, and foods to multiculturalize their instruction are being dreadfully shortsighted. Furthermore, they are miseducating our students to the real values of various cultural/ethnic groups.

The Texas Education Agency in 1972, in its revised Standards for Teacher Education and Certification included the following:

> E. Multicultural Emphasis
>
>   The institution seeking approval for
>   undergraduate level teacher preparation
>   shall design its program of general
>   education so that each student recommended

for certification shall have a
knowledge and understanding of
the multicultural society of which
he is a part. To verify this
standard, the institution shall
present evidence that:

1. its program of general
education is designed to give
emphasis to the multicultural
aspects of society.

2. each student recommended
for certification has a knowledge and understanding of our
multicultural society.[3]

Perhaps no other single factor provided the impetus

for the incorporation of multicultural experiences in the

preservice and inservice teacher training program or

additional certification programs than the Texas Education

Agency revised Standards for Teacher Education and

Certification. The revised TEA standards, as standards are

normally, were just an impetus, a catalyst or a requirement.

Also, after the "debated dust" began to settle, some of us

in a more somber state raised the following questions: How

do you train teachers for multicultural education? How do

you operationalize the process of multicultural education so

that its acquisition and implementation is feasible to

teachers?

The significance of the two previous questions is quite

obvious when one realizes that the reason for the multicultural

education movement is because of the promises many of us

believe it holds for contributing to or facilitating

educational equity for all students. Therefore, its

incorporation into classroom instruction, regardless to the

magnitude of the task is of paramount importance. We believe
it is not debatable that the process of multiculturalizing
classroom instruction is sin qua non to educational equity.

Now to return to the first of our two questions: How
do you train teachers for multicultural education? We
support a delivery system (i. e., teacher training system)
that is characterized by clear cut objectives and specific
alternative processes. Conceptually we are referring
to a competency based delivery system; for, as indicated
at the beginning of this paper, there is enough haziness and
vagueness surrounding multicultural education, that we can
ill afford to couch it in a fuzzy delivery system. However,
it is beyond the scope of this paper to rationalize the
competency based delivery system. We, along with other
authors - Hunter[4], Grant[5], have already made a case for the
relationship of multicultural education and competency
based education.

Of course a major component of a competency based program
are the competencies. During our seven years of training
teachers for multicultural education, we have identified
eighteen generic competencies. Eleven are cognitive and eight
are affective. Generic in the sense that any teacher
(elementary and secondary) must acquire these competencies
if he or she desires to effectively multiculturalize his or
her classroom instruction.

The teacher for multicultural education should demonstrate
the ability to:

1. acquire a knowledge of the cultural experience in both contemporary and historical setting of any two ethnic, racial, or cultural groups;

2. demonstrate a basic knowledge of the contributions of minority groups in America to our society;

3. assess relevance and feasibility of existing models that afford groups a way of gaining inclusion into today's society;

4. identify current biases and deficiencies in existing curriculum and in both commercial and teacher-prepared materials of instruction;

5. recognize potential linguistic and cultural biases of existing assessment instruments and procedures when prescribing a program of testing for the learner;

6. acquire a thorough knowledge of the philosophy and theory concerning bilingual education and its application;

7. acquire, evaluate, adapt, and develop materials appropriate to the multiculture classroom;

8. critique an educational environment to the extent of the measurable evidence of the environment representing a multicultural approach to education;

9. acquire the skills for effective participation and utilization of the community;

10. design, develop, and implement an instructional module using strategies and materials which will produce a module or unit that is multicultural, multiethnic, and multiracial;

11. develop a rationale or model for the development
and implementation of a curriculum reflective of cultural
pluralism within the K-12 school and be able to defend
it on a psychological, sociological, and cultural basis.

The teacher for multicultural education is a person who
can:

1. develop an awareness in the learners of the value
of cultural diversity;

2. assist the learners to maintain and extend
identification with and pride in the mother culture;

3. assist and prepare the learners to interact
successfully in a crosscultural setting;

4. assist all to respond positively to the diversity
of behavior involved in cross-cultural school
environments;

5. recognize both the similarities and differences
between Anglo-American and other cultures and both
the potential conflicts and opportunities they may
create for students;

6. recognize and accept the language variety of the
home and a standard variety as valid systems of
communication, each with its own legitimate functions;

7. recognize and accept different patterns of child
development within and between cultures in order to
formulate realistic objectives;

8. recognize and accept differences in social structure,
including familial organization and patterns of authority,
and their significance for the educational environment.

Teachers who acquire these competencies and incorporate them into their classroom instruction will be taking a giant step toward providing educational equity for all of their students. Acquisition of these competencies by teachers will facilitate them in becoming more multiethnic (see Baptiste and Ford's article) in their attitudes and behavior. Furthermore, acquisition of these competencies assures the recognition of multicultural education as a process of education. That is a process and not a series of fragmented, unrelated attempts at multiculturalizing which will be too limited in focus and impact to bring about real change in classroom instruction for educational equity.

The multicultural process includes diversifying the subject matter content as well as humanizing teaching strategies. Much has been written about diversifying subject matter content. This has caused us to overlook the humanizing component of the multicultural process. That part of the process which deals with the interaction of teacher and student can facilitate the creation of a supportive learning environment in the classroom. The teacher should make a constant conscientious effort to create a teaching/learning environment reflective of power sharing, equality, and decision making. It is important for the teacher to realize that shared power and decision making flow in two directions between teacher and students. Designing learning activities which will enable the student to explore his/her self concept

is often the beginning stage for the multicultural processes.
Self-esteem and worthiness are undeniably linked to the
feeling of having some control over one's environment.
A real voice in decision making is fundamental for the
student to acquire a positive self-esteem. Many subject
areas such as art, drama, music, language, social studies,
and sociology can be used by teachers to facilitate the
positive growth of the students' self-esteem.

There are no curriculum guides, no material kits,
no pre- or post tests, no objectives, and no teacher
editions available for one to plug into the existing
courses for Multicultural Education. The consequent
objective for material effectiveness is evaluated by the
teacher not only in terms of students' gains in understandings
and knowledge of other people, but in the reduction and
resolution of conflicts.

A classroom teacher who implements the multicultural
process must utilize his/her training/preparation from
the suggested competencies. The development of a rationale
by each teacher for institutionalizing the philosophy of
cultural pluralism provides a personal frame of reference for
the individual teacher as he/she begins to construct the
learning activities.

a) The teacher should select a subject area or topic
that he or she is knowledgeable and is comfortable with in

the teaching/learning situation. A strong interest in a topic or subject is helpful, but not sufficient for effective multiculturalizing.

b) The teacher should select concepts or topics that are regularly taught in the curriculum as a part of the multicultural process.

c) An integrated subject area or interdisciplinary approach can facilitate the implementation of the multicultural process.

d) Acquisition of the contributions and knowledge production and cultural values of the various minority ethnic groups is essential for implementing multicultural education as a process in classroom instruction.

e) Teaming with colleagues will provide a support system and a larger knowledge base to draw upon for diversifying and humanizing your classroom instruction.

f) The utilization of community resources can provide you with catalytic rich and ethnically/culturally divergent resources for adrenalyzying the multicultural process.

g) Know yourself (affectively).

C I T E D   R E F E R E N C E S

1. "No One Model American," in Journal of Teacher Education, No. 4, Winter, 1973.

2. Tomas A. Arciniega, "The Thrust Toward Pluralism: What Progress?" Educational Leadership, 33, No. 3, (December, 1975), p. 163.

3. "Standards for Teacher Education in Texas," Bulletin 651 (Austin: Texas Education Agency, June, 1972).

4. Hunter, William, ed., Multicultural Education through Competency-Based Teacher Education, American Association of Colleges for Teacher Education, Washington D. C., 1974.

5. Grant, Carl A., ed., Sifting and Winnowing: An Exploration of the Relationship Between Multicultural Education and CBTE, Teacher Corps Associates, University of Wisconsin-Madison, Madison, Wisconsin, 1975.

APPENDICES

AFFECTIVE COMPETENCIES

1. Developing an awareness in the learners of the value of cultural diversity.

2. Assisting the learners to maintain and extend identification with and pride in the mother culture.

3. Assisting and preparing the learners to interact successfully in a cross-cultural setting.

4. Assisting all to respond positively to the diversity of behavior involved in cross-cultural school environments.

5. Recognizing both the similarities and differences between Anglo-American and other cultures and both the potential conflicts and opportunities they may create for students.

6. Recognizing and accepting the language variety of the home and a standard variety as valid systems of communication, each with its own legitimate functions.

7. Recognizing and accepting different patterns of child development within and between cultures in order to formulate realistic objectives.

8. Recognizing and accepting differences in social structure, including familial organization and patterns of authority, and their significance for the educational environment.

GLOSSARY

ACCULTURATION - It is the interchange or process of intercultural borrowing between diverse peoples resulting in new and blended patterns of living, learning, assessing.

AFRO AMERICAN - An individual who is a member of the Negroid race (especially the African branch) distinguished from members of other races by physical features. These physical features do not include factors such as language and mental capabilities. Further, the identification as a Black American includes a racial pride which emphasizes sociological and psychological strengths gained as a result of "self-system examinations" in recent times. Identification as a Afro Black American frequently rejects identification as a Negro-and this rejection is based on specific philosophical differences constituting ethnicity.

For years, Americans of Negroid descent preferred to be identified as Negroes. This was an anthropological substitution to describe persons of black skin. Because many people perceived black color in negative terms, Negro was an accepted substitution. With the onset of desegregation, there is decreased rejection of black identity and preference for the use of the term black rather than Negro. The use of the term Negro frequently denoted a rejection of self while Black American identification is total acceptance of self including one's ethnic heritage.

Black American is synonymous with Afro American. The term further emphasizes the African ethnic identity.

ASSIMILATION - Assimilation, in many ways, is philosophically synonymous with the melting pot theory. It presupposes that all persons would like a common perception, a common curriculum, a common set of practices on which lives are based.

BILINGUAL EDUCATION - Bilingual education is the offering of formal and informal instruction in two languages-one of which is the native language of the predominant ethnic group undergoing instruction. Both languages are emphasized equally, and learners are encouraged to speak and write in both languages. The positive contribution of bilingual education is that learners develop the skill of expressing themselves in two languages rather than one. Most important, students are instructed in the language or vernacular most familiar to them. Bilingual education, therefore is not foreign language instruction in two languages; it is instruction in the language of the student as well as instruction about the official language of the country. Countries such as Mexico, Canada, India, and the USSR have traditionally used the bilingual format in their public schools.

CULTURAL DEMOCRACY - Cultural democracy is the legal and moral right of an individual to maintain his own ethnic identity and at the same time learn and accept the values of mainstream society.

CULTURAL PLURALISM - Cultural Pluralism is the social, economic, and political variation in a given society and the anthropological patterns accompanying the variation - the autonomous freedom of cultural variation among entities in the American milieu.

CULTURE - Culture is a lifestyle pattern shared by members of a society - knowledge, beliefs, values, attitudes and morals - and united by a common language.

DEFACTO SEGREGATION - Separation of races which is not the result of law, but the result of common practice and prevailing circumstances such as poverty and neighborhood composition.

DEJURE SEGREGATION - Separation of races enforced by law; the separation of people in social-political-educational contexts according to accepted "laws of the enforcing groups."

DESEGREGATION - Desegregation is a physical arrangement whereby persons of different racial-ethnic backgrounds work, learn and live in the same setting.

DISCRIMINATION - Discrimination is an action of demonstrating unequal treatment of individuals or groups.

ELITISM - Elitism is the idea that one group (usually an economic group) is better than another based on the value judgments of that group regarding their attributes and characteristics. Elitism involves the concept of social superiority because of economic advancement and it incorporates the idea that one group in society is better able to govern and, therefore, should hold the political power.

ETHNIC GROUP - An ethnic group is a group of people with a common heritage, such as a geographic heritage (Poles, Swedes, Italians) which can be distinguished due to cultural and sociological traits. It may also be defined to include factors such as religion, language, folklore, and group activity.

ETHNICITY - Ethnicity is the awareness of the uniqueness of one's ethnic identity by the individual members of the group. Such awareness also reflects itself in the pride which one takes in his-her ethnic identity. It also involves the potency of the identity expressed by members of that group, and these expressions are transmitted through the culture.

ETHNOLOGY - Ethnology is a science that studies the division of people into groups based on their origin, distribution, relations and characteristics.

INTEGRATION - Integration is a broader concept than desegregation, in that it involves the social acceptance as equals of persons who are racially-ethnically different, the social process of accepting and respecting the rights of individuals, regardless of racial, ethnic or cultural differences.

MEXICAN AMERICAN - The generic term used to describe an individual in America
whose ancestors or parents come from Mexico or Spain. The
term encompasses the broad spectrum of a diverse ethnic
group, the largest bilingual (Spanish-English) ethnic group
in the country. There are at least three sub-groups among
Mexican Americans. The Hispano is an individual whose
ancestors were the original colonizers in the Southwest.
Juan Onate and other Spanish colonists first settled the Rio
Grande Valley of the Southwest during the 16th Century;
these Hispanos represented a cultural identification with
Spanish traditions and customs. The Mejicano is an individual
whose ancestors remained in or migrated to the Southwest
after Mexican traditions and customs, which consist of both
Indo (Mexican Indian) and Spanish influences. The Migrant
is an individual, either Hispano or Mejicano, who earns his
living in the agricultural fields of this country. The
Mexican American migrant stream begins in the Southwest
(Southern Texas, New Mexico, Arizona, California) and goes
north to Kansas through the Midwest to Michigan or north up
the West Coast and the Imperial Valley of California.

The obvious indicant of the Mexican American is his bilingualism.
He speaks American English and a dialect of Spanish, a calo,
which combines Castilian, Mexican, and some English language
forms. Ethnocentric labels for the Calo have been "Tex-Mex"
or "pocho," but in recent years linguists and anthropologists
have recognized the calo as a rich, complex, rule-governed
dialect indigenous to this country. The vitality of the calo
also indicates the vitality of the Mexican American culture.

Chicano is a term that describes a person who is Mexican
American as well as a philosophic orientation. The term
traces its derivation back to the last part of the word
Mejicano as pronounced by the Aztecs-Meshicano. From the
ending of Meshicano comes "shicano" or chicano." Chicano
is an ingroup term used to show unity and nationalism among
its members, and was at first associated with the militant or
low economic Mexican segment, but it is gaining acceptance
among various elements of the total Mexican American group
as well as the Anglo society.

NATIVE AMERICAN - An individual whose ancestors were native inhabitants of the
territory known as the United States - the original occupants
of America.

PREJUDICE - Prejudice is an unfavorable feeling or attitude toward a person
or group. Prejudice most often involves prejudging without having
significant facts to support one's attitude.

PUERTO RICAN - An individual whose ancestors came from the island called
Boriquen that was later named Puerto Rico. The Taino Indians
lived on the island, but Spaniards and Africans settled there
and began families. Today, a Puerto Rican may have either
Indian, African, or Spanish ancestry, or combinations of
these. Because (at a later time) the French, Italian, and
Irish also migrated to the island, Puerto Ricans of today may
reflect part of that ancestry as well.

RACIAL GROUP - A racial group is a division of people possessing traits that are transmissable by descent and sufficient to characterize it as a distinct human type. A racial group actually includes a complex distinction of degrees of human traits that are physical, linguistic, and cultural and psychological.

RACISM - Racism is the belief that race is the primary determinant of human traits and capacities and that racial differences produce the inherent superiority or inferiority of a particular race.

SEGREGATION - Segregation is the separation of an entity or group of individuals based on some identifiable characteristic which is frequently physical.

SEXISM - Sexism is the belief that one sex (male or female) is inherently superior to the other.

STEREOTYPE - A standardized mental picture that is held in common by many members of one group about another-and that represents an oversimplified opinion, affective attitude, or uncritical judgement. It is a preconceived or pre-judged idea about a group of people with diverse membership. While there are positive stereotypes, the most frequent reference is to those reflecting undesirable characteristics. While this concept usually has ethnic or racial connotations stereotypes could also refer to other characteristics, such as "bookworm," "egghead," etc.

VALUES - Values are acquired attitudes and standards of judgment held by various groups (i.e., racial, religious, ethnic) about what things are important, desirable, and right. There is also variation in value priorities that differ from one group to another.

University of Houston
Houston, Texas
LRC Resources

LRC SAT.
NUMBER: TITLE:

3263   Multicultural Education through CBTE (1974)
Shelf D

3266   Cross Cultural Research Methods   (1973)
Shelf D

3276   Teaching Multicultural Populations
Shelf D

4036   Cultural Democracy Biocognitive Developement &
                Education (1974)

4101   A Mexican American Chronicle (1967)
Shelf H

4102   Teaching Ethnic Studies   (1973)
Shelf H

4103   Urban Education   (1971)
Shelf H

4104   Bibliografia de Aztlan (1971)
Shelf H

4105   Mexican Americans (1972)
Shelf H

4106   Principal (Nov. 1970)
Shelf H

4107   Multicultural Curriculum in the Elementary School
Shelf H

4108   Black Education in America (1970)
Shelf H

4109   Phi Delta Kappan (Jan. 1972)
Shelf H

4110   IRCD Bulletin (1969)
Shelf H

4111   Afro-American History: Primary Education (1970)
Shelf H

4112   The American Immigration Collection (1970)
Shelf H

LRC SAT. NUMBER	TITLE:
4113 Shelf H	Teaching Strategies for Ethnic Studies (1975)
4114 Shelf H	Mexican-Americans in School: A History of Educational Neglect (1970)
4115 Shelf H	The Black American (1967)
4116 Shelf H	Racial Crisis in American Education (1969)
4117 Shelf H	Mexican Americans (Moore) (1970)
4118 Shelf H	A Documentary History of the Mexican American (1971)
4119 Shelf H	Counseling and the Black Student (1970)
4120 Shelf H	Ethnic Modification of the Curriculum (1970)
4144 Shelf I	The Schools and Prejudice: Findings (1969)
4145 Shelf I	Adolescent Prejudice (1975)
4178 Shelf H	Educational Leadership (April 1974)
4179 Shelf H	Educational Leadership (Oct. 1974)
5248 Shelf H	A Handbook of Bilingual Education (1974)
5249 Shelf H	The Afton Falls Case (1974)
5250 Shelf H	Cultural Pluralism: The Comic Imagination (1975)
5251 Shelf H	Interrelating Cultural Pluralism through A Language-Experience (1974)
5252 Shelf H	Science History Module: Scientific and Technical Contributions (1974)
5254 Shelf H	A Self-Awareness Module (1974)

LRC SAT. NUMBER:	TITLE:
4181 Shelf I	A Better Chance to Learn: Bilingual-Bicultural Education
4182 Shelf I	Bilingual Schooling in the U. S. Vol II
4183 Shelf I	Bilingual Schooling in the U. S. Vol. I
4184 Shelf I	Educational Leadership Vol.32, No. 1
4185 Shelf I	Educational Leadership Vol. 31, No. 7
4186 Shelf I	Phi Delta Kappan Vol. LIII, No. 5 The Imperatives of Ethnic Education
4187 Shelf I	The National Elementary Principal Vol. L, No. 2

4188
Shelf I
	Articles Pertaining to Multicultural Education (5)
	    Teachers for Multicultural Education
	    "No One Model American"
	    Mano a Mano -- "Multicultural Education"
	    Mano a Mano -- "Multicultural Eduction - Who am I?
	    Mano a Mano -- "The Myth of the Melting Pot
	        Gives Rise to Multiculture Education"

LRC NUMBER:	TITLE:

LRC 18	Fostering Ethnic Values
	    by Child Care Information Center
	    (audio tape presentation)

LRC 120	New Concepts for Teaching the Multiculture Experience (audio cassette)
LRC 156	Dick Gregory: The Light Side, The Dark Side, Parts I&II (audio cassette) 1973

LRC 262	Bread and Butterflies
	    National Instructional Television Center
	    (2 video cassette tapes)

LRC 449	Dr. Reywell Parkins Black Seminar Conference (audio cassette)
LRC 498 A&B	Barbara Sizemore (video cassette)

LRC 512	Perspectives on Multicultural Education
	    by Dr. H. P. Baptiste, Jr. (1976)
	    (video tape)

BIBLIOGRAPHY

Banks, James, ed., Teaching Ethnic Studies, National Council for Social Studies, 1973.

Banks, James. Teaching Strategies for Ethnic Studies, Allyn and Bacon, Inc., 2nd edition, 1979.

Brislin, R., et.al., Cross-Cultural Research Methods, John Wiley and Sons, 1973.

Brown, Dee. Bury My Heart at Wounded Knee, Holt, Rinehart, and Winston, 1970.

Carter, Thomas P., Mexican Americans in School: A History of Educational Neglect, College Entrance Examination Board, Princeton, 1970.

Curriculum Guidelines for Multiethnic Education, Position Statement, National Council for the Social Studies, Arlington, Virginia, 1976.

Dora and House, eds., Education for An Open Society, Association for Supervision and Curriculum Development, 1974.

Dunfee, Maxine, ed., Eliminating Ethnic Bias, A.S.C.C., 1974.

Epps, Edgar, ed., Cultural Pluralism, McCutchan Company, 1974.

Freire, Paulo, Pedagogy of the Oppressed, Herder and Herder Publishers, New York, 1971.

Glazer and Moynohan, Beyond the Melting Pot, The M.T.T. Press, 1970.

Gold, Milton, Grant, Carl, Rivlin, Harry, In Praise of Diversity: A Resource Book for Multicultural Education, Teacher Corporations Association of Teacher Educators, Washington, D.C., 1977.

Goodman, Mary E., Race Awareness in Young Children, Collier Books, 1964.

Goodman, Mary E., The Culture of Childhood, Teachers College Press, 1970.

Grant, Carl, ed., Multicultural Education: Commitments, Issues, and Applications, Association for Supervision and Curriculum Development, Washington, D.C., 1977.

Grebler, Leo, et.al., The Mexican-American People, MacMillan Company, 1970.

Green, Robert, ed., Racial Crisis in American People, MacMillan Company, 1970.

Harrington, M., The Other America, Pelican Books, 1971.

Hunter, W., ed., Multicultural Education Through Competency-Based Teacher Education, AACTE, 1974.

Illich, Ivan, Deschooling Society, Harper and Row, Publisher, 1970.

Jencks, Christopher, <u>Inequality: A Reassessment of the Effect of Family and Schooling in America</u>, Harper and Row, Publishers, 1972.

Klassen, Frank and Gollnick, Donna, eds., <u>Pluralism and The American Teacher: Issues and Case Studies</u>, AACTE, Washington, D.C., 1977.

Ladner, Joyce, ed., <u>The Death of White Sociology</u>, Vintage Books, 1973.

Lambert, W. E., and G. I. Tucker, <u>Bilingual Education of Children</u>, Newbury House Publishers, 1972.

McDaniel, Clyde, <u>Research Methodology</u>, Kendall/Hunt Publishing Company, 1974.

Montagu, Ashley, <u>Man's Most Dangerous Myth: The Fallacy of Race</u>, Oxford University Press, 1974.

Myrdal, Gunner, <u>An American Dilemma</u>, Volumes I and II, Harper and Row, 1944, 1962.

Novak, Michael, <u>The Rise of the Unmeltable Ethnics</u>, MacMillan Publishing Company, 1973.

Poblano, Ralph, ed., <u>Ghosts in the Barric</u>, Leswing Press: San Rafael, California, 1973.

Ramirez and Castaneda, Cultural Democracy, <u>Bicognitive Development, and Education</u>, Academic Press, 1971.

Robertson, Wilmot, <u>The Dispossessed Majority</u>, Howard Allen Company, 1973.

Rose, Arnold, <u>The Negro in America</u>, Harper and Row, 1964.

Smith, Arthur, <u>Transracial Communication</u>, Prentice-Hall, Inc., 1973.

Steinfield, Melvin, eds., <u>Cracks in the Melting Pot</u>, Glencoe Press, 1973.

Stent, M. et.al., eds., <u>Cultural Pluralism in Education</u>, Appleton-Century-Crofts, 1973.

Stone and DeNevi, eds., <u>Teaching Multicultural Populations</u>, Van Nostrand Reinhold Company, 1971.

Turner, Paul R., ed., <u>Bilingualism in the Southwest</u>, University of Arizona Press, 1973.